From The FRONTLINE

From The
FRONTLINE

From The FRONTLINE

The Extraordinary Life of
SIR BASIL CLARKE

Richard Evans

For Abigail

First published 2013
by Spellmount, an imprint of The History Press
The Mill, Brimscombe Port
Stroud, Gloucestershire, GL5 2QG
www.thehistorypress.co.uk

British Library Cataloguing in Publication Data.
A catalogue record for this book is available from the British Library.

isbn 978 0 7524 9429 6
Typesetting and origination by The History Press
Printed in Great Britain

Contents

Acknowledgements

Writing this book would have been impossible without the support of many people and I would like to say thank you to some of them. Most of all, I am grateful to Abigail Evans, my beautiful wife and the love of my life, who has been a huge support over the three years I spent writing it. It was just the two of us when I started and by the time it was completed our two wonderful children, Evelyn and Orson, had arrived, which gives an idea of what Abigail has taken on while I was spending days in libraries and archives or in front of a computer.

I would like to thank Jo DeVries and the team at The History Press for their faith in and support for the book, as well as Kathy Turner, David Gleed; Sandra Gleed; Lisa Day; Sheena Craig; and Lucie Jordon for reading various drafts and offering valuable advice. I am also extremely grateful for how Basil Clarke's relatives Richard, Angela and Jim Hartley have been so generous in welcoming me into their home and giving me access to photographs and letters and a previously unknown first draft of his memoirs. Relatives from another branch of the family, Roger and Annie Bibbings, have also kindly given me photographs and documents and talked to me about Clarke, as have Colin Clarke and John Southworth.

I am also grateful for the help of staff at archives and libraries, including the British Library (the St Pancras site and the newspaper library at Colindale); the National Archives; the John Rylands Library in Manchester; the Royal Society of Arts; Manchester Grammar School; the Churchill Archives Centre in Cambridge; the Parliamentary Archives, King's College London's Archives and Special Collections; the Bodleian Library; the University of Oxford; the London Metropolitan Archives; and the Halifax and Canford School. Thanks, also, to

Peter Howlett of the London School of Economics and the historian Judith Moore for their information and guidance.

And a very special mention goes to my mum and dad, Dee and Brian Evans. Not only did they both read the book and suggest changes, but without their huge support throughout my life I would never have got around to writing it. I hope it goes part of the way towards making up for the mess I made of my history degree.

Prologue:
'The Austrians Are Here'

'Get up, get up, sir! The Austrians are here!'
Basil Clarke heard the voice coming into his dream and then a few seconds later was woken suddenly by the feeling of hot wax hitting his wrist. It had dripped from the candle that the night porter was holding over him.

As his eyes adjusted to the light, his Romanian assistant Dobias came running into the room. 'Get up, get up!' he shouted frantically. 'What can you be dreaming of, to lie still so? You will get me murdered and yourself, too, if you don't make haste!'

Clarke tried to get them to tell him how long ago the Austrians had arrived but both men were incoherent with panic. So he got out of bed and began to dress, doing so deliberately slowly in the hope that this might help calm Dobias. Looking back on the incident later, though, he would admit that 'I was pretty scared, too, inwardly'.[1]

★★★

It was February 1915. Clarke and Dobias were in Chernivtsi, a city in present-day Ukraine that had already changed hands between the Austrians and the Russians several times during the first seven months of the First World War.

When they had arrived the previous day, Chernivtsi had been under Russian control but was gripped by an atmosphere of 'brooding uncertainty' because of a rumour that the Russians, who were fighting on the side of Britain and France, were about to withdraw and let the Austrians retake the city.

Clarke and Dobias visited the Russian Army headquarters to try to discover if the rumour was true, but the first official they asked was unable to give them any useful information. Clarke noted with concern, though, how he would abruptly stop speaking in the middle of a sentence to listen to the sound of the Austrian guns in the distance, as if trying to judge how far away they were. But a Russian soldier later assured him that as a newspaper correspondent he would be told in advance about any order to withdraw and so he and Dobias found a hotel for the night.

Clarke planned to spend the evening in the city after dropping off their luggage, but they were stopped at the front door of the hotel by a Russian sentry with a bayonet who told them that no one was allowed outside after 6.00 p.m. The hotel did not have a restaurant so they ate ham and bread with a bottle of Austrian wine in Clarke's room and then Dobias returned to his own room while Clarke stayed up writing by candlelight until 11.00 p.m. Just before he went to bed he visited the night porter, whom he gave a large tip in exchange for a promise to wake him immediately at any sign of movement of troops or shooting in the streets.

But the night porter fell asleep and by the time he woke up the Russians had withdrawn and the Austrians were already starting to arrive in the city. This meant Clarke was now behind enemy lines.

He and Dobias hurriedly paid their hotel bill and the night porter ushered them to the front door, opening it but then quickly closing it again at the sound of movement outside. The three men looked through the glass panels of the door and saw snow-covered soldiers marching past. The night porter waited until the soldiers had passed before opening the door again, looking up and down the street and then pushing Clarke and Dobias down the steps and closing the door behind them. They were on their own.

They decided to head north towards the River Prut, as this was the way the Russians were likely to have left the city. But after a few hundred yards there was a large explosion in the distance ahead of them that they thought must be the Russians blowing up the bridge. So with that escape route now closed to them, they instead began to head in the direction of the Romanian border, from where they had arrived the previous day. After seeing a man who they thought was carrying a bayonet, they decided it would be safest to stay off the roads and so they climbed over fences and ran through fields and gardens until there was just countryside between them and Marmornitza, the border village they had come from.

Marmornitza was less than 10 miles from Chernivtsi but the journey meant trudging through snow that was so deep that they were only able to keep to the road by following the telegraph poles in front of them. As well as the threat of capture by the Austrians, Clarke and Dobias spent the journey anxiously looking out for the wolves they had been told roamed the area. In the event, the only animal they encountered was an angry farm dog whom they took turns fending off with a stick while the other man lowered a bucket into a well to get a drink of water.

It was morning when they finally arrived at the Romanian border after five hours of walking and, tired and hungry, they went straight to a restaurant to get breakfast. By the time they finished their meal, just an hour after crossing the border, they returned to see that hundreds of Austrian soldiers were now on the other side.

★★★

Just a year before, Clarke had been the *Daily Mail*'s northern England correspondent, writing about subjects as mundane as the trend for built-in furniture[2] and the increasing popularity of communal living as a way of minimising housework.[3]

But though the war was less than a year old, he was already well-used to living by his wits by the time he came to make escape from the Austrian Army in the middle of the night. He had been hardened by the experience of living as a fugitive in Belgium and France during the first few months of the war, under the dual threat of arrest by the Allies and sudden death from a German shell. While the period he had spent in Flanders as what he described as a 'journalistic outlaw' may have only lasted some three months, it had exposed him to more danger and hardship than most journalists face in their entire careers.

Notes

1   *The War Illustrated*, 2 December 1916, p.363–4, Also Basil Clarke, *My Round of the War*, London 1917, pp.128–30. In some versions of this story, he and Dobias were chased by two Austrian soldiers during the last part of the journey.

2   *Daily Mail*, 3 March 1914, p.6.

3   *Daily Mail*, 9 February 1914, p.6.

1

Into Journalism

As the son of a shepherd, it was a considerable achievement that by the time James Clarke came to having children of his own in the 1870s, he and his wife Sarah were running a chemist's shop in the affluent Cheshire town of Altrincham and were comfortable enough to employ two servants.

It was the third of their five children, a boy born on 11 August 1879, who would go on to complete the family's vertiginous social rise by becoming both a celebrated journalist and pioneer of a new profession that would change the nature of journalism itself.

When considering those who have led remarkable lives, there is always the temptation to over-interpret aspects of their childhood that might mark them out as special. Certainly, there was nothing about the circumstances Thomas Basil Clarke was born into that hinted at what lay ahead of him.

Yet from an early age, Clarke was undoubtedly different. For his parents, this difference lay in his musicality: while still a toddler he would play tunes by ear on the family piano and sing songs in local shops in exchange for sweets. The historian, on the other hand, may be more likely to see his early wanderlust – as a young child he boarded a train on his own that took him as far as Manchester and a few weeks later sneaked onto a steam boat at Blackpool – as the reason for the extraordinary course of his life.[1]

But for Clarke himself, what gave him the strong feeling of being set apart from other children was the fact that he only had one eye. The disfigurement bestowed him with a kind of celebrity, as children would be either sympathetic because of the incorrect assumption that having an empty eye socket must be painful, or curious to discover how the eye had been lost. Clarke himself never learned the truth of what had happened because he had been too young to remember and his parents would change the subject whenever he asked about it. He was not, though, about to let his lack of knowledge on the subject detract from the attention it brought him and he would invent far-fetched stories about it; one particularly fanciful version was so heart-rending that it reduced a pretty classmate to tears and led to an invitation to her house for tea.

The loss of an eye never caused Clarke any great difficulties, though it did mean that at the age of six he had to endure having a glass eye fitted. The trau-matic memory of an elderly man with shaky hands trying to fit lots of different glass eyes to find one that was the right size and colour would stay with him for the rest of his life. It was the ones that were too big that were worst, causing Clarke to cry out in pain as the old man tried to push them into the socket. Eventually, his father ended the ordeal by opting for the more expensive option of having some specially made.

His new glass eye only added to Clarke's local fame, with people regularly stopping him in the street to ask to see it. He was usually happy to oblige, though it proved an expensive form of showing off as his inability to keep a firm grip meant that, as he later wrote, 'more than one dainty sample of the shaky-fingered old gentleman's fragile wares has gone tinkling to the pave-ment to smash into a thousand fragments'.

His disfigurement may have made him feel special as a young boy, but his experience of the education system led to him feeling singled out in a less pleasant way. His father was passionate about the importance of education – he paid for lessons with a local teacher just so that he would be able to talk to his children about their studies – and when Clarke reached the age of eleven he was sent to Manchester Grammar School as a day boarder.

It was a standard of schooling his family could barely afford, but the money they spent on it was largely wasted. His first day got off to a bad start when the teacher told the class that 'all Clarkes are knaves' and then proceeded to publicly ridicule his attempts at Latin. This humiliation set the tone for a school career in which Clarke defied authority as much as possible and was haunted by what he described as an 'indefinable but never-easing load on the mind and bleakness of prospect before me'. Not surprisingly, this resulted in an inconsistent school record. He enjoyed sport and music, both of which he showed a real talent for, and he managed to show some academic promise by coming second out of fifteen boys in Latin in his first two terms, and top of his form in physics at the age of fourteen. But at the same time as he was excelling at physics, he had fallen to twenty-first out of twenty-two boys in Latin and even in English, the subject most closely associated with journalism, he finished bottom of his form in both the summer and winter of 1894.[2]

Even half a century later and with a successful career behind him to insulate him against the memory of it, Clarke would still feel bitter about the way he was treated on that first day at Manchester Grammar School.

'I find it difficult … to look back with anything but contempt on the man who could so self-satisfiedly knock the heart and zest out of a small ill-taught boy,' he wrote. 'I can see now that this teacher had a disastrous effect on my school life and character.'

Given how focused Clarke's father was on his children's education, it is not surprising that he was disappointed by Clarke's attitude towards school and Clarke later admitted that 'it must have nearly broke his heart to see me frittering away opportunities'.

***

For reasons Clarke never discovered, his father had a visceral loathing of the banking profession that was so intense he would often refer to a job in a bank as a kind of shorthand when talking about professional and personal failure. When he was given news about Clarke's rebellious attitude at school, for example, he would warn him that 'I shall certainly see you with a pen behind your ear perched on a banker's high stool one of these days, my boy'. So it was with a sense of shame that, on leaving school at the age of sixteen in the summer of 1896, Clarke took a job as a junior clerk at a Manchester branch of Paris Bank Limited,[3] although his acceptance of it was as much to do with the modest working hours giving him time to practice music as it was the result of his poor school record. His father did not live to see what would have been, to him at least, Clarke's disgrace. He had died the previous year.

Clarke hated the job in the bank, finding it not only boring but also physically exhausting because it involved carrying heavy bags filled with ledgers and coins. There were, though, other things to occupy his mind. As well as playing for Manchester Rugby Club, in 1897 he started a long-distance degree in music and classics at Oxford University that gave him the chance to study under Sir John Stainer, best known for his arrangements of Christmas carols such as *God Rest Ye Merry, Gentlemen*, and Sir Hubert Parry, who composed the popular hymn *Jerusalem*. There is no record of Clarke completing any exams during his time at Oxford; he would later claim that he dropped out as a result of his father's death,[4] though this seems unlikely as his father had actually died two years before he started his degree.

Perhaps the real reason was that he was unable to mix the demands of a degree with a draining full-time job, though the work at the bank did become easier when he was transferred to a small branch where his manager was the only other employee. As well as the work not being as physically tough, he discovered that he and his manager shared a mutual love of Gilbert and Sullivan and they eased the boredom by inventing a game where one man would sing a line and then the other would have to sing the line that came next. It may have passed the time, though Clarke later admitted that 'these little interludes, though cheery enough, were hardly conducive to accuracy of work'. Eventually, he was transferred again to another branch and his relationship with his new manager was much less amiable; he was fired after responding to the manager's rebuke that he was an 'impudent young man' by telling him that it was preferable to being 'a foolish old one'.

A job at the City of Glasgow Assurance Company in Manchester followed, but this proved no more successful in instilling in him a love of banking and he left after a year, complaining that he found it 'uncongenial'.[5] With no job apart from a part-time position as an organist in a local church, he started sending music he had written to publishers in the hope of becoming a professional composer. He even tried his hand as a travelling salesman by trying to sell sheet music of a song he had previously had published at his own expense. Called 'Morning Song', it was a poem by the nineteenth-century poet Allan Cunningham that Clarke had set to music. Though he never made his money back on it, the expense was justified some years later when he was walking past a house and felt a great thrill when he heard it being played on the piano inside.

It was around this time, on 14 April 1902 and with Clarke now twenty-two, that his sweetheart Alice Camden gave birth to a baby boy they called Arthur. The arrival of their first child meant Clarke's need for a job was all the more pressing, and so when Arthur was just under a year old Clarke travelled to London for the first time to try to secure a job playing piano at a West End theatre. He was unsuccessful, but during his stay in the capital he met a German man who was looking for people to teach English in Germany.

Clarke was initially sceptical, not least because his inability to speak German made him question how useful he was likely to be, but his prospective employer assured him this would actually be an advantage and so Clarke took a boat to the Netherlands and then travelled on by train to Hirschberg in Germany. There, he made his way to the Bokert Academy, an establishment whose rather grand-sounding name belied the fact that it was based in a small house, and met its French proprietors, two men called Bokert and Prunier who Clarke took an instant dislike to.

Perhaps surprisingly, there was actually a job for him there, though shortly after he started work he began to wonder how Bokert and Prunier were able to afford his wages given the small number of students he taught. He was right to be worried; before long his employment came to a bizarre end, and one he came to believe was engineered as a pretext for getting him off the payroll, when Prunier accused him of knocking on doors in the town and running away.

In the confrontation that followed, Clarke gave Prunier a 'flat-handed clout' and Prunier retaliated with a kick to the head that Clarke described as a 'dangerous little sample of the "savat" fighting for which you have always to keep a bright lookout when exchanging fisticuffs with a Frenchman'. Though the kick was sufficiently powerful for Clarke to think 'it would probably have broken my jaw had it landed', he managed to catch his opponent's heel and the momentum of the kick, aided by a shove from Clarke, sent Prunier onto his back, smashing a glass door in the process. Bokert, who had been watching the fight, left the room and returned a moment later with a gun and shouted at Clarke to 'allez'.

'I have done many silly things in my life,' Clarke later wrote, 'but I have never yet argued against a revolver.'

He left, though he did return later to demand his unpaid wages. He threatened to go to the police if they refused and they eventually gave him the money they owed him, though only after deducting the cost of a new pane for the glass door.

Clarke's fight with Prunier is the first known example of the violent temper that would be a feature of his adult life, but it was not his only confrontation during his time in Germany. No one could accuse him of picking on easy targets. He was later told he was lucky not to have been put through with a sword after he insulted a drunken German officer, while on another occasion he was attacked and thrown in a river by some German soldiers he had got into an argument with.

After the job at the Bokert Academy ended, he continued teaching English but made such little money that he could barely afford food and cigarettes, and paying for a ticket back to England was out of the question. But things improved when he got a job playing piano in a small theatre orchestra and he also started giving swimming lessons. Then when the summer ended and it got colder, he ended the swimming lessons and started teaching boxing instead.[6]

He described living abroad as a 'good life', though it was more the existence of a young man without responsibilities than that of the father of a young son. Perhaps it was the inevitable fulfilment of the need to travel that he had felt since he had boarded the train to Manchester as a toddler. Certainly, looking after children on her own was something that Alice would have to get used to. She and Clarke would go on to have a large family and his thirst for adventure, probably more so than the demands of his career, meant he spent long periods of their upbringing away from home.

★★★

Clarke returned from Germany near the end of 1903. The time spent apart from Alice does not seem to have diminished his feelings for her and as soon as was practically possible, on 4 February 1904, the couple married in Altrincham.

A plain-talking woman, Alice responded to his proposal of marriage with a characteristically matter-of-fact 'all right'.[7] There is little doubt that her acceptance of his proposal was one of the best things that ever happened to Clarke. Alice would be a loving – and sometimes long-suffering, given the amount of time he spent overseas – companion until the end of his life and was known for her kindness and warmth.

One of the witnesses at the wedding was Clarke's friend Herbert Sidebotham, who he had met at Manchester Grammar School when Sidebotham had been a prefect and Clarke had thrown a screwed up piece of paper at his head. Sidebotham's decision that calling Clarke a 'silly ass' was sufficient punishment proved to be the start of a lifelong friendship.[8]

Sidebotham, a scholarly figure who studied at Balliol College before becoming a journalist for the *Manchester Guardian*, would go on to play an important role in setting the direction of Clarke's career. But Clarke's initial brush with journalism happened entirely by accident.

He had re-joined Manchester Rugby Club shortly after arriving back in England and was at an evening team selection meeting in a local hotel when three men who had just finished dining began to sing a quartet from Gilbert and Sullivan's Mikado. Clarke realised that the lack of a fourth singer meant most of the chords were missing a note and, knowing the words to Gilbert and Sullivan's oeuvre almost by heart, he decided to join in. When the song was finished, one of the men thanked Clarke and in the conversation that followed Clarke mentioned he was a church organist. The man replied that he was editor of Manchester's *Evening Chronicle* and asked Clarke if he would be interested in writing an article for it.

Clarke had never before even considered the possibility of a career in journalism and, somewhat shocked by the offer, asked what the article should be about.

'Write it, my boy, on good music and how to appreciate it,' the editor replied. 'Just write me a column saying simply and clearly what you feel you'd like to say about it to someone you liked. And ... let me have it in my office by ... noon tomorrow without fail.'

It was already gone 10.00 p.m., so Clarke went straight home and, fuelled by large quantities of coffee, began to write. He finished the first draft of the article at around 3.00 a.m. but he was not happy with it and so started again from scratch. The sun was already beginning to rise when he completed the second draft but he was still not satisfied and so began a third and, it transpired, final draft, which he delivered to the *Evening Chronicle*'s office with just 10 minutes to spare before the midday deadline.

Clarke bought the newspaper the following evening and saw his work, barely changed, on the page with the initials 'B.C.' at the bottom. It gave him a huge amount of pride. 'That "first-article-in-print" feeling,' he later wrote, 'surely it is the masculine counterpart of the feminine "first baby" complex.'

But as great as the sense of achievement he felt at becoming a published writer may have been, it might not have led anywhere had it not been for Sidebotham. The two men were taking an afternoon walk about two weeks later when Sidebotham suddenly turned to him.

'Basil,' he said, 'I've been thinking that we ought to make a journalist of you.'

Clarke was surprised and more than a little flattered that someone he respected as much as Sidebotham thought he had the potential to be a successful journalist. As well as boosting his confidence, Sidebotham also gave him the practical advice that he should get six months' experience on any newspaper that would have him and to then come and see him.

After a number of unsuccessful requests to newspapers in London to employ him on a nominal salary, Clarke managed to persuade the Conservative Party-supporting *Manchester Courier* to give him a job as a volunteer sub-editor.[9] On his first day, he was given an article and told to 'revise and shove some headlines on that'. And that is broadly what he did for the next six months, learning the skills of sub-editing as he turned journalists' raw copy into the finished product that appeared on the page. He found that he enjoyed life in a newspaper office. He appreciated the fact that his fellow sub-editors were experienced and talented newspapermen and he also relished the camaraderie of life in a newsroom; after working through the night he and his colleagues would often stop at the pub on the way home for a 6.00 a.m. pint of beer.

By the end of his placement, he had made a good impression on his colleagues. His news editor praised his 'enthusiasm, assiduity, and adaptability' and congratulated him on the speed with which he had learned the sub-editors' craft.[10] He was offered a permanent job but Sidebotham advised him to aim higher and to instead apply for a position at the more prestigious *Manchester Guardian*.

After years of aimless drifting, Clarke's career finally had a sense of direction. His family life was going well too, as he and Alice had another son, John, who would be followed a year later by a third son, whom they named Basil Camden but called Pip to distinguish him from his father.

Fatherhood suited Clarke; his friend James Lansdale Hodson later wrote that 'if a lad had the choosing of a father I cannot think of a better one than Basil'.[11] There is no doubt he adored his children. 'What married people get, in return for not having kiddies I don't know,' he wrote home to Alice on one of his many trips abroad, 'but whatever it is, whether fame or position or pleasure or merely wealth, it is jolly well not worth it.'[12]

Notes

1 These two stories come from a previously unknown draft of Clarke's autobiography. It has been kindly given to the author by the Hartley family, who are descendants of Clarke. Its contents are being made public here for the first time. Unless otherwise stated, all the personal information about Clarke's early life comes from this source.
2 Details of Clarke's academic record were previously unknown and are from correspondence between the author and Manchester Grammar School's archive.
3 *Financial Times*, 10 March 1923, p.4. This article contains details, not included in Clarke's autobiography, of his start date at the bank.
4 Manchester University: John Rylands Library, A/C55/4/500, letter from Clarke to the *Manchester Guardian*, 14 June 1904.
5 Ibid.
6 *Sheffield Independent*, 5 September 1919, p.4.
7 Basil Clarke, *Unfinished Autobiography*, p.63.
8 *Daily Sketch*, 20 March 1940, p.10.
9 Manchester University: John Rylands Library, A/C55/8, Letter from Clarke to C.P. Scott, 11 October 1916.
10 Manchester University: John Rylands Library, A/C55/1, Testimonial from F.J. Coller, news editor of the *Manchester Courier*, to Clarke.
11 James Lansdale Hodson, Home Front, London, 1944, p.118.
12 Letter from Clarke to Alice, Amsterdam, 11 October, 1915. This letter is the property of the Hartley family and its contents are being made public here for the first time.

2

The Manchester Guardian

T he *Manchester Guardian* started life in 1821 as a local newspaper that was established in response to the Peterloo Massacre and the campaign for the repeal of the Corn Laws. But by the time Clarke applied for a job there, it was already a significant way through the transformation that would see it move to London in 1964 – it truncated its name to *The Guardian* – and with the advent of the Internet become one of the most widely read English-language newspapers in the world.

A large part of the reason for this remarkable journey was C.P. Scott, the legendary editor and owner who presided over it for more than half a century and whose bust is still displayed at *The Guardian's* office today.

It was Scott that the 24-year-old Clarke wrote to in 1904 to apply for a position as a sub-editor, supplementing his application letter with references from the *Manchester Courier* and from Herbert Sidebotham.

'I have formed a very high opinion of Mr Basil Clarke's natural ability,' Sidebotham wrote, before going on to describe him as 'a man who in my opinion might go very far indeed in journalism' because of his 'remarkable capacity for assimilating new ideas' and the 'industry and zeal which come from keen interest in his work'. Clarke had 'direct personal knowledge of men and things,' Sidebotham added, along with 'ready sympathies and a keen eye for the human side of current affairs'.[1]

Given such effusive praise from an existing member of staff, it is not surprising that Clarke got the job. He joined the sub-editors' room and, though he found the work challenging and the expectations high, he quickly grew to love the idealistic spirit that characterised the *Manchester Guardian* and which still sets *The Guardian* apart from the rest of the newspaper industry today.

He also enjoyed being surrounded by men of intelligence and culture – his fellow employees included the future Poet Laureate John Masefield – and he welcomed the chance to work with some of the finest sub-editors in the country. And he and his fellow sub-editors got on so well that they would often go walking together or play tennis before work, and on Saturday evenings would congregate at one of their homes.

As well as editing the work of others, Clarke also got the opportunity to write occasional articles of his own. In 1906, for example, he wrote about his experience of having to appear at Manchester Police Court after his chimney caught fire and the smoke attracted the attention of a zealous police officer. The article was a whimsical account of what it was like to stand in the dock alongside criminals, and it was so well-received that he got a bonus that not only covered his fine but left him with enough money to take Alice for tea and cakes at a fashionable restaurant.[2] The tone of the article was mostly light-hearted, but it also contained the alarming admission that when a 'small-eyed youth with lower jaw hung like a rag' arrogantly asked him why he was in court, 'an impulse seized me to dash him to the floor', suggesting that a steady career and a settled home life had not made Clarke any less combative.[3]

This and the other articles he wrote appear to have given him a taste for it and in 1907 he wrote to C.P. Scott to ask to switch to a reporting role. 'I might eventually go further as a reporter than as a sub-editor,' he suggested. 'Mr Sidebotham says that my individuality would have better scope.'[4] But Clarke, who found Scott a 'formidable and rather terrifying' figure,[5] was also careful to avoid creating the impression that he was unhappy with life as a sub-editor. 'I am very comfortable in the sub-editors room and have no reason for dissatisfaction of any kind,' he insisted. 'My relations with everyone are of the happiest and the work is quite congenial.'

The reply from Scott must have expressed concern about his lack of shorthand because, two days later, Clarke wrote to him again promising to 'make all the haste I can to become proficient'. 'Till then I could be given engagements that did not demand much verbatim note-taking,' he suggested. 'I might get along all right, I think.'[6]

This second letter was enough to secure him a reporter's job and if his lack of shorthand meant the appointment was a gamble, it was one that paid off. While the claim by one of his colleagues that Clarke was 'one of the *Manchester Guardian*'s most brilliant special correspondents'[7] may have been an exaggeration, he was certainly successful and became known for his descriptive writing ability in particular. When he visited Edinburgh for the first time to report on a rugby match, for example, he devoted as much space in his match report to describing his impressions of the city as he did to the rugby, including the memorable line that Princes Street was 'the vision of an architect not past his dreaming days'.[8] When the article was published, a Scottish colleague wrote to Clarke to congratulate him on it, joking that Clarke had done a better job of capturing the appeal of Edinburgh in a single morning than he had managed in his entire career.[9]

Equally, Clarke's news reporting style was clear and to the point, thanks in part to Sidebotham's advice to him that everything he wrote should meet three tests:

> Is that exactly what I meant to say, neither more nor less? Could any person – wise man, knave or fool – construe it to mean anything different from what I meant to say, either more or less? Could I have made it more easy for the reader to understand what I meant him to understand?

It was this diligence that led to him making a success of an interview with Ernest Rutherford, the Nobel Prize-winning physicist who later became the first person to split the atom. On meeting Clarke, Rutherford told him to 'ask me questions in schoolboy language and I will reply in schoolboy language', which suggested he did not have much confidence in Clarke's ability to grasp the finer points of his work. But the first draft of the article Clarke sent him to check its accuracy impressed him enough that he did not change a single word.[10]

As accomplished as Clarke's writing may have been, it was not something that came easily. One of his colleagues wrote:

> His stuff is clean and direct and is the product of great painstaking. I have known him to write and rewrite passages in his articles over and over again until he was satisfied with them. He once spent nine or 10 hours on a back-pager. They are usually very laborious but they succeed – they are finished and don't show the traces of his labour. None of his writing with us was ever spoiled by hasty or slipshod work: he is about the only man I ever knew who set out deliberately from nothing to become a good descriptive writer and succeeded out-and-out.[11]

★★★

As well as standing out for the quality of his writing, Clarke also had the resourcefulness and tenacity needed to be a successful reporter. For example, when the Midlands Railways Company refused to comment on rumours that it was secretly employing men to act as strike breakers, Clarke got a tip off from a railway worker over a pint of beer and, after a cross-country horse and carriage ride and a scramble up the banks of a railway line, he eventually found a camp where the men were staying.[12]

It was these qualities that led to a meeting with a future Prime Minister. David Lloyd George, who was then making a formidable reputation for himself as President of the Board of Trade in Henry Campbell-Bannerman's Liberal Government, was in Manchester to negotiate with striking cotton workers.[13] There had been no sign of an agreement and at 12.30 a.m. C.P. Scott appeared 'almost shyly' in the reporter's room – it was the only time Clarke ever saw him there – and told Clarke he did not want to leave for the night if Lloyd George was about to secure a deal.

'I hardly like to go home leaving him still at it,' Scott said. 'You'll never know what that amazing man will pull off or when he'll do it.'

So Clarke was sent to the hotel where Lloyd George was staying to find out if an agreement was likely to be reached that night. He arrived to find about thirty reporters waiting for news, but rather than joining them he asked at reception for Lloyd George's room number and, surprisingly, they gave it to him. So he went to the fourth-floor room and knocked on the door.

'Come in,' came a voice from inside. Clarke opened the door and was confronted by a man he later described as a 'little dapper secretary person' who he assumed was a civil servant.

'Who are you?' the man screamed.

Clarke explained he was a journalist.

'How dare you come into Mr Lloyd George's room?' the man shouted. 'How dare you?'

At this point, Lloyd George rose from the chair he was sitting in and walked across the room towards Clarke.

'What is it, my boy?' he asked.

Clarke told him how Scott had sent him to find out if an agreement was imminent.

'Tell him with my compliments that I don't think there is any chance whatever of that tonight,' Lloyd George replied.

He put a hand on Clarke's shoulder. 'My boy, don't be upset about what my colleague said as you came in,' he said. 'We've had a very tiring day. And my boy, you'll make a very good reporter.'

★★★

Clarke may have taken the rebuke from the civil servant in his stride, but another industrial dispute once again showed his pugnacity.

On the same day the *Manchester Guardian* published an article by Clarke that he admitted contained some 'very plain' comments about the employers in a dispute, he telephoned the company's chairman to get some more information.

'Are you the man who wrote that article about the strike in this morning's *Manchester Guardian?*' the chairman asked.

Clarke replied that he was.

'Well if you ever come within reach of me, I'll knock your bloody head off,' the chairman replied.

It is not especially unusual for journalists to be threatened with violence by those they write about and the normal response is to try to stay out of the person's way until they calm down. Instead, Clarke found the nearest taxi and went straight to the chairman's home to confront him.

He knocked confidently on the door, assuming that the chairman would not be a match for him in a fight. But when it opened he was surprised to discover that the chairman was a 'wild-looking, outsized Irishman'.

'I feared the worst,' he later recalled. 'He glared at me for some minutes, then he asked me to sit down ... and have some tea! And nothing was said, or done, about my head.'[14]

The two men ended up discussing possible solutions to the industrial dispute and Clarke put forward an idea for a compromise that might suit both parties. The chairman said he would submit it to his fellow employers and this promise gave Clarke another story as he broke the news of a 'possible way out'.[15]

★★★

While Clarke covered a wide range of subjects for the *Manchester Guardian,* his main interest was in aviation. The early twentieth century was a period of great technological advance and in no field was progress more exciting than that of powered flight. It had first been achieved by the Wright brothers in 1903 – the year Clarke had travelled to Germany – and the first powered flight in Britain was in 1908, the year after Clarke became a reporter.

Its combination of danger and sense of wonder meant aviation was well-suited to Clarke's descriptive writing style. Air travel may seem mundane today, but Clarke's description of French pilot Louis Paulhan negotiating strong winds at a hugely anticipated air show in Blackpool in 1909 captured the sense of awe the new technology inspired:

What a strange and admirable sight to see a man poising himself among the winds and sailing on that tempestuous highway perched only on the edge of certain square feet of canvas stretched on bars of wood, with emptiness in front and behind, and the wind whistling among the wires and struts which hold him together from destruction!

And all this vigilance in balance, all this battle with air currents, is carried on by a single lever moving every way at Paulhan's right hand. On the strain endured by one arm – and to move the planes when winds are against you is not done without some force – depends the safety of M Paulhan and his machine.[16]

It was this article that first brought Clarke to the attention of Lord Northcliffe, the owner of the *Daily Mail* and the man who had first suggested the idea of an aviation week to Blackpool Town Hall after being inspired by a similar event in France. 'We ought to have that man on our paper,' Northcliffe is said to have remarked about Clarke when he read it.[17]

★★★

On 12 July 1910, nine months after his article about Paulhan, Clarke attended an air show at Bournemouth. He probably saw the assignment as little more than another chance to showcase his descriptive writing skills, but it proved to be by far his biggest story for the *Manchester Guardian*.

Among those flying was Charles Rolls, the 32-year-old co-founder of the luxury car manufacturer Rolls-Royce. Aviation had by now replaced the auto mobile as Rolls's main interest, and shortly before the Bournemouth show he had become the first man to complete a non-stop double crossing of the English Channel.

A few days before the show, Clarke saw Rolls in a hangar in Wolverhampton and spoke to him as he worked on his aeroplane with a spanner.

'Making all tight?' Clarke asked him.

'Yes. Never take any risks that I can help. Would you?'

While careful preparation could minimise the risks, it could not eliminate them and Clarke would have known that all the pilots taking part in the Bournemouth air show were risking their lives in doing so.

One of the displays at the air show saw pilots compete against each other by trying to land their aeroplanes nearest to a given spot. On his first attempt Rolls landed 20 feet from the target, beating an effort by Claude Grahame-White by 10 feet. But rather than wait to see if this was enough to give him victory, Rolls decided to try to get closer still.

His second attempt began normally but started to go wrong when one of the bars of his aeroplane buckled as he lifted it to clear some railings. Clarke wrote in the *Manchester Guardian*:

His machine rose nevertheless and cleared the fencing. With its upward momentum too it rose on the apex of its curve. But the collapse of the hinder plane had destroyed the whole balance of the machine. Its weight was thrown all to one end. You might compare it almost to a seesaw when the boy at one end has fallen off. Instead of completing the curve through the air with a glide to earth the machine reached the apex of the curve only, and then, after an instant's dead pause, turned tail up and fell sheer down, Rolls on the front of it.

Rolls landed clear of his aeroplane and Clarke was one of a group of people who joined hands to form a circle around him to stop the crowd that swarmed forward. The line of arms was broken to let stretcher-bearers through, and as they lifted Rolls onto the stretcher Clarke noticed a man holding a camera.

'With cold deliberation he pointed it at the brown stretcher sheet,' Clarke wrote. 'A fist dashed it from his grasp, and an angry heel crushed through screen and plates.'

Rolls was carried away but he was already dead. He had become the first British fatality in an aeroplane accident. In itself, this was a tragic landmark in the history of British aviation. Combined with Rolls's celebrity, it meant Clarke had witnessed one of the biggest stories of the age unfold in front of him.

In the *Manchester Guardian* the following day, Clarke began his article with the understated power characteristic of the best news reporting:

> Mr C.S. Rolls, one of the two or three most capable and distinguished of British flying men, met with his death on the aviation ground here this afternoon.

> His aeroplane broke, and fell some thirty feet straight down, he with it, and the fall killed him instantly. He dropped clear of his machine and lay still on the turf on his back, his neck broken. It was a terrible sight.

Clarke's article went on to describe his impressions of the tragedy:

> One cannot forget the sounds of that accident. First the crackling of the rear plane as it broke. It was like that of a fire of damp sticks. Then the grinding of wood and iron, the dull pizzicatos of snapping wires, and their whirring hiss as they curled up like watch-springs.

> Then that tense moment of stillness, more terrible than noise, when the biplane lay poised in the air deciding whether to fall tail first or head. The head had it. The planes turned slowly from horizontal to vertical; then down came the whole thing, thud on the grass ... Tail and head, skids, sides, engine, and all lay in one low heap of wreckage, with Rolls beside it, his face to the sky, a hand palm upwards on his chest.[18]

It was a powerful piece of journalism, and when he left the *Manchester Guardian* it was this article that C.P. Scott mentioned when he said some kind parting words to him.[19]

★★★

Witnessing Rolls's death did not diminish Clarke's interest in flying, and soon afterwards he even played his own small role in aviation history when the actor and aviator Robert Loraine invited him to travel with his mechanics in the support car that helped him prepare for the first ever flight over the Irish sea.[20]

Then just a month later he was given the chance to experience flight for himself when Claude Grahame-White, one of the pilots Rolls had been competing against when he died, offered to take him up in his Farman biplane.

Clarke accepted the offer but as he walked onto the airfield near Blackpool he noticed the wreck of an aeroplane lying 100 yards away. It brought back images of 'Rolls quiet on the grass', which he later recalled was not the 'most comfortable prelude to a first essay in flight'.

When he reached the aeroplane, he found Grahame-White already inside, looking up at the sky.

'Bit windy, don't you think?' Grahame-White said. 'Suppose I just try first by myself and see what it's like, you don't mind?'

'Just as you think,' said Clarke, trying his best to sound relaxed as he felt the strong wind against him and imagined how much more powerful it would be high above the ground.

'Very well, then,' said Grahame-White, impressed by what he thought was Clarke's nonchalance. 'Clamber up behind.'

Clarke climbed over Grahame-White's shoulder and sat behind him, where he took comfort from the illusion of control he felt at being able to see what his pilot's hands were doing.

'Quite comfy?' a man on the ground shouted at Clarke above the noise of the propellers.

Clarke made an affirmative gesture and the man signalled to four other men who were holding the back of the aeroplane. They released their grips and Clarke felt it begin to move forward. It rattled at first, but as they continued the rattling became steadily quieter until Clarke looked over the side and suddenly realised they were high above the ground. He wrote:

> At what point we left it I could not say, for I had felt no sudden heave upwards, such as an aeroplane seems to make in rising when seen from below. We were in the air. Yet nothing had altered. But for the fact that the wind was whistling past my ears and that the sound of the engine seemed much more remote than it

had been, there was nothing much to show that we were not still standing on the ground with the engine running. I found, however, on watching an earth-object for a moment, that we were rising at one steady angle. Yet so still and comfortable were things that the extraordinary fierceness of the wind seemed out of place. It was like having your head out of an express train window. It went like a brush over your head (I was without a hat), and forced a way like something solid into your mouth did you happen to open it ever so little.

They had been flying for a few minutes when the aeroplane tilted ominously and suddenly lost altitude. Grahame-White did not seem especially worried but was unhappy enough with the aeroplane's performance to take it back in to land. 'She's not pulling well,' he shouted to his mechanics when they were back on the ground. 'Just have a look what's up.'

Grahame-White climbed out and he and the crew worked on the aeroplane for about a minute. Then when he was satisfied he climbed back into the pilot's seat and they were soon back in the air.

'By this time I had become more used to the inner life of the aeroplane and was able to take fuller notice of things further afield, of the crowds below, of the country and sea outside the aerodrome, my range growing ever wider as we mounted,' Clarke wrote. 'And I don't remember having the slightest concern as to the machine and its safety.'

As they flew over farms and fields, Clarke looked down on the earth below and in the article he tried to describe a feeling that had then only been experienced by a handful of people:

It is not in the distant prospect that lies the uniqueness of a flying machine as a view point. Were this all, a peep from a tower top would serve almost as well. It is the addition of motion to your height that makes your view point the rare thing it is.

And it is in the nearer rather than the remoter prospect that the strangeness of this view is to be noticed most. There was something very extraordinary, for instance, in watching a forty-foot pylon, with flag at its peak, gradually foreshorten and foreshorten till eventually, as we passed high over the top of it, it was nothing but a little white square with a red streak across it. In the same way a man of the crowd gradually dwarfed down till he became a pair of shoulders with an upturned face inset between them; a woman till she became just a black circle – a hat.

When it was time to land, Grahame-White turned off the engine and pointed the aeroplane downwards. They descended alarmingly quickly until they were only about 50 feet from the ground and then the aeroplane suddenly levelled off and they safely eased towards the ground.[21]

Looking back on his career towards the end of his life, Clarke would describe his three years as a reporter for the *Manchester Guardian* as 'the happiest of my journalistic life'. 'One was on tiptoes all the time, it is true,' he wrote, 'but surely it is the on-tiptoes moments of life and work that are the most worthwhile, memorable and pleasant.' Above all, he enjoyed working for a newspaper his fellow reporters were so passionate about, writing that 'no gathering of wom-enfolk ever discussed hats and fashions with more earnestness and zest than we of the M.G. Reporters' room discussed that mornings paper and one's own and one's colleagues contributions to it'.[22]

So when he was sounded out for a job with the *Daily Mail* in 1910, he was not particularly interested and responded with a salary demand he assumed would be prohibitively large.[23] But to his surprise, the *Daily Mail* agreed to pay him close to what he had asked for, along with the promise that he would never have to write anything that went against his political beliefs.[24]

Clarke accepted the offer. When he wrote to C.P. Scott to give his notice, he told him that 'if I am to do as well for my own kiddies as I was done by I must earn more money during the next 10 years or so'.[25] It was true that Clarke was now thirty and had four children to care for – Alice had given birth to another boy, who they called George, in 1908 – but he later admitted that 'it was not that I greatly needed more money and was short of it, or that I liked money unduly for its own sake'. Yet it was purely the prospect of extra money that made him leave the *Manchester Guardian*. Later in life, he wrote that he found it difficult 'to realise why that constituted an adequate inducement – a sufficient lure and bait to attract me from what I was fully conscious at the time was more of a primrose path than a "job of work"'.

As well as his sadness at leaving his beloved *Manchester Guardian*, he also felt trepidation at moving to the *Daily Mail*, which he regarded as 'more com-mercial and mundane in its editorial outlook'[26] and which had a reputation among journalists for 'not being too nice in its treatment of its staff'. But as brash and aggressive as the *Daily Mail* may have been in its editorial style, it was also phenomenally successful. He must have known that if he could meet the demanding expectations of his new job, it had the potential to take him to the very summit of British journalism.

Notes

1   Manchester University: John Rylands Library, A/C55/2, Testimonial from Herbert Sidebotham to Clarke.
2   Basil Clarke, *Unfinished Autobiography*, pp.65–6.

3 *Manchester Guardian*, 9 March 1906, p.12 (Clarke made it clear in his *Unfinished Autobiography* that he was the author).

4 Manchester University: John Rylands Library, A/C55/6, letter from Clarke to C.P. Scott, 19 April 1907. In his *Unfinished Autobiography*, Clarke wrote that C.P. Scott asked him to apply for the job after being impressed by his occasional articles. But there is nothing that suggests this from Clarke's application letter, and it is likely that, looking back at least thirty years later, Clarke misremembered what had happened.

5 Basil Clarke, *Unfinished Autobiography*, p.72.

6 Manchester University: John Rylands Library 127/84, letter from Clarke to C.P. Scott, 21 April 1907.

7 Tom Clarke, Northcliffe in History, An Intimate Study of Press Power, London, 1950, p.165.

8 *Manchester Guardian*, 21 March 1910, p.16 (Clarke makes it clear in his *Unfinished Autobiography* that he wrote this article).

9 Basil Clarke, *Unfinished Autobiography*, p.85.

10 *The Practice of Journalism*, Ed. John Dodge and George Viner, London, 1963, p.60. The reference to Clarke's interview with Rutherford was in a chapter entitled 'A Reporter's Memoir', by Maurice Fagence.

11 Manchester University: John Rylands Library, A/C55/9, Memo from William Percival Crozier to C.P. Scott, 15 October 1916.

12 Basil Clarke, *Unfinished Autobiography*, pp.74–5.

13 Sir Basil Clarke, A Reporter's Memories of Lloyd George, The Journal, Institute of Journalists, May 1945, p.62.

14 Basil Clarke, *My Round of the War*, London 1917, p.82. In Clarke's account the words 'head off' were preceded by a blank, to indicate a swear word without actually stating what this was. But he uses the word 'bloody' when relating the same story in his *Unfinished Autobiography*.

15 Basil Clarke, *Unfinished Autobiography*, pp.78–9.

16 *Manchester Guardian*, 20 October 1909, p.7. The article is not by-lined, but his colleague at the *Daily Mail*, Tom Clarke, made it clear that Clarke was the author (Northcliffe in History, An Intimate Study of Press Power, London, 1950, p.165).

17 Tom Clarke, *Northcliffe in History, An Intimate Study of Press Power*, London, 1950, p.165

18 *Manchester Guardian*, 13 July 1910, p.7. The article is not by-lined, but in a letter to C.P. Scott some years after he left the *Manchester Guardian*, Clarke reminds him about kind remarks Scott had made about Clarke's coverage of the tragedy.

19 Manchester University: John Rylands Library, A/C55/8, Letter from Clarke to C.P. Scott, 11 October 1916.

20 Basil Clarke, Unifnished Autobiography, pp.86–7.

21 *Manchester Guardian*, 16 August 1910, p.7.

22 Basil Clarke, *Unfinished Autobiography*, p.83.

23 Ibid.

24 NUT, Schoolmaster, 10 October 1935.

25 Manchester University: John Rylands Library, A/C55/7a, Letter from Clarke to C.P. Scott, 26 October 1910.

26 *Daily Sketch*, 20 March 1940, p.10

3

The Daily Mail

By any measure, the career of Lord Northcliffe was remarkable. Hugely ambitious and driven, he became editor of *Bicycling News* at the age of just twenty in 1885 and within six years he owned a string of magazines and newspapers.

It was the launch of the *Daily Mail* in 1896 that established him as one of the most influential people in the country. Filling a gap in the market for a serious newspaper that cost less than the penny journals, by the turn of the century it had become the best-selling newspaper in the world[1] and confirmed Northcliffe's reputation for possessing 'the common mind to an uncommon degree'.[2]

Northcliffe went on to establish the *Daily Mirror* – founded as a women's newspaper in 1903 but quickly re-launched with a pictorial focus when that concept failed – and to buy *The Times* and *The Observer*. So when Clarke accepted a job at the *Daily Mail* in October 1910,[3] he was joining not just a successful newspaper but a media empire that exerted massive political influence. During the First World War, for example, the Government was so concerned about the effect of the Northcliffe press on public opinion that it offered Northcliffe control of the Air Ministry in the hope of making his newspapers less critical. He not only rejected the offer but did so in an open letter published in *The Times*.[4]

Clarke became the *Daily Mail*'s Special Commissioner for the North of England, a title that Clarke took pride in, though he later admitted his role was 'nothing more than [a] plain, honest-to-goodness reporter with perhaps a little higher salary'. He and Alice were, though, now well-off enough to afford a servant.

Clarke was based at the newspaper's Manchester office and James Lansdale Hodson, who worked there with him, later remembered how they were 'crowded into a small room, and about six o'clock we were commonly busy writing, tearing out hair, and eating tea and toast and marmalade, and asking one another how the devil you said this or that.'[5] Being based in Manchester meant he did not have to relocate, which suited Clarke because he enjoyed Manchester's social life – he was president of the Manchester Press Club and played piano on club nights[6] – and just after he joined the *Daily Mail*, on 17 January 1911, Alice gave birth to another baby boy. They named their fifth successive son James, though he was known by his middle name of Alan.

★★★

After a relatively quiet first couple of months at the *Daily Mail*, Clarke was at home on Christmas Eve when he received a call from the office. There had been a train crash in Cumbria in the early hours of the morning and his news desk wanted him to go there immediately.

The Hawes Junction rail disaster, in which twelve people died after a collision between two trains, may have disrupted Clarke's Christmas but it presented him with the chance to show his new employers what he could do.

He arrived at the remote crash site after a pony trap ride of many hours and saw three engines lying on their side. Clarke looked on the track and found charred coins and a watch. 'The pockets in which they had rested, the fingers which had last touched them – of these things there was no trace,' he wrote in the *Daily Mail*. 'The fire had done its work too well for that.'[7]

He was lucky enough to find some local people who had seen the tragedy unfold and were able to describe it articulately. The timing of the disaster also worked in Clarke's favour. The fact that newspapers did not publish on Christmas Day meant that instead of rushing to send the bare facts in time to meet that evening's deadline, Clarke was able to check into a local hotel and take his time in weaving what the eyewitnesses had told him into an account of the disaster that was so vivid that it is still difficult to read even a century later.

He described the desperate effort to rescue passengers trapped inside as the fire slowly worked its way through the carriages. A man he spoke to had tried to rescue a passenger trapped between two seats, hacking at the carriage with an axe as the man he was trying to get to pleaded with him to hurry. Then an explosion forced the rescuers back and they watched helplessly as the man cried out. With his last words he asked them to find his mother and tell her what had happened. 'She lives in Ayr,' he shouted. Then there was silence. Clarke also told the story of how a 5-month-old baby was trapped under a fallen seat. Its parents were unable to get it out and they became increasingly terror-stricken as the fire progressed towards them; the carriage with the baby still inside was eventually destroyed by the fire as its mother stood screaming helplessly at the door.

Clarke wired his article through to London on Christmas morning and the following day the *Daily Mail* printed it almost in its entirety. He arrived at work that day to find telegrams of congratulation from Thomas Marlowe, the editor of the *Daily Mail*, and from Northcliffe, who offered Clarke his 'heartiest thanks' for ensuring the *Daily Mail* outperformed its rivals on such a big story.[8]

Clarke later believed his coverage of Hawes Junction 'did me more good professionally than any other reporting I ever did' and that day the *Daily Mail*'s Northern Editor predicted to Clarke that 'before a month is through the Chief will want to see you in London'. He was almost right; just over a month later he was invited to Northcliffe's London home.

His first meeting with Northcliffe, though, did not get off to a good start. The press baron irritated Clarke by complaining that he had been working on too many 'petty-fogging' assignments and Clarke began to lose his temper and forcefully defended the quality of the work he had been doing. But Northcliffe assured him he was not criticising his work but instead suggesting his skills were not being properly used.

'You must go about with a bomb in your fist, my boy, and make them give you better work,' Northcliffe told him. 'A bomb in each fist if need be and let them have it till they give you better work.'

When they had finished talking about work, Northcliffe asked Clarke about his family and was astonished to learn Clarke had five sons.

'Five boys!' he exclaimed, violently slamming his fist down on the arm of his chair. 'God, if I'd only one!'

The fact of Clarke's large brood stuck with Northcliffe and in the years that followed he would often mention it when they saw each other.

'How many squirrels in your house now, Clarke?' he once shouted to him as they passed in the office corridor.[9]

Northcliffe was a controversial figure whose forceful personality would eventually descend into megalomania, but Clarke's first meeting with him marked the start of a good relationship between the two men and Clarke would later write that 'he was always good to me, always appreciative for a boss, very human and extremely generous'. This relationship would only have been aided by the role Clarke played in the *Daily Mail* campaign, very much the brainchild of Northcliffe himself and now one of the most celebrated campaigns in newspaper history, to improve the nutritional quality of the nation's bread by promoting the benefits of a 'standard' wholemeal loaf over the more popular white bread. Clarke travelled to Dublin and managed to secure the support of the Earl of Aberdeen, who was then Lord Lieutenant of Ireland, for the campaign.[10]

Northcliffe also seems to have been as impressed by Clarke's willingness to stand up for himself as he was by his ability to procreate. It was because of this combativeness, together with his physical bravery, that Northcliffe began calling Clarke 'my pig-headed Lancashire man' (he had actually been born just inside Cheshire).[11] While not a sobriquet Clarke would have chosen, he came to appreciate that it was a term of endearment that alluded to the fact that Northcliffe thought he could be relied on for even the most difficult assignments.

For example, it was Clarke who was chosen to report on the August 1911 rioting in Liverpool, from which he later wrote that he was lucky to escape with 'nothing worse than a kick on the leg, some barked knuckles, and a split straw hat'.

Clarke arrived in the Scotland Road area of the city to see children swearing at 'a miserable slut of a woman as shabby as themselves', though when they noticed Clarke they stopped shouting at the woman and began to throw stones at him, 'egged on by the smiles of their filthy mothers who sat in hordes with armsful of babies on every doorstep'.

Characteristically, Clarke seems to have responded to the provocation he received in Liverpool with physical violence. His reports on the riots did not contain any details of fights he took part in, but his detailed knowledge of the 'Liverpool hooligan's' approach to fighting strongly suggests that he made good use of his boxing skills:

> He is not much good with his fists, but he can kick and he can sling stones with a remarkable speed and accuracy. He prefers to fight with stones because it does not entail action at too close quarters. Corner a hooligan in some act of violence and he will first threaten you with some blood-curling threats and then he will whine horribly and drag the deities and many holy things into his protestations of innocence. Thump him, as he deserves, and you give him the one punishment he hates, namely physical pain.

★★★

Hawes Junction was not Clarke's only notable story from his early days at the *Daily Mail*. He also secured a significant scoop about David Davies, a habitual criminal whose cause was taken up by David Lloyd George (by now the Chancellor of the Exchequer) after he was jailed for thirteen years for stealing just 2s. Partly because of Lloyd George's intervention, Davies was released and given a job on a farm on condition that he did not leave it without permission. He absconded after just two days.

The authorities kept the location of the farm secret, presumably because of the embarrassment the episode caused. Yet Clarke managed to find it about 10 miles from Wrexham and he persuaded a woman who lived there to give him an exclusive interview. She told him Davies had been as 'quiet spoken and jolly as could be, with his tales and his talk'. He had spent the Saturday evening sitting by the fire telling his hosts stories from prison but then they had woken the following Monday morning to find him gone.

As well as producing news stories, Clarke also wrote articles that gave an insight into the minutiae of daily life in the North of England. He introduced his readers to the concept of 'barrow walks', where men challenged each other to see who could push a wheelbarrow 30 miles most quickly. He also reported on how men would bet on who could walk furthest while carrying a brick between their thumb and forefinger, which quickly became excruciatingly painful.[12]

As fascinating as some of his early articles at the *Daily Mail* were, others were less impressive. He wrote an exceptionally dull piece, for example, about how Liverpool's streets were superior to those in London, while an article about the Unionist movement in Liverpool was embarrassingly sycophantic.

He also wrote two articles about the Chinese communities in Liverpool[13] and Cardiff[14] that, from a modern perspective, make uncomfortable reading. They pandered to racial stereotypes and made dark references to allegations against the Chinese community, particularly in Liverpool, that are never spelled out but that hint at child prostitution. The two articles about the Chinese communities did contain some interesting details, such as the story of how the police could not understand why a particular Chinese shop in Cardiff was so popular until they finally learned that its Chinese sign simply said: 'Gambling now on'. He also affectionately recorded how the Chinese sailors 'add a keen zest to life ashore by getting, as sailors will, into the maximum of mischief in a minimum of time'.

But perhaps Clarke's most memorable early article for the *Daily Mail* – for all the wrong reasons – was about which city had the most attractive women.

Apparently undeterred by the 'filthy mothers' he had seen there during the riots, he thought Liverpool was the most obvious candidate because of its 'abnormally high standard of beauty' and so started writing the article. As he typed, a friend looked over his shoulder and saw the title. 'The city of fair women?' he asked. 'Why, that must be Liverpool, surely!'

This suggested to Clarke that he had stumbled upon a subject on which people had strong views, so he decided to delay writing the article to give himself the chance to consult more widely. He debated the issue around the fire of his club with a barrister, a story-writer, a playwright, two artists and several journalists. All but one of them agreed Liverpool was a worthy winner, with the only dissenting voice being that of an Irishman, who made the case for Dublin.

'I do not think there is much doubt about it,' wrote Clarke, his tone all the more authoritative now that it was supported by market research. His article set out the evidence for why this was the case:

People who know the English cities well and have eyes that notice must be struck by the high average of beauty that is to be seen in Liverpool – an average not equalled even in London itself. Walk along Bold Street or Lord Street or Church Street when the wives and daughters of all the Mersey-side suburbs are busy shopping … or stand on the long promenade by the riverside some Sunday morning and judge for yourself!

And judge not for mere shapeliness of feature alone, but for the clearness and texture of skin, for brightness of eye and lustre of hair; also for grace and ease of movement; also – and this is important – for that happiness of expression which does as much to enhance a pretty face as its finest features. In these things I think you will admit the women of Liverpool pre-eminent.

If he had stopped there, the article would have been embarrassing but harmless. But Clarke then went on to explain why women in other cities did not come up to Liverpool's exacting standard.

London fared reasonably well. Its women had 'a more sophisticated beauty,' Clarke wrote, but were let down by their tendency to follow fashion too slavishly:

The hair of London's beauties is suspiciously sensitive to prevailing fashions. Let copper-red be the fashionable hue of the moment and London's prevailing hair colour is copper-red. I have often been struck by the unanimity of London's hair colours.

Nor is there about London's women quite the same free buoyancy of carriage, and certainly there is not the same joyousness of expression. The beauty of London is more serious, more careworn; just a little more tired and deep-eyed than that of Liverpool.

As for Dublin, the men around the fire agreed its women were certainly beautiful but they ranked it second to Liverpool because of a lack of diversity, with too many of its women being of the same oval-faced and dark-eyed type. Women in Birmingham and Glasgow were dismissed as 'undistinguished' and Aberdeen's women were 'bright-cheeked' but were marked down because Scotland 'will not clothe its beauty well'.

But Clarke saved his harshest criticism for Manchester, despite the fact that it was virtually his home town. 'Manchester, alas! is low down in the scale,' he wrote. 'Beauty is rare. Forms are often too thin and angular, complexions murky. And in a futile effort to atone for lack of beauty, Manchester women are often tempted to overdress – a sad result.'[15]

It could have been this article that C.P. Scott was reading when he unkindly remarked to colleagues at the *Manchester Guardian* that they had had 'a very lucky escape' in Clarke leaving them.[16] But while Scott may have been unimpressed by his former employee's work for the *Daily Mail*, Northcliffe had no regrets about acquiring his services.

'I have been following your interesting work with great pleasure,' he wrote to him in December 1912.[17] But as pleasing as Northcliffe may have found his output, within two years of him writing this note a combination of Clarke's sense of initiative and events that were without precedent in world history would ensure his work would become infinitely more interesting.

Notes

1 J. Lee Thompson, *Northcliffe: Press Baron in Politics 1865–1922*, London, 2000, p.69.
2 Kevin Williams, *Read All About It! A History of the British Newspaper*, Abingdon, 2010, p.126.
3 Manchester University: John Rylands Library, A/C55/8, Letter from Clarke to C.P. Scott, 11 October 1916. In it, he refers to having left the Manchester Guardian 'six years ago this month'.
4 J. Lee Thompson, *Northcliffe: Press Baron in Politics 1865–1922*, London, 2000, p.292.
5 James Lansdale Hodson, *Home Front*, London, 1944, p.118.
6 *Manchester Guardian*, 24 February 1913, p.3.
7 *Daily Mail*, 26 December 1910, p.6
8 Basil Clarke, *Unfinished Autobiography*, p.92.
9 Ibid., pp.92–5.
10 Ibid., pp.98–100.
11 Ibid., p.97.
12 *Daily Mail*, 28 October 1913, p.8.
13 *Daily Mail*, 16 March 1911, p.6.
14 *Daily Mail*, 23 March 1911, p.4.
15 *Daily Mail*, 24 February 1914, p.4.
16 David Ayerst, *Guardian – Biography of a Newspaper*, Collins, London, 1971, p.421.
17 Northcliffe to Clarke, 8 December 1912. This is the property of the Hartley family and its contents are being published here for the first time.

4

Canada

On 25 April 1914, Clarke boarded a boat at Glasgow that was bound for Quebec; in doing so he became one of the many Britons who made the journey to Canada during the early part of the twentieth century.

In 1913, an all-time record 400,000 people arrived in Canada and as many as 40 per cent of them were from Britain,[1] a huge increase since the turn of the century when barely 1,000 Britons a year had made the journey.

This increase was partly because charities such as the Salvation Army actively encouraged poor people to move there, but was also because of the Canadian Government's establishment of an immigration office in London in response to political pressure to retain the country's British character.[2]

While Clarke's fellow passengers were attracted by the chance to improve their standard of living or to escape the rigid class system of home,[3] he was travelling undercover as part of an assignment. In 1911, he had written an article about the effect that a 'great outpouring of people' was having on rural communities in Scotland and had reported that the attraction of emigration to Canada was so great that while he was in Forfar a Canadian agent told him: 'If I could only grant free passages, I could half-empty Scotland tomorrow.'[4]

Clarke's article was so well-received that he was asked to write about the subject again. The only follow-up he could think of was to travel to Canada to see the conditions that awaited emigrants for himself and discover how easy it was for them to find work; the *Daily Mail* editor Thomas Marlowe took the idea one step further by suggesting that he assume the identity of a work-seeking migrant and write about his own experiences of trying to get a job there.[5]

The assignment was personally approved by Lord Northcliffe, who agreed to pay Clarke £50 (about £3,000 today)[6] towards expenses and three guineas (about £60 today) for each article.[7] And so, going under the name of a Scottish labourer called Ben McLaren, he bought a ticket in the steerage section of the boat.

The steerage section was least expensive and so had the most basic amenities, which included having to share a cabin with three other men. Despite the lack of privacy, his article about the voyage emphasised the camaraderie that existed among the passengers. He reported how they entertained themselves by playing the bagpipes, accordion and fiddle, while the Russian passengers used reed instruments to play what he described as 'melodies that are no doubt accounted cheerful in Russia'.

When they were not playing music, he reported that he and his fellow migrants braved the cutting winds to play rounders and football on the decks from early in the morning until bedtime. The energy expended during the day's activities apparently meant he found himself 'consulting the day's menu on the steerage wall with an interest that ordinary life at home but seldom provokes'.[8]

But while his article may have presented the experience as one of wholesome enjoyment, a letter he wrote to Alice from the deck of the ship painted a rather different picture. In contrast to the conviviality depicted in his article, the letter accused his fellow passengers of being 'the limit for swinish habits' because of the unsanitary condition of the toilets, while he also complained about the 'filthy hogs' who when suffering from sea sickness would 'spew all over themselves rather than lean forward or go to the side'. The ship stewards, meanwhile, were 'unshaven dirty beasts whom you see mopping up spew one minute and half an hour later waiting at table in the same filthy white coats'.[9]

His complaints may have simply been a case of Clarke venting his spleen at a low moment when his thoughts would have naturally turned to how much he was missing his family. But a more likely explanation for the discrepancy is that his aim of producing a light-hearted and cheery series of articles about Canada led him to gloss over the less pleasant aspects of it.

★★★

Ten days after leaving Glasgow, the boat arrived at Quebec and Clarke stood on the deck as it pushed past blocks of ice to get to the dockside. Once it had docked, he and his fellow passengers said their goodbyes to the staff and made their way to the customs and immigration desks. Clarke went through customs unimpeded and then while waiting for the immigration check he noted how the 'very miserable' attitudes of the Russians and the Poles contrasted with that of the Britons among the group, who saw the time spent waiting as 'ripe … for the exercise of humour and mirth' and began to sing 'some song about "bonny lasses" and the like'.

When his turn came, Clarke was given a cursory medical examination and then walked on to a wicker gate where immigrants had to show how much money they were carrying. The minimum required for entry was $25 and many of the men did not have this much and so had to borrow from their fellow passengers. Clarke had no such problems and showed the man the $100 he had with him. 'Pass on, Rockefeller,' the man said with a smile. From there, he picked up his luggage and walked on to the railway station, free to travel anywhere in the country.[10]

Clarke had already decided to travel west to Winnipeg, which he had heard was a kind of 'clearing house' for labour in Western Canada and so would be a good place to start his search for work.

He bought his ticket and then after buying some supplies he boarded the train, where he was pleased to find a friendly atmosphere among the passengers, as people would sit talking to each other and invite each other to their section of the train for tea. 'Thus you entertained and were entertained,' he wrote. 'Things were primitive sometimes, and perhaps you put milk into your tea direct from the Swiss milk tin without any mediation from a spoon. But whatever the method, the hospitality itself was always of the heartiest.'

But while the days on the train were quite enjoyable, for many passengers the nights involved sleeping on bare boards. Sometimes in the night Clarke, who slept on a sleeping rack suspended by chains over his seat, would look out to see his fellow passengers 'turning and twisting in all contortions of discomfort' and hear people moaning in pain. Two French couples on the train suffered so badly that they took to adding brandy to their morning coffee and seemed surprised when Clarke rejected their offer to join them. But he had had the forethought to buy a straw mattress and a rug in Quebec, which made the journey much more comfortable.

> Truth to tell – and I felt almost a brute for it, I slept a solid eight hours every night, and woke up in admirable fettle. I felt that had I only been able to get my clothes off and to have a bath I could have lived in a colonist car for a month.[11]

After travelling through the frozen landscapes of Quebec and Ontario for two days and three nights, the train reached Winnipeg.

Despite arriving in the early hours of the morning, a few thousand people were waiting to greet the train and Clarke was fascinated to watch the reunions of husbands and wives and children and parents, many of whom had not seen each other for years.

'I shall not forget the sight,' he wrote. 'Tired and train-weary you might be, but this strange pageant of reunion fascinated one's mind and eyes and goaded one into interest. Right by me on the station as I left the platform was a man virtually enveloped in loving kith and kin. A wife's arms were around his neck, her cheek against his; children, big and little, were around his legs and body – all striving to hug him at once.'

He noticed two young women in the crowd who were looking anxiously at the faces of the passengers as they passed. Eventually, a young man touched one of them on the arm and she turned and looked at him coldly.

'Aren't you Jenny Mylrea and Mary?' he asked them with a smile.

'Yes,' said one of the women, still looking severe.

'Well don't you know your brother Alec?' the man asked.

'He had been a lad when they left home to go to Canada,' Clarke wrote. 'Now he was a big fellow with a moustache. Great moments in life are moments such as those meetings at Winnipeg Station, moments you can envy people. "Tears of joy" I always thought as something of a figure of speech till then – when I saw them.'

Once the crowd had dispersed, Clarke found a room in a Main Street hotel for a dollar and a quarter a night. The next morning he woke planning to start his search for work but he was told by local people that the 'great freeze-up' of December 1913 had lasted into the New Year and that the continuing cold weather – it had been the worst winter for a decade – meant there was little work for artisans and labourers. The result was that Winnipeg's streets were filled with unemployed men who spent their days sitting in saloons or standing idly in the street.

Most of these men, Clarke discovered, came from places such as Germany, Russia and Scandinavia and so spoke little English. They were known locally as 'earth-shifters' because they were only qualified to do the lowest form of labour and they had lost out to the English speakers when it had come to allocating the winter jobs.

Clarke could understand why it might be difficult for non-English speakers to find work, but he had little sympathy for the few British among them. 'Amusing as some of them were, I came to the conclusion that they were rather a shiftless crew, likely to be out of work in any country,' he wrote. 'They "cadged" for money and tobacco, hung about the bars waiting for drink, and had as their chief topic of conversation the rottenness of the country.'

Undeterred by the unappealing state of the labour market, Clarke began looking for a job. [12] His first stop was the local employment office, but he found a long queue outside it. Then he saw a passing streetcar that had an advert with the words: 'Arbor day. Citizens, clean up'. Clarke thought this would probably involve tree planting and tidying the city and so, thinking there might be work available, he headed to the town hall. He had guessed correctly; the town hall was hiring men to clean up Winnipeg's suburbs and a crowd of some 500 men had gathered to try to get a job.

Clarke approached an official. 'Any chance of a job, boss?' he asked, having been told this was the standard phrase used by men seeking work in Canada.

The official looked him up and down. 'You'll do,' he said eventually. 'Go inside the hall.'

He had managed to find a job in under an hour. 'I felt a little guilty in taking this work when so many men were in greater need than I,' he wrote, 'but I had come as an emigrant – to get work; to keep my head above water; and what is the virtue in getting work if you wait till everyone else is served?'

Clarke joined a team led by a large Yorkshireman with a big moustache who told them to meet at 7.00 a.m. the following Monday morning. But when the day came, Clarke was the only worker who did not have a shovel and a rake. He worried he might be sacked for not having tools but the Yorkshireman explained that he would not need them because his was to be a management role.

'We're to work in two gangs,' the Yorkshireman told him. 'I'll take one half the bunch and you are to take the other. You've got to keep 'em moving good.'

'I was immensely tickled,' Clarke later wrote. 'I, a foreman, who had never handled anything heavier than a pen for a living in my life!'

The Yorkshireman took six men and left Clarke with the rest. It was only when the other group had gone that Clarke realised none of his group spoke any English. They were tasked with clearing old timber, cans and other rubbish from the land near the railway, but first Clarke had to work out how to communicate with them. None of the men understood him when he spoke in English or French, though he had more success when he tried German. But the language barrier was not his only problem, as he quickly discovered the men did not like hard work and would slowly walk long distances just to pick up a single stick. In the end, he found the only way to get them to work at a reasonable pace was to set them an example by joining in himself. By midday he was so tired he 'could willingly have gone to sleep on the grass where we stood' and by the end of the day his back and thighs ached unbearably.

When he woke at 5.00 a.m. the next morning his body felt stiff and sore and when he looked outside he saw it was raining, which meant he spent the day working in soaking wet clothes. Then the following day he and his team had to work in such muddy conditions that at times it was a struggle just to move their feet.

Despite the toughness of the work and the poor attitude of his team, Clarke clearly made a good impression, as on his sixth day he was recommended for a permanent job. He was told he would be able to advance quickly if he did well, with the potential to become a clerk or a sanitary inspector. Meanwhile, another man who had heard him speaking German arranged a trial for him as a correspondence clerk with a firm of dealers.

But instead of taking these jobs, Clarke decided to move on. He had proved that it was relatively easy to find work in Winnipeg. Now he wanted to see if this was also true for the rest of the country.

***

From Winnipeg, Clarke headed west to Calgary. But while the aim of his assignment was to experience the life of an ordinary emigrant, there was nothing ordinary about Calgary in May 1914.

On 14 May, shortly after Clarke arrived in the city, he was sitting in the common room of the Third Avenue boarding house where he was staying when a young Scot ran into the room, shouting that oil had been discovered. 'I can see him now,' Clarke later wrote, 'with his knotted woollen jacket of brown and green, his arms aloft, and his bright blue eyes sparkling with excitement and delight.'

A wave of euphoria swept the city following the announcement of the discovery of oil, as many of its inhabitants, even those in menial jobs, had been investing in oil companies over the previous few months and so made large amounts of money almost overnight. That evening, Clarke and his companion went into the city to see the reaction to the news, which he reported in the *Daily Mail*:

> I saw men shaking hands wildly for minutes together, others whooping with delight, others actually skipping and dancing in the street … One may see scenes such as this in England perhaps on a "Cup-tie" night in some chance footballing town, or possibly on a racecourse when the favourite has got home, but I never remember anything of the sort to have been set afoot by a commercial project – and a speculative one at that.

The next day Clarke heard there had been a surge in interest in oil company shares. Shops that usually sold clothes or sweets suddenly became oil share exchanges and in many cases people queued out of the doors of shops to buy shares.

Clarke thought there must be employment opportunities in this and he bought a shirt and collar and made his way through the crowds outside a real estate office that was promoting an oil company. Once he had managed to get inside, he saw that the clerical staff could not process the shares quickly enough to keep up with demand.

'You want another clerk?' he asked a man who seemed to be in charge.

'Ya,' the man replied, hardly looking at him. 'There's a pen and things. Sit at that table and make out receipts.'

Clarke got straight to work and sat processing the shares for hour after hour. He was so busy that at mealtimes he would eat a sandwich from a paper bag with a pen still in his other hand.

He earned 14*s* (about £40 today) for his first day's work and thought he was likely to be offered a permanent job. But he had heard that share salesmen were making 5 per cent commission and so thought this might be an even better chance to make money. He set himself up as an independent street broker, which involved being approached by people who wanted shares in a particular company and then finding someone willing to sell at the right price. The deals were made in an atmosphere of confusion, with no one seeming to know the exact price of a share at any given moment and the same shares being sold for different prices at the same time.

As hectic as being a street dealer was, it proved easy money. On Clarke's first day he made £12 (about £1,000 today) and the following day made another £7. One of his customers was an Englishman who suggested Clarke get a stockbroking license, promising to recommend him if he did so.

'But for a fidelity to my work, I, an immigrant without friends or influence here, might have been permanently established in Calgary now as a stockbroker,' he wrote. But he recognised that Calgary's oil boom was an exceptional situation and therefore unlikely to give a meaningful insight into the job prospects for those emigrating from Britain[13] and so after two days he gave up street dealing and once again began looking for work. It did not take him long to find a job at a receiver's office and on his first evening he was set to work changing light bulbs, a task made more difficult by the fact they were too high to reach even if he stood on a chair. But determined to make a good impression, he was able to change the bulbs by putting one chair on top of another and then climbing on top of them. 'I was agreeably surprised that I broke neither the globe [bulb] nor my neck,' he wrote.

After fitting the bulbs, Clarke spent the rest of the evening filling in share certificates and did well enough to be offered more work. He did another shift and then the next day worked solidly from Friday morning right through to Saturday night. By the time he had finished his marathon shift, he had been promoted to the share transfer department and after two days there was offered regular work.

Clarke declined the offer, mindful that he was in Canada to find work rather than to keep it. But his employer was insistent. 'I don't want to lose you,' he said. 'I've got another job. I want a safe man to look after a confectionery factory. It's in the creditors' hands and they are running it. He would have to take charge on their behalf and see that their interests are looked after.'

Despite not wanting permanent work, the appeal of running a sweet factory was too great to resist. So barely a month into his stay in Canada, he was in charge of a factory that produced chocolate, sweets, chewing gum and ice cream. He could smell the vanilla from the glass office where he worked, while he had the added perk of having to sample the ice cream every morning to check its quality. Yet as much as he enjoyed his new job, he soon gave it up to work on a ranch some miles outside Calgary that was owned by William Munro, a farmer who supplied the factory with cream.[14]

At the ranch, Clarke shared a shack with two other working men and, on seeing the shack only had two beds, he realised he would have to share a bed. His two room-mates were Charlie Sample, a thick-set Canadian with cold green eyes and a brick-red face, and Warren Stretton, an Englishman who Clarke described as 'a good thirteen stone of bone and muscle'. As he shook hands with Stretton, Clarke got the feeling he had seen him before and Stretton also thought Clarke seemed familiar.

'Kind of feeling I've met you already,' Stretton told him. 'Never happened to be in Burton-on-Trent, did you?'

Clarke replied that he had been there once to play a rugby match.

'For which club?'

'Manchester Rugby Club.'

'Why, that's it,' said Stretton, grabbing Clarke's hand and shaking it again. 'Why, I played against you for Burton. I remember you now quite well. Why, you licked us that day by 40 points.'

Stretton's eyes sparkled at the memory of it and Clarke found that he, too, began to remember details of the match. When they had finished reminiscing, Stretton found Clarke a clean towel and, noticing Clarke's overalls were torn, he offered to mend them. He also told Clarke he was welcome to share his bed.

'To play in opposition football teams will hardly constitute basis enough even for an acquaintance at home,' Clarke wrote, 'but after four years life on the prairie such as Stretton has lived, without seeing a soul from home, it may prove basis enough for a friendship.'

★★★

On his first evening at the ranch, Clarke and the other labourers dined with the family and then one of Munro's daughters played a record on the gramophone while another daughter accompanied it on the organ.[15] Then the next morning Clarke was woken at 5.00 a.m. for his first day as a ranch labourer and was asked by Munro's youngest daughter to chop some wood. She disappeared before he could ask her where he could find either an axe or some wood, though he eventually he found a large pile of wood in one of the ranch buildings and an axe in a bull shed that he had to push his way past a bull to get to.

Clarke had never chopped wood before; his first swing lodged the axe into the wood and it took him some two minutes to get it out. When he finally managed to do so, he inspected the wood and saw that he had barely dented it.

He carried on swinging away at the wood and before long he was wiping the sweat from his forehead and undoing the collar of his shirt. Yet all he had achieved was to criss-cross the log with shallow lines and so, feeling frustrated, he steadied himself to swing the axe as hard as he could. But instead of having any great effect on the wood, the impact caused the axe head to fly off and the axe handle to split. To make matters worse, he looked behind him to see Munro watching him.

'Good morning,' Clarke said weakly.

'Guess they burned only gas fires around your infant cradle,' Munro said.

The ranch owner walked away, returning a few minutes later with another axe. Clarke apologised for breaking the axe, but was told not to worry and that it was just a question of learning the right technique.

'You'll split lots of axe-hafts your way, and, maybe, your back, but no wood,' said Munro, as he picked up a log from the pile, set it down and split it with one swing of the axe. He repeated the action again and again, each time explaining what he was doing. 'Hit them on the edge, son, not in the middle,' he said. 'Hit him in the middle and he's tough as a bronco. Hit him on the edge and he splits as smooth and crisp as the pie mother made.'

Once Clarke had learned the correct technique, Munro left him to carry on. He spent the next two hours splitting logs and then he and the other workmen joined the family for a breakfast of porridge and bacon and eggs followed by fruit with cream. After breakfast, it was back to work; after an exhausting day of physical exertion the workers and the family shared a meal and then played baseball on the lawn in front of the ranch house as the sun set.

It was not just at the ranch that the workers and the family mixed socially. One day Munro's daughter, Ethel, heard Clarke singing while he worked and was sufficiently impressed to invite him to join her church choir. Clarke did not feel he had much choice and so on the evening the choir met he washed and put on his Sunday suit and he, Ethel, and two other members of the choir squeezed into a buggy that a horse pulled the 6 miles to a small church at the junction of four prairie roads.

The choir was conducted by a 'severe, elderly lady' who joined in the singing herself and Clarke thought that this, together with the fact she seemed hard of hearing, was the reason they escaped the criticism the quality of their singing deserved.

The other members of the choir had no idea the ranch worker singing with them had studied music at Oxford University. But despite the other singers' comparative lack of ability, Clarke saw the humour in the situation:

Our organist, a rancher's daughter, with short, stubby fingers, had a cheerful innocence of "ear". If the right note was "at the top" any old chord was good enough to go with it. Her time, too, was miraculous. She most blithely played "God Save the King" … in "four" time while we sang it in the normal "three" time. Still, we, the choristers, sang heartily, if nothing more, and the choir-mistress, good old soul, sang on, and seemed satisfied with us.'[16]

It was partly the fact that the Munro family did not seem to regard the ranch workers as socially inferior that meant Clarke enjoyed working there despite how physically exhausting he found the work. But the end of his time in Canada was approaching and he regretfully told Munro he was leaving. After spending the previous few weeks looking at the Rockies in the distance, it was time to see them up close.

He took a four-hour train journey through the mountains and then, thinking it would be good to walk part of the Rockies on foot, left the train at a small station and after buying sandwiches set off in the direction of a railway camp he had been told was about 12 miles away.

After two hours without seeing another person, he met a man walking in the opposite direction who carried a small bundle tied in a carpet and rope on his back. The man told Clarke he had been unable to find work in Vancouver and so was heading to Calgary to try his luck there.

Clarke asked him if he planned to walk the whole way.

'Between jumps,' the man replied.

Clarke did not understand what he meant, so the man explained that he rode freight trains without having a ticket, which was an attractive option for men who did not have much money because prosecutions were rare and those who were caught were not usually mistreated.

Clarke gave the man one of his sandwiches and his companion was halfway through eating it when he suddenly stopped chewing to listen to a sound in the distance. It was a train that was struggling to make its way up a hill.

'I'll have to leave you,' he said, putting what was left of the sandwich into his pocket and running to a hiding place in some nearby rocks.

Clarke watched the man keep out of sight until the middle of the train was level with him. Then he emerged from his hiding place and stood next to the train, looking at the carriages and waiting for his chance before grabbing onto a bar with both hands and pulling himself up until he was lying on top of the carriage. Clarke saw his legs sticking out from the train for a few seconds and then he repositioned himself so he was lying in the middle of the carriage. Then he turned to look at Clarke, smiling and blowing him a kiss as the train carried him into the distance towards Calgary.

About another mile along the railway line, Clarke met two men who had been ejected from the same train. He shared a drink with them but declined their invitation to spend the evening with them as they swore almost constantly and he thought they 'were not quite safe company for the night time'.

After three more miles he arrived at the camp, where he found that work had stopped for the day. The workers offered Clarke some bread and bully beef, a slice of raisin pie and a mug of tea,[17] but any ideas he had of getting a job there were instantly forgotten when he noticed signs of an infestation of insects in the sleeping quarters. 'Small crawly things, and especially when associated with bedding or sleeping quarters, make me shudder,' he wrote. Instead, he walked to a nearby village and got a room in a hotel.

The next morning he boarded a train to Vancouver, where he found what he later described as 'the nicest job I ever had' as the pianist in a cinema. He was given a grand piano and allowed to play whatever he liked as long as it fitted with the mood of the film. But after several happy days, he was playing one afternoon when two pairs of hands suddenly came down heavily on his own, bringing his playing to an end with a loud and discordant sound.

'Are you a member of the Musicians' Union?' a voice asked him.

'No,' said Clarke. 'Go to blazes!'

The two men who had interrupted his playing grabbed his piano stool and carried it, with him still on it, out of the room. He protested angrily but on getting a proper look at the two men he saw that they were 'likely-looking young fellows whom it would probably have been a hospital job for me to take on single-handed'. So rather than fighting them, he appealed for help to the cinema manager, who had heard the noise and come to see what was happening. But the manager told him there was nothing he could do. Not seeing that he had any other options, Clarke offered to pay to join the union, but was told they were not accepting new members because they already had too many pianists who could not find work.[18]

★★★

It was around this time that Clarke decided to bring his Canadian adventure to an end. He bought new clothes, sold his working clothes and, remembering that Lord Northcliffe had once advised him to see America if he ever had the chance, he decided to travel back to the east coast through the United States, where he would sail from New York back to England. From Vancouver, he took a boat to Seattle, which he thought seemed like a cross between Liverpool and Paris and where he spent many hours on the quay watching the ships. He then travelled 230 miles east to the city of Spokane, where he watched 'with mingled thoughts' both male and female Japanese labourers working in the orchards.

From there, he travelled to Chicago, which he thought was a beautiful city, but was left with a feeling of 'appalling depression' after a visit to the stockyards and packing-houses because of the miserable working conditions there that he thought seemed to be robbing the workers of 'all heart, if not of soul'.[19]

Clarke's stopover in Chicago was some years before Al Capone became synonymous with the city, but it was already notorious for its organised crime. It was because of the reputation of Chicago's criminals that Clarke decided to visit the local prison so he could, as he put it, 'examine the genus at close-quarters safely immured'. During the visit, he gave a cigarette to one of the prisoners and after the man thanked him he asked Clarke to visit his sister to tell her he was in prison. Clarke found himself agreeing to the request before he had time to think about it and the man gave him an address where he would find his sister, emphasising that Clarke was not to give the message to anyone but her.

So later that night, Clarke walked into a drinking establishment he thought seemed 'very low' and asked at the bar if the prisoner's sister was there. The barman went to speak to another man and they whispered to each other for some time before the second man came from behind the counter and demanded to know why Clarke wanted to see his wife. Clarke replied that he had a message for her, but this only made the man angrier and as he started to shout and swear Clarke sensed the crowd in the bar beginning to turn hostile. When the man grabbed Clarke's lapel as if to hit him, he decided it was time to leave.

'I have not often since attaining what are called "years of discretion" deliberately dodged a fight with a man of reasonable size and weight,' he later wrote, 'but I funked this one – though from the feel of his arm as I wrenched it from my coat I believe I could have killed the fellow in five minutes. Still, the thing to do in this mob was to get out.'

With the other drinkers crowding in and jostling him, Clarke fell back on the skills he had learned on the rugby field by getting his head and shoulders as low as possible and charging towards the exit. He managed to get to the door and to make his escape, giving one of his assailants a 'beautiful hack on the shin' in the process and leaving another winded on the floor after hitting him in the stomach with his shoulder.[20]

Clarke then travelled from Chicago to Buffalo, which he dismissed as 'a rather grim town', before arriving in New York. There, he boarded the 24,000-ton liner that was to take him back to Britain.[21]

Throughout his time away, Clarke wrote regular articles about his experiences, with the first one appearing just over two weeks after he had set sail. His articles seem to have been followed with interest by Lord Northcliffe; following the publication of Clarke's account of his first day working in Winnipeg,

Northcliffe asked for the *Daily Mail* editor Thomas Marlowe to make it more obvious in the articles that Clarke was a member of the newspaper's staff.[22]

From quite early in the series of articles, Clarke made it clear he was impressed by the life Canada offered those seeking work:

> I know pretty well the conditions of work and living in most parts of Great Britain, and I can say safely that the Canadian artisan has the pull over his British brother in every way. He has a better home, better food, better clothes, better working conditions, and with all three advantages he has another – he has a better bank balance ...

> There is one other advantage which is hardly to be put in terms either of money or comfort. It lies in this. Here the worker is as good as anybody. Work, no matter how humble its kind, carries no stigmas ... Socially there is no difference between the bosses and his hired man.

Clarke wrote the last article of the series on the deck of the ship during his voyage home and in it he reflected on the opportunities Canada offered the working man. He pointed out that he had arrived there with no relevant experience and at a time when the job market was worse than it had been for many years. 'But bad as the times were they were good enough so far as I was concerned,' he wrote. 'I had never much trouble to get work. I was offered many more jobs than I could take.'

Even more than its employment opportunities, Clarke was impressed by Canada itself. 'Its vastness, its richness, the infinity of possibilities, my mind is still groping for a full conception,' he wrote. 'There is a true home there for a working man – a home with true freedom, with social fairness, with all that the country has both of wealth and of honours open to the man with the abilities and character to attain them. If I were a working man I would go far to get to a country like that.'

But just as Clarke had put a positive gloss on life in the steerage section of the boat from Glasgow to Quebec, his gushing portrayal did not give a fully rounded view of the welcome that awaited immigrants. He admitted some years later that he had noticed Canadians were 'a little fed-up' with English people because they 'found fault with the Mother Country's more-than-matronly slowness in moving, with her dullness to new ideas, with her passive resistance to improvements and up-to-dateness'.[23] This reflected the experience of the *Evening Standard* journalist H.R. Whates, who on arriving in Canada in 1905 had been told that 'the Englishman is too cocksure ... he thinks he knows everything and he won't try to learn our ways'.[24]

In fact, the English were held in such low regard that Clarke saw some job adverts that warned 'no Englishmen need apply', which meant that he may have been lucky the identity he had assumed was that of a Scottish labourer. And while he may not have faced any great difficulty in finding work, his background as a journalist meant he was always likely to find it easier than the average labourer. It was a point the *Calgary Daily Herald* made when it described his Canadian experiences as 'illuminating, but not altogether convincing', because as 'a trained newspaperman, he was possessed of a wit and ingenuity above the average, calculated to see opportunity where others less fortunately endowed would miss it, and to make opportunity where it was non-existent'.[25]

This final article marked the end of Clarke's first big foreign assignment and it was well-received, at least within the *Daily Mail*. Lord Northcliffe later told Clarke his Canadian articles were the 'cheapest set of page-fours we've ever had; good stuff too' and gave him a bonus for them, telling him to 'buy madam a new hat and those boys of yours a cricket bat'.[26]

But as entertaining as his articles may have been, as the series progressed their light and witty tone began to feel increasingly out of step with the mood of a Britain that was watching the rapidly deteriorating political situation in Europe with increasing alarm.

Clarke's final article about Canada was published on 29 July 1914, the day after Austria-Hungary declared war on Serbia in retaliation for the assassination of Archduke Franz Ferdinand a month earlier. On the very same page as Clarke's eulogising about the life awaiting emigrants to Canada, the *Daily Mail*'s leader column told its readers that discussions in St Petersburg between Russia and Austria offered a 'ray of hope, that … the extension of this conflict may yet be averted'. 'If they take a favourable turn the war may be localised,' it suggested. 'If not, Europe is face to face with the greatest catastrophe in human history.'[27]

As he sat in a deckchair on the promenade deck of the ship back to Britain, eating French soup under a blue sky and looking out onto a calm Atlantic Ocean, Clarke could hardly have imagined that the boat was carrying him towards that catastrophe – a war that would cause unimaginable death and destruction and change the course of his own life forever.

Notes

1   Bill Freeman and Richard Nielsen, *Far from Home: Canadians in the First World War*, Canada, 1999, p.6.
2   Valerie Knowles, *Strangers at our Gates: Canadian Immigration and Immigration Policy*, 1540–2006, Canada, 2007, pp.94–5.

3   Ibid.

4   *Times of India*, 31 May 1911, p.8 (quoting from Clarke's article in the *Daily Mail*).

5   Basil Clarke, *Unfinished Autobiography*, p.103.

6   This, along with all other financial equivalents included in this book, has been calculated using the National Archives Currency Converter, which can be accessed online at http://www.nationalarchives.gov.uk/currency/ (accessed December 2012).

7   British Library, Northcliffe Papers and Diaries, Add 62199/6, letter on behalf of Northcliffe to Thomas Marlowe, 15 April 1914.

8   *Daily Mail*, 13 May 1914, p.6.

9   Clarke to Alice, RMS Corsica, 23 April 1914. This is the property of the Hartley family and its contents are being published here for the first time.

10 *Daily Mail*, 20 May 1914, p.6.

11 *Daily Mail*, 21 May 1914, p.4.

12 *Daily Mail*, 3 June 1914, p.6.

13 *Daily Mail*, 8 June 1914, p.6.

14 Basil Clarke, *Unfinished Autobiography*, pp.112–17.

15 *Daily Mail*, 10 July 1914, p.6.

16 *Daily Mail*, 15 July 1914, p.6.

17 *Daily Mail*, 22 July 1914, p.6.

18 Basil Clarke, *Unfinished Autobiography*, pp.132–3. Interestingly, this was not included in his articles for the *Daily Mail*, whose only mention of his time in Vancouver was a day he spent feeding ice into an ice breaking machine for a fish packer.

19 *The Times*, 23 April 1923, p.17.

20 Basil Clarke, *Unfinished Autobiography*, pp.135–7.

21 *Daily Mail*, 29 July 1914, p.6.

22 British Library, Northcliffe Papers, Add 62199/9, Northcliffe to Marlowe, 3 June 1914.

23 *The War Illustrated*, 6 April 1918, p.159.

24 Valerie Knowles, *Strangers at our Gates: Canadian Immigration and Immigration Policy, 1540–2006*, Canada, 2007, p.95.

25 *Calgary Daily Herald*, 14 August 1914, p.6.

26 Basil Clarke, *Unfinished Autobiography*, p.97.

27 *Daily Mail*, 29 July 1914, p.6.

5

To War

As the boat from New York arrived at the Liverpool docks, Clarke scanned the faces of the waiting crowd and saw Alice and their young son George. As much as he had made a success of his time away, he had missed his family to an extent he later admitted 'can only be counted as a weakness' for a journalist, and he struggled to contain his tears as he watched George looking proud in his sailor's suit and Alice with her head bowed to hide her own tears.

He intended his arrival home to mark the start of a period of settled family life with Alice and their five sons, but this ambition was to be thwarted by world events as, in a tragic escalation, the dispute between Austria-Hungary and Serbia was joined first by Russia and then by Germany and France. Then on 4 August 1914, Britain declared war on Germany after it refused to guarantee Belgium's neutrality.

It was immediately clear that the declaration of war was not just the biggest story of Clarke's career but one of the most significant events in world history. And it had an immediate impact on Clarke in that a telegram arrived ordering him to report for duty at the *Daily Mail's* London office the following Monday morning.[1] Clarke went down on his own, with Alice and the children following him down shortly afterwards and, judging by the tone of a letter Clarke wrote to her, Alice was far from enthusiastic about having to relocate to the capital. 'We must go into it light-heartedly and in hope,' he urged her. 'Don't go and worry your little self or you'll make us both miserable.'[2]

It was probably while he was waiting for his family to join him in London that Clarke was in a hotel and heard a tune being played that he immediately thought notable for being 'energetic, tuneful and good'. It made such an impression on him that he found a piano in a nearby room and began to try to play it. He had just managed to work out the tune when the door of the room was suddenly opened and he was confronted by an angry looking young man.

'How dare you play that tune?' the man demanded.

'What's to prevent me?' Clarke snapped back at him. 'I shall play any tune I jolly well like to play and you won't stop me.' Then to further antagonise him, Clarke thumped out the first few bars of the tune again, as noisily as he could.

'Well, you've no right to play it,' said the young man.

Clarke repented that he could play whatever he liked.

'Well I do wish you wouldn't,' the man said, speaking more softly now. 'The darn thing is not published yet; and I don't want it all over the place before it is.'

He then walked out of the room, shutting the door quietly behind him. Clarke, perhaps feeling guilty for being so abrupt, stopped playing.

A few weeks later Clarke heard it again, this time along with the rest of the country. It was the tune to *Keep the Home Fires Burning* and he discovered that the young man he had argued with was Ivor Novello. The song became a huge hit and, perhaps more than any other song, encapsulated the mood of the nation at the outbreak of the First World War.[3]

★★★

On arriving in London, Clarke's first task was to represent the *Daily Mail* at the Press Bureau that was established at Charing Cross to issue war news and censor newspaper articles.[4] On his first day there, he met Lord Kitchener, the military hero who was made Secretary of State for War at the start of the conflict and who is best known today for appearing on the iconic 'Wants You' recruitment posters. They were introduced by F.E. Smith, the MP who was in charge of the Press Bureau, and Kitchener went to shake Clarke's hand but then pulled his hand away at the last moment, apparently thinking better of it.

'Very nice indeed,' Kitchener said awkwardly and then turned around and walked out of the room. Clarke thought Kitchener's comment was 'inane and fatuous' and it left such a negative impression of him that he later admitted: 'I thought him rather stupid'.[5]

Neither was Clarke impressed by the Press Bureau's facilities. He later remembered it as a place where 'chaos reigned', with up to thirty reporters crammed inside its cramped offices at any one time and the entrance crowded with messengers waiting to take news back to Fleet Street. The quality of its news rarely justified the disagreeable working conditions. 'The amount of news issued to the Press was of the smallest; its news value of the poorest,' Clarke wrote, adding that much of it amounted to little more than free publicity for the work of government departments. In fact, the Press Bureau became known among journalists as the 'Suppress Bureau' for the way it proved more interested in censoring news than in supplying it.

As well as collecting news reports, Clarke acted on the *Daily Mail's* behalf in negotiating with censors. It was on this that his time at the Press Bureau was most productively spent.

'One or two of the censors were pompous people who sought to cut down war news by every pretext,' he later remembered. 'Others were quite reasonable men who tried, each according to his lights, to deal fairly with "copy" – so far as the curious and ill-defined rules which had been given to them allowed them to do so. It is actual fact that news deleted totally by one censor would often be passed without question by his successor on the censors' rota.'

Clarke was at the Press Bureau on 15 October 1914 when he received a call instructing him to return to the *Daily Mail's* office immediately. When he got there, his news editor told him the Germans were about to take Ostend in Belgium and he wanted him to try to reach the city before it fell into enemy hands. After spending the first two months of the war protecting the work of his colleagues from the hands of the censors, here was the chance to finally experience war reporting for himself.

'Get there first and send us a tip-top story,' his news editor told him as he handed him the paper bag filled with 100 gold sovereigns that was to be his expense account. 'Run it to a page if you like.'

War reporting has always been one of the most challenging types of journalism, but working as a war correspondent in the first few months of the First World War was especially difficult because journalists were not allowed at the Front. According to the historian J. Lee Thompson, Kitchener had 'contempt for the press' because he believed newspaper coverage of Omdurman and the Boer War had damaged his reputation and this antipathy towards journalists was exacerbated when, barely a week into the war, a private remark he made to *The Times's* military correspondent was printed in the newspaper.[6] So he decided to ban war correspondents[7] and for the needs of newspapers to be met instead by establishing the Press Bureau and by appointing Sir Ernest Swinton – a British Army officer today best known for coining the term 'no man's land' and for his role in the development of the tank – as a kind of official war correspondent.

The fact that Kitchener thought these measures might be acceptable to newspapers shows he lacked any real understanding of the press, and unsurprisingly both Swinton and the Press Bureau proved to be inadequate replacements for newspapers having their own reporters in the war zone. One editor complained to Clarke that Swinton's work was 'magnificently uninformative',[8] while at the Press Bureau even F.E. Smith quickly became exasperated by Kitchener's uncompromising approach to journalists.[9]

He rather thinks he is in Egypt where the press is represented by a dozen mangy newspaper correspondents whom he can throw in the Nile if they object to the way they are treated,' Smith said.[9]

The *Daily Mail* was among the newspapers that criticised the ban on reporters, urging the Government to 'have the great courage to tell the British people the truth'.[10] Clarke was also personally opposed to what he believed was a 'short-sighted and brutal policy'. 'If Britons and Allies died in their thousands,' he wrote, 'their fathers, mothers and sweethearts, and the countries that gave them, were entitled to know some little of the work they did, for which they often lay down their lives.'[11]

The ban made it difficult for journalists to report from the Front, but it is to the credit of the independent-minded nature of the press that a number of reporters used their guile to get to the war zone and send news back to London. They would often be helped – or at least a blind eye would be turned – by members of the military who thought the restrictions were unnecessarily draconian, but the ban still meant that during the early days of the war the ability of war correspondents to evade capture was at least as important as the traditional journalistic skills of finding news and writing articles.

Dozens of British journalists were apparently arrested and sent home[12] and while most of them were treated well, being arrested was not without danger. One of Clarke's *Daily Mail* colleagues claimed Kitchener 'talked wildly about having the reporters shot if they could be caught',[13] while Philip Gibbs of the *Daily Chronicle* was held under arrest for ten days and warned that he would be put against a wall and shot if he dared to return to France.[14]

★★★

As Clarke received his instructions to go to Ostend, he still had on the bowler hat and Burberry coat he had worn to the Press Bureau that day. He had no idea how long he would be away, but there was no time to say goodbye to his family and so collected the small suitcase he kept packed in the office and headed straight to Dover. He would later wonder if he was the only journalist ever to have gone to war in a bowler hat.

At Dover, he was told that no boats were going to Belgium and so he took a cab to Folkestone to see if he could get one from there. As he waited at Folkestone, boats began to arrive that were crammed full of Belgian refugees and he spoke to some of them and was told that they had come from Ostend and that the Germans had already taken the city. He was too late.[15]

The German occupation of Ostend meant that completing his news editor's instructions was now impossible, so the obvious course of action was to return to the office. But instead, Clarke made a life-changing decision that was extraordinary both in its impetuosity and its recklessness. Despite having a young family, he was so eager to see the war for himself that he decided to risk both his life and the ire of his employers by taking the first boat heading to Europe and, using his bag of gold sovereigns to pay his way, see what he could of the war. He gambled that he might be able to retrospectively justify his decision to his newsdesk if he was successful in getting news back from the Front. And so began the three months Clarke spent as what he described as a 'journalistic outlaw', when he lived outside the law and survived day by day by using his cunning to evade arrest in what was a 'labour greater and more complex than anything I have ever undertaken in journalistic work'.

Clarke took a steamer to Calais, where he explained to a British Consul that he wanted to head towards the war zone but was told not to leave town unless it was to return to England. Clarke also tried to get French officials to help him but they all refused to give him a 'laisser-passer' to anywhere in the direction of the fighting.

'I chafed exceedingly at this refusal of Authority to yield me a chance of doing my work,' he wrote. 'Years of Press privileges in England had made me used to going where I wanted, and to being helped rather than hindered. And now to be stopped at the very outset of the greatest journalistic adventure!'

Clarke was determined to circumvent the intransigence of officialdom and he headed to the train station despite not having the necessary paperwork. But when he arrived he saw that its doors were guarded by soldiers with bayonets and so he instead decided to try to leave town by road. He had identified Dunkirk as a potential base because of its relative convenience for getting copy back to London and, given that it was just over 20 miles from Calais, he thought he might be able to walk there.

On the outskirts of Calais he came to a sentry box and the soldier inside refused to let him pass. Feeling tired and dejected, he stopped at a roadside café filled with soldiers. There, he struck up a conversation with a soldier who had been a printer on a French newspaper before the war and who remembered reading Clarke's work in the Paris edition of the *Daily Mail*. He said that he would shortly be leaving on a train that would stop at Dunkirk and agreed to help Clarke board the train. So Clarke headed back to the station, where he found that the door to the station restaurant was unguarded and he was able to walk through the restaurant and straight onto the platform, where the soldier was waiting for him.

They boarded a train full of French soldiers and as they made their way towards Dunkirk they passed such large numbers of Belgians either trudging in the opposite direction or crammed into trains that it seemed to Clarke to be 'a stream of outcast humanity as few live to see'.[16] He saw trains that were so overcrowded that men were lying on the roof or holding on between the carriages, and at one point he saw women being pulled out unconscious. 'All Belgium seemed to be pouring into France,' he wrote.[17]

When they stopped just outside Dunkirk's station, Clarke decided to leave the train in the hope of avoiding the officials who would be guarding the station. He grabbed his suitcase, said goodbye to the soldiers and jumped down onto the track. But there was no obvious way to get off the track and as he looked for an exit he noticed he was being watched by a soldier with a bayonet. Anxious not to attract any more attention, he started walking towards the station platform and then through to the main hall. Both exits were guarded by a soldier, a police officer and a ticket inspector.

Fearing he was about to be arrested or sent back to Britain, he noticed the refreshment buffet. To delay facing the officials, and reasoning that if he had to spend the night in jail then it would be better not to do so on an empty stomach, he went inside and got a meal.

And then his luck changed. As he ate, a train full of Belgian refugees arrived and the platform was suddenly full of hundreds of people who all seemed to want to get to Calais.

'There are no more trains tonight,' Clarke overheard a station official telling the refugees. 'Tomorrow, perhaps.'

Someone else said they had heard there were no vacant rooms left in Dunkirk that night and news of the accommodation shortage led to a rush towards the station door. Clarke realised this was his chance and so he joined the crowd that was now surging forward.

The pushing and shoving became worse as Clarke got near the exit and he was pushed onto a woman holding two small children. He lifted one of the children, a girl aged three or four, onto his shoulders to protect her from the crush, and just then the half-open station door suddenly burst open under the pressure of the crowd and Clarke was carried past the gesticulating officials and out onto the street. When he gathered himself, he realised he still had the girl but could not see her mother or the other child. He decided to wait for them and sat on his suitcase among the refugees outside the station and did his best to comfort the crying girl.

Half an hour later, the girl's mother finally appeared. She told Clarke she had been left inside the station when the staff shut the door and feared he had run off with the girl. Clarke could see she had been crying and she had also lost her luggage in the crush. He assured her she would find the luggage later but did not offer to help look for it because he thought going back inside the station might lead to his arrest. Instead, he bought some warm milk for the children and a coffee for the woman, which they drank sitting on the cobbled stones of the square outside the station. After finishing their drinks, they found a nearby furniture store whose owners let the woman and the children sleep on the floor for the night.

Clarke said goodbye and returned to the station square, wondering how he himself might be able to find a bed. But as he considered his options he was noticed by a police officer who asked him where he was from.

A wrong answer could have meant an abrupt end to his ambition of becoming a war reporter. So instead of answering the police officer's question, he asked him when the next train for Calais was leaving, hoping to change the subject. The tactic worked. The police officer gesticulated as he explained it would be impossible to get a train to Calais that evening and Clarke managed to further distract him from his original question by insisting that he was surely wrong and that there must be another train to Calais that night.

'You can never do more towards making the ordinary man talk and forget his original line of question than by contradicting him, and letting him convince you he is right,' Clarke later wrote.

The police officer ended a long explanation by concluding that Clarke's only option was to spend the night in in Dunkirk. Clarke thanked him for his advice and said goodbye.[18]

He then tried some of the nearby hotels but without success, though he eventually got talking to a barber's assistant who arranged for him to stay in a room in a nearby café. Clarke was pleased with the find. He thought the small number of guests there made it less conspicuous than a large hotel and he ended up staying there for some weeks before eventually deciding to leave after a police officer showed too much interest in him.

★★★

After spending his first night in Dunkirk, Clarke woke early the next morning and, intent on getting to the Front as soon as possible, walked to the gates of the city. There, he found a guard-house that was manned by soldiers and he confidently walked up to it and asked the soldiers the way to the nearby city of Furnes.

'Your laisser-passer, monsieur?' said one of the soldiers.

Knowing he did not have the correct documentation, Clarke ignored the request and instead repeated his question. But the soldier again demanded that Clarke produce his papers, more aggressively this time. Clarke took out the documentation giving him permission to go as far as Calais and showed it to the soldier.

'What is this?' the soldier asked.

At this point, Clarke decided to tell the truth and explained that he was a journalist who wanted to get to the Front but had not been able to get a permit. The soldier told him that he would not be allowed outside the city gates, but as they continued talking the tone of the conversation became friendlier. The soldier mentioned he had once lived in London and remembered reading the *Daily Mail*.

'If you let me through that gate,' Clarke said, sensing an opportunity, 'I'll undertake to show you some of my writing in the *Daily Mail* in a day or two from now. Possibly it will have my name on it and then you will know it is mine, but to prevent accidents I will tell you when I return through this gate tonight what I am going to write and then when it appears in the paper you will be certain.'

The soldier laughed. 'It is not allowed to leave the gate, monsieur,' he said in a conspiratorial tone, 'unless one wants to pay a visit to the cemetery which you see over there. The same road leads to Furnes and Ypres and the Front. If monsieur, now, would say he would like to see the cemetery, I should be able to let him through the town gate.'

Clarke said he would love to see the cemetery and the soldier winked at him and let him through.

By the time Clarke returned to the gate it was dusk and he had had his first experience of war reporting.[19] On Sunday, 18 October 1914, three days after leaving to try to get to Ostend, he sent his first despatch back to London. Just thirty-eight words, it appeared in the *Daily Mail* the following day:

> Severe fighting is taking place today near Nieuport (south of Ostend). Very heavy firing has been heard at Dunkirk since eight this morning. It is suggested that torpedo-boats or gun boats are being used in the canals.[20]

As Clarke became more settled in Dunkirk, the fear of arrest that initially 'weighed like a nightmare' on him gradually eased as he found that, with the exception of a few 'jacks-in-offices', the presence of journalists was generally tolerated. 'Many a soldier and sailor, officer and man, would go out of his way to help you, or would at least be friendly enough to ignore your presence in that prohibited area,' Clarke later wrote.[21] In fact, he often relied on friendly soldiers for news, and his presence was so open during a visit to a treatment centre for wounded soldiers in November 1914 that he acted as a translator between the medical staff and German prisoners.[22]

It was on the road to the Front that he most appreciated the benevolence of the military. The journey would take many hours on foot, so he was greatly relieved when he started being offered lifts in an assortment of military vehicles that varied from the back of a cart and horse[23] to officers' limousines.[24]

The problem of getting to the Front was just one of the ways Clarke found the most basic elements of journalism now presented new difficulties. One of the greatest challenges was getting stories back to London.

Of all the reporters who stayed illegally in France and Belgium during the early days of the war, it was Philip Gibbs of the *Daily Chronicle* who came up with perhaps the most audacious method of sending his stories home.

He would simply stride confidently up to an official courier and give him an envelope marked 'The Daily Chronicle, care of the War Office – URGENT', telling him to take it back to London. Once it arrived at the War Office in London, another messenger would unassumingly rush it to the *Daily Chronicle*'s office.[25]

To get his own stories home, Clarke used a telegraph office for urgent news, but he worried that this might alert the authorities to his presence, and so in most cases he gave his articles to a French courier or even to friendly British soldiers who were about to go home on leave.[26]

The challenges of war reporting could be more basic still. On one occasion, Clarke was stranded in a village for the night and could not find a light to write by; it was only when he gave the owner of the hotel he was staying in two francs as an incentive that she was able to find a candle for him. The next day he discovered it was the birthday candle of the young girl who brought him coffee in the morning and through her tears she told him she had planned to take it to church that day. Having already used half of it, Clarke confessed what had happened and attempted to make it up to her by using a knife to make the candle look new, albeit considerably shorter, and giving her a franc to put in the church's poor box.[27]

★★★

Clarke's first significant story during his time as a war correspondent came to him by chance a few days after arriving in Dunkirk. While waiting for a lift to the Front, he recognised one of the soldiers in a passing armoured car as Richard Reading, who six weeks previously had been editor of the *Sporting Chronicle* in Manchester and who was a fine singer who Clarke had accompanied on the piano during musical nights at the Manchester Press Club.

Reading recognised Clarke, calling for the car to stop and getting out and greeting him warmly. He told Clarke he had applied to join a force of British volunteers after, as Clarke put it, 'the war and a roving spirit and a hardy manhood all tugged at him'.[28] But he became impatient with how long it was taking to process his application and so applied to join the Belgian Army instead.

Reading was now a corporal in the Belgian Army and Clarke's article about him gave the impression that he was enjoying a romantic adventure. 'A machine gun, a steel-plated motor car, and all the roads in France and Flanders and all the Germans in them at his disposal,' Clarke wrote. 'What a life!'

The two men arranged to meet for lunch that day at Les Arcades hotel in Dunkirk, and Reading arrived at the meal with his lieutenant. 'You may think it odd, perhaps, that a corporal should lunch his lieutenant,' Clarke wrote. 'But you did not see those two. They were a pair. You could see it at once.

Deep black eyes, with the same quick flash in them; a laugh as ready and as careless as a boy's, humour, energy, "go" – all these things, the common possession of both men, bespoke as happy-go-lucky, stop-at-nothing a pair of dare-devils as ever went looking for mischief.'

As they drank Dubonnet over lunch, Clarke asked Reading how many Germans he had killed. 'Some other time,' Reading replied, apparently reluctant to talk about it. But when Reading left the room his lieutenant explained how the former sports journalist was 'mad to fight' and had recently chased two armed Germans across the Belgian countryside despite being unarmed. When he returned 45 minutes later, he had one of the Germans with him and was carrying the rifle he had taken from him.

Later, Clarke asked Reading how he had managed to capture the German soldier and Reading laughingly explained what had happened:

> I clean forgot I was unarmed. When one bolted into an inn I knew I'd got him. I thought I'd better make certain of one, so I let the other alone and went into the inn.

> The German was in the middle of the kitchen, blown and frightened to death, his rifle in his hand. The inn people were all around, very scared too. I went for him and grabbed his rifle. He was quiet after that.

Reading had finished his story, but Clarke pressed him to tell him what had happened next.

He laughed. 'Why, I stood him a drink.'

'To chase one's prey a mile,' Clarke wrote in the *Daily Mail*, 'catch him, disarm him, take him prisoner – and then buy him a drink! It was Richard all over.'

Reading's exploits, at least as Clarke described them, encapsulated the spirit of adventure-seeking that was typical of the attitudes of many Britons during the early part of the war.

In his article, Clarke reported that Reading was still using the German rifle he had taken because he preferred it to the one the Belgian Army had issued him with. 'It is a beauty,' Clarke quoted him as saying, 'as comfortable and easy-firing as you could wish. The only thing is, I've got to catch a German blighter or two every few days to keep myself supplied with ammunition that will fit it.'

'His ammunition supply has not failed so far,' Clarke wrote, as he ended the article. But just as the country's enthusiasm for the conflict would give way to weariness and grief in the face of the reality of modern warfare, Reading's own war was about to come to a sudden and violent end.

Less than a week after their lunch, Reading and his comrades got out of their armoured car at what appeared to be a quiet turn in the road and were ambushed by German soldiers. Four of Reading's colleagues were able to get back into the car, but with his legs having been riddled with bullets – twenty were later removed from his body[29] – Reading was unable to get inside before it drove off. He did, though, manage to cling to its back springs and this probably saved his life, though both his legs were broken as he was dragged along the road for 600 yards before his colleagues were able to pull him into the car.[30] Despite having sustained horrific injuries, he still displayed apparently inexhaustible reserves of cheeriness; a nurse who treated him later remembered how he was smoking a cigar and laughing as he was carried into hospital.[31]

This was not the end of Reading's remarkable story. He spent the next two years in hospital before moving to Australia to continue his recuperation. But the ship carrying him was sunk by a submarine off the coast of India and his legs were further damaged in the blast. He and some fellow passengers managed to get into a lifeboat and it took them over seven hours to get to the coast, from where they endured an arduous trek before finally reaching safety.[32]

Reading became known as the 'Man Who Would Not Die' and those who knew him in Australia spoke of the 'indomitable courage' with which he bore his injuries, as he worked first as an oyster farmer and then as a sub-editor in Melbourne. Following his death in 1929, Clarke wrote a tender newspaper tribute to him:

A beautiful man was Dick – a beautiful body, a handsome face, and the simplest and kindliest of minds ... It was good to have known him, and if the best riches of life lie in the happy memories one has stored up in the course of it, then I and a good many journalists are the richer for Dick's days among us.[33]

The way Clarke's lunch with Reading introduced him to his lieutenant is an example of how Clarke built a network of contacts, as the next morning he saw the lieutenant again and was offered a lift in his armoured car. It was an uncomfortable journey because the car was already full and so Clarke had to lie on the floor next to the driver's pedal. But while unpleasant, it led to a remarkable insight into the war as, after driving past beet fields and through tiny hamlets, they arrived in the town square in Furnes to find it full of soldiers and military vehicles.[34] Their car stopped in the middle of the square and when Clarke clambered out he looked up to see a man in a dark blue and gold uniform standing at a window of the town hall. It was Albert, the King of Belgium.

King Albert had already played an important role in the war in that his refusal to allow Germany to move its army through Belgium to attack France

– he had responded that 'I rule a nation, not a road' – had provoked the German invasion.

Now in personal command of the Belgian Army, Albert stood above Clarke with his head on his hand as he looked down on the French and Belgian troops below. Clarke thought he seemed 'pale-faced and sad looking' as 'the wind flicked his light hair about'. A conductor gave an order and a small band of trumpeters began to play, their music competing with the sound of the guns in the distance. Clarke wrote the music on an envelope so it might be preserved for history. Years later, he described how Albert had watched the soldiers salute him and then march off in the direction of the guns:

> His eyes and his mien were sad. Perhaps he was wondering, as I was, how many of those sturdy Chasseurs of France would ever come back again along that road leading from the old town square of Furnes. He waited till the last of them had left the square, then stood silently looking after them. Then he quietly shut the window.[35]

Notes

1 Basil Clarke, *Unfinished Autobiography*, p.146.
2 Clarke to Alice, 10 Sep 1914. The property of the Hartley family, this is being published here for the first time.
3 Basil Clarke, *Unfinished Autobiography*, pp.79–80. The exact circumstances of this story are unclear. In Clarke's autobiography, written towards the end of his life, he recalls it as occurring while he was attending a Welsh National Eisteddfod in Colwyn Bay on behalf of the *Manchester Guardian*. However, in Clarke's autobiography he admits that 'memory may be at fault' as to the timing and location, and the last time the Eisteddfod would have been held in Colwyn Bay was 1910 and no Eisteddfod was held in 1914, despite all the evidence suggesting that Novello wrote the song after the outbreak of war. So while the confrontation with Novello probably did happen, and the early days of the war is the most likely timing, we cannot be sure. This is a story that has also been passed down through Clarke's family.
4 Basil Clarke, *Unfinished Autobiography*, p.146.
5 Ibid., pp.147–8.
6 J. Lee Thompson, *Northcliffe: Press Baron in Politics 1865–1922*, London, 2000, p.225.
7 Ibid.
8 John Terraine, *Impacts of War 1914 & 1918*, London, 1970, p.99.
9 J. Lee Thompson, *Northcliffe: Press Baron in Politics 1865–1922*, London, 2000, p.226.
10 Ibid.
11 Basil Clarke, *My Round of the War*, London 1917, Preface.
12 *The War Illustrated*, 18 November 1916, p.314.
13 Hamilton Fyfe, *Sixty Years of Fleet Street*, London, 1949, p.175.

14 Phillip Knightley, *The First Casualty: The War Correspondent as Hero, Propagandist, and Myth-Maker*, London, 1978, p.94.
15 Basil Clarke, *My Round of the War*, London 1917, p.4.
16 *Daily Mail*, 21 October 1914, p.5.
17 Basil Clarke, *My Round of the War*, London 1917, p.6.
18 Ibid., pp.7–11. This account differs slightly from the one given in the *Daily Mail* (17 October 1914, p.5), but given he later admitted inserting inaccuracies about his whereabouts to help evade capture, it seems more likely that it is the account in *My Round of the War* that is more reliable.
19 Ibid., pp.14–16.
20 *Daily Mail*, 19 October 1914, p.5.
21 Basil Clarke, *My Round of the War*, London 1917, p.12.
22 *Daily Mail*, 17 November 1914, p.4.
23 *The War Illustrated*, 18 November 1916, p.314.
24 Basil Clarke, *My Round of the War*, London 1917, pp.16–17.
25 Phillip Knightley, *The First Casualty: The War Correspondent as Hero, Propagandist, and Myth-Maker*, London, 1978, p.94.
26 *World's Press News*, 15 November 1934, p.2.
27 *Daily Mail*, 8 December 1914, p.8.
28 *Daily Mail*, 24 October 1914, p.4.
29 Sarah Macnaughtan, *My War Experiences in Two Continents*, London, 1919, p.44.
30 *Daily Mail*, 27 October 1914, p.5.
31 Sarah Macnaughtan, *My War Experiences in Two Continents*, London, 1919, p.44.
32 *Times of India*, 4 July 1917, p.7.
33 *Northern Star*, Lismore, New South Wales, 25 December, 1929, p.2. This quotes from an article Clarke wrote for the *Daily News*.
34 Basil Clarke, *My Round of the War*, London 1917, pp.22–3.
35 Ibid., pp.22–5.

6

'A Sort of Nightmare'

Clarke's first few weeks on the Western Front were dominated by the Battle of the Yser, a desperate struggle in which the Belgians and the French defiantly tried to prevent a German advance across the Yser Canal. Up to this point, readers of the *Daily Mail* probably most associated Clarke with the light-hearted writing style of his Canadian articles, but he proved equally adept at producing raw and compelling accounts of the fighting. His report about a German attempt to cross the canal in late October 1914 gives an example:

> There were 2,500 German bodies in the Yser Canal this morning after the fighting in the night. Many of them had been drowned, others bayoneted. The very water itself was bloody. Dixmude's streets were strewn thick with dead.[1]

Clarke's ability to pick out telling details meant his copy was powerful without having to rely on excessive use of adjectives. In the same article, he described how 'men even wrestled and died by drowning each other in the canal's waters' and told the story of a 'huge Belgian … [who] used his rifle like an axe … and felled man after man till a bullet took him through the thigh bone and fetched him down'.

But as vividly as he described the fighting, his articles could not be said to offer a full picture of the conflict. For one thing, he avoided spelling out the true horror of the war out of concern for the families of those fighting. 'The way the wounded are when they get here to Dunkirk is awful,' he wrote in a letter home to Alice. 'One simply can't write about it. They've lain in their clothes for days in all sorts of … filth and the stench could make you heave …

War is a ghastly thing and no one could realise how ghastly till they saw something of it.'[2]

But even more fundamentally, the censoring of his work meant it often failed to reflect the truth of how the Battle of the Yser was progressing. His reports described the German Army as 'despairing', for example, and claimed the presence of old men and 16-year-old boys in its ranks was a sign of 'an approach to the end of Germany's tether in Northern Belgium'.[3] But those willing to read between the lines may have guessed from the muted tone of some of his reporting that the outlook was less promising. 'In spite of many scares, prospects in the Yser battle are still quite hopeful,' he reported on 29 October. 'The Germans can hardly meet with a more stubborn resistance than they have met with during the past week, for the Belgians have been simply wonderful in their doggedness.'

As this hinted, in reality the mood in Dunkirk was increasingly pessimistic and its inhabitants feared that the Germans might overrun the Allied lines at any moment. Looking back at this time some years later, Clarke was candid about just how imminent a German breakthrough had seemed:

I look over my diary and dispatches for that period and they bring back vividly to me the awfulness of those days, the silken slimness of the margin by which the struggling Allies avoided disaster.

Have you ever lived for days on tenterhooks that kept your brain and thoughts on the stretch all day and made your very awakening in the morning a return to a sort of nightmare – a nightmare of anxiety and foreboding? The people of this country, owing to an all-embracing censorship, were spared those tenterhooks, but over in Flanders in those days of the war there was no merciful anaesthetic of this sort, and people there who were in close touch with affairs knew the cruel truth. It was touch-and-go with our Army, the French Army, the Belgian Army; they were near the end of their tether. Any day might see them flung forward before German hordes and into the sea.

Clarke would lean out of his hotel window at night to listen to the sound of the guns and watch the flashes in the sky and the fires burning in the distance. As he looked at the fires, he wondered blackly if he was watching the Germans breaking through the Allied lines. Then in the morning he would visit the Yser Canal and see the bodies of those killed the previous night.

Many people in Dunkirk began to contemplate leaving and Clarke knew a jeweller who buried his stock in the sand dunes to prevent it being looted when the Germans took the city. But perhaps the strongest indication of the precariousness of the situation was when an officer offered Clarke a place on a boat that was to leave if the Germans broke through. 'It would be unpleasant for you if the Germans collared you,' he told Clarke with a grim smile. 'If the Boches are here tonight slip down there and get aboard slick … I've not mentioned it to you before, but I thought I'd better today because things are getting tight.'

The same day, Clarke met a Canadian officer in the Belgian Army as he arrived back in Dunkirk from the fighting. He was bleeding from the head and covered in mud. 'It's pretty well all over,' he told Clarke. 'My poor devils have been licked to Hell. They're through.'

Clarke watched the fires and flashes from the window of his hotel room that night with particular anxiety, thinking they seemed even closer than the previous night. Then the next morning a friend in the Belgian Flying Corps told him the Germans had got through the line at one or two points and it was now a question of whether the Allies could cut off those who had broken through or whether they would be overrun.

'It looks like a "bad egg", as your boys say,' his friend told him, and this seemed to be confirmed later that day when Clarke heard that the Germans were progressing towards Furnes and Dunkirk and resistance was crumbling.

Clarke did not sleep that night and before dawn he climbed the tower of Dunkirk's cathedral. He was looking out onto the sea as the sun started to rise, and with the break of day he was greeted with the comforting sight of British ships firing at the Germans on the coast. It gave him hope that perhaps Dunkirk would be safe after all.

But it was actually a bold decision by the Belgians to open the canal locks at Nieuwpoort to try to flood the German trenches that turned the Battle of the Yser in the favour of the Allies. It meant flooding large areas of Belgian countryside but it forced the Germans to launch an all-out assault on the Belgian trenches, which were on higher ground. Despite enjoying some initial success, the Germans were eventually pushed back and so were forced to abandon the idea of crossing the Yser.

Clarke's article about the German retreat contained a palpable sense of relief as he described the Germans as having been 'smashed like a fallen wine glass', and those *Daily Mail* readers who had not realised anything was wrong must have been surprised by the giddiness of his reporting on the jubilation in Dunkirk:

The Germans in Northern Belgium are on the run and Dunkirk feels safe at last. Calais, too, and all the little towns and hamlets round about. You need to have lived in the midst of alarms such as the Dunkirk region has known this past month to realise the relief that is felt, the intolerable load that is lifted.

Picture a like state of things about your quiet English home. Imagine waking each morning to the solemn thud of guns – every day louder and nearer than the day before; imagine from daylight to dark, and even after that, a steady stream along the high road, past your very garden gate, perhaps, of men and women, houseless through the war, but with household salvage on their backs, and children tugging at their skirts – children weary with walking and want of sleep. And punctuate this crowd at near intervals with motor loads, van loads, cab loads, cart loads of wounded men …

Twenty days of this life (each with some special alarm of its own) and 20 wakeful nights, listening to the thud of the guns and wondering what moment might bring down your own bedroom ceiling with a crash upon you – and you in your cosy English home would begin to know something of what Northern Belgium and France have known of late.

And then suddenly to find the cloud lifted, the guns gone, the enemy in frenzied, grovelling retreat, your home safe after all! The relief of it! Such a relief is Northern Belgium's now. Can you wonder that the people laugh again, that they stop their hardy, mud-caked soldiers in the streets and clap them on the back?[4]

This article was, like much of Clarke's coverage from Flanders, highly partisan in favour of the Allies. But it is to his credit that his reporting avoided the casual xenophobia of much of the *Daily Mail*'s war coverage, which variously described Germans as 'barbarians'[5] and 'Huns'.[6] In fact, Clarke was so fair-minded that one of his articles even included details of German gallantry. 'It is an actual fact – and a fact that in fairness should be reported,' Clarke wrote, 'that the enemy have in this part of the line even carried Belgian wounded to the Belgian trenches and handed them over to safe keeping. On the last occasion they did this men of the two opposing armies exchanged coat-buttons as souvenirs and shook hands, and the Germans went back to their trenches.'[7] Clarke's admirable attitude towards the Germans did not, though, extend to questions of good taste. When a Belgian soldier offered him the helmet of a German soldier he had killed, Clarke not only enthusiastically accepted the macabre gift but, on returning to England, he hung it on his wall as a souvenir of his time in Flanders.[8]

★★★

The German retreat was a turning point in Clarke's time in Dunkirk. Firstly, the fact that the Allies now had the upper hand meant that his copy was less severely censored, while the end of the imminent threat to Dunkirk made life much more tolerable. It did not, though, mean an end to danger altogether, as his visits to the Front still involved placing himself at considerable risk. There was one incident, in particular, where he experienced the terror of being faced with imminent death.

Clarke had spent the day visiting Allied trenches and gun posts with a Belgian official and they were driving back to Dunkirk in a limousine in the middle of the afternoon. 'It seems a pity to go home so early,' the Belgian said to Clarke. 'How would you like to turn aside and see a bit of the Boches' work in one of the ruined villages about here?'

Clarke eagerly accepted the offer to see the effect of German bombing up close and so the Belgian gave some instructions to the driver and they turned into a lane that took them to Zuydschoote, a deserted village that heavy shelling had reduced to what Clarke described as 'a jagged wreck of a village'.

On arriving in Zuydschoote, the two men went into the roofless village church and then Clarke left his companion to wander through some nearby ruined houses. In one of them he found a bayonet whose blade had speared a partly toasted piece of bread and he was wondering why it might have been left like that when he heard a faint whining noise that was followed by the sound of a shell bursting outside the house. Clarke looked out through a hole in the wall and saw the earth, stones and bricks that the shell had flung high into the air landing just 60 yards away. He rushed back into the street to find the Belgian official.

'The Boche have found us, monsieur,' said the Belgian with a smile.

'Evidently,' Clarke replied, trying to maintain his composure.

Standing in the road, they again heard a faint whine that was similar, Clarke thought, to the 'whimpering drone of some distant dragon-fly', and a second later another shell landed. This time the chimney of a nearby cottage collapsed. The Belgian flicked away some pink brick dust from his tunic.

'This is not agreeable,' he said.

'What do you suggest, monsieur?' Clarke asked, as calmly as he could. 'Had we better take cover or make a bolt for the car?'

'Better take cover for a while, monsieur. Perhaps they are only seeing whether there is anyone in the village or not, and will drop their tricks after this.'

They went into the most solid-looking house they could find and Clarke absent-mindedly picked up a photo album that had been left there. As he looked through the pages, a third shell hit the church and then a fourth hit the street. Then silence.

'Yes, it's all over,' said the Belgian. 'They will not shell a deserted village any more. We can go.'

But as they reached the door of the cottage, three more shells exploded in quick succession. The last of them hit the cottage next to theirs and would have buried them in bricks if they had not leapt clear of the building and into the street.

'We will bolt for the motor car,' said the Belgian.

They ran towards the car as more shells exploded around them. They were running past a sow that had been disturbed by the shelling and was waddling down the street when another shell exploded near them and this time the sound was so loud that Clarke thought it seemed to be 'right against my very ear-drums'. He felt a sharp smack against his neck and put a hand to where he had felt the impact. He pulled it away and it was with a sense of horror that he saw it was covered in blood.

'You are wounded! You are wounded!' shouted the Belgian.

'My first thoughts on the blood were that I had received my death blow from that shell,' Clarke later remembered. 'Grim thoughts of wounds I had heard of which cause no real pain but only quick death flashed through my brain. Yet I wondered that I did not *feel* wounded.'

He touched his neck again and he finally convinced himself that despite the blood he was not actually wounded. He looked around and saw the sow lying on the floor, nearly dead. It was with great relief that he suddenly realised the shell had torn a piece of flesh from the sow and it was this that had hit his neck.

'It is not I who am wounded, but poor old Madame la Pig there,' he jubilantly told the Belgian as he pointed to the pig.

The Belgian laughed and they ran back to the car. The driver already had the engine running and they quickly got in and started to drive away. But one of the car's back wheels became stuck just outside the village and then the engine stopped and they had to endure an anxious wait as the driver struggled to restart it with shellfire exploding around them. Eventually, the engine responded and they were able to drive to safety.

★★★

Clarke had dinner with an officer friend in Furnes that evening and told him what had happened and how scared he had been. Clarke's words seemed to have an effect on the officer, who, it transpired, had spent a lot of time thinking about the concept of fear. He told Clarke that while it was the instinct of self-preservation, some men find that their imagination adds to this instinctive reaction 'until it creates a grand structure of horror that yields an exquisite torture'.

'I am one of those men,' the officer said solemnly, before falling silent and looking thoughtfully at the flames of the candles on the mantelpiece. After sitting quietly for some time, the officer began to tell Clarke about his own experiences: how the first time he had come under shellfire he had responded by standing still and staring up at the sky, but that finding a woman with two children and a baby had made his fear almost vanish because he became preoccupied with getting them to safety.

'From this I deduced that personal fear lessens before anxiety for the safety of others and before some task which occupies the mind,' the officer told Clarke. 'I find that men notice rifle and shell fire much less when they are doing something. It is the sitting idle and having time to see and listen and think – to imagine, in short – that is most disconcerting. Many a time when the shell fire has been especially hot and close I've made the men get out their trenching tools and do something or other to the trench just to give them something to do. When their minds are busy it's amazing how little place fear has … Give them a job to do and it can rain fire and bricks and iron round them and they don't seem to notice it.'

As the officer talked, Clarke realised he was listening to a remarkable account of what it is like to cope with fear in the face of death. He turned it into an article for the *Daily Mail* that stood out from much of the shallow jingoism of British newspaper coverage of the war because of the realistic way it presented the psychological reality of trench warfare. Perhaps the most memorable part of the article was the officer's description of how he had fought at close quarters with German soldiers after taking part in a charge against a German trench:

> One fellow was so scared that he would be killed that he pulled a photograph of his wife and kiddies from his pocket and held it up before his face for our boys to see. That was blue funk if you like. He'd too much imagination, you see. He was thinking of his wife and kiddies instead of bravery – the deliberate controlling of one's funk.[9]

A week after being shelled at Zuydschoote, Clarke heard that the Belgian official who had been with him had been telling the story of the 'phlegmatic Englishman' who had looked through photo albums and made jokes as shells fell around them, while the official himself had been 'fremissant' (shivering) with fear.

Clarke was bemused by the suggestion that he had been fearless under shell-fire. 'This was my first intimation to me that he [the Belgian] had been even disturbed by the shell fire,' Clarke wrote, 'while, for myself, I know quite well that, whatever I may have said or done during those moments of stress, I too, was as "fremissant" as he, and as ever I care to be.'[10]

Notes

1 *Daily Mail*, 27 October 1914, p.5.
2 Clarke to Alice, Dunkirk, 22 November 1914. The property of the Hartley family, its contents are published here for the first time.
3 *Daily Mail*, 28 October 1914, p.6.
4 *Daily Mail*, 6 November 1914, p.6.
5 *Daily Mail*, 29 September 1914, p.10.
6 *Daily Mail*, 17 October 1914, p.8.
7 *Daily Mail*, 21 December 1914, p.7.
8 Basil Clarke, *My Round of the War*, London, 1917, pp.44–9.
9 *Daily Mail*, 2 January 1915, p.4.
10 *The War Illustrated*, 14 October 1916, pp.194–6.

7

Ypres

With the Battle of the Yser now over, attention turned to the strategically important city of Ypres. About 25 miles from Dunkirk, its position as the last city before the coast meant it was important for protecting the Allied supply route, while for the Germans the Front near Ypres was the last defence before its railway network.

Even considering the bloody standards of the First World War, the Battle of Ypres was exceptional. It would be remembered in Britain for the British Expeditionary Force's valiant battle to defend the city, while in Germany it became known as the 'Slaughter of the Innocents' and would later feature in Nazi propaganda because of Adolf Hitler's participation in it.[1]

Despite the intensity of the fighting, Ypres itself was at first relatively unscathed by the battle. But at the beginning of November the Germans began shelling the city, and then two weeks later sent a stream of shells directly into the city centre.

Clarke initially suspected the bombardment was designed to conceal a repositioning of the German forces,[2] but he later came to believe it was motivated by malice. 'Finding that with all their men and all their guns and all their struggles and their sacrifice of lives they could not take it, they set out to break it,' he wrote. 'Peevish children are sometimes like that.'[3]

The bombing devastated Ypres's historic city centre and destroyed its cathedral and its ancient Cloth Hall; the damage was so severe that even today the rebuilt city is one of the main symbols of the tragedy of the war. The bombing was also perhaps the pinnacle of Clarke's journalistic career. He was the first reporter to get into the deserted city centre after it was set ablaze and he later thought his eyewitness account of it was his 'best exclusive'.[4]

Accompanied by a Belgian official who gave him a lift there, he made his way through the smouldering ruins and met a young woman who was looking at the damage. She told them her father ran a café in Ypres and had refused to leave despite the bombing, and so she had stayed to look after him. She explained how on the night the bombing had intensified, her father had climbed onto the roof to protect his home. 'All that night the firing went on, and sparks and fire and burning wood were thrown on to our houses from houses near us that were hit,' she said. 'Some of these houses caught fire, and we should have been burned down, but father stayed on the roof, getting here and there with a fire extinguisher, putting out every bit of fire he could see.'

After listening to the woman's story, Clarke went to take a closer look at the destruction. As he had done with his article about the threat to Dunkirk, when he came to reporting on what he had seen, he imagined what the English equivalent might have been:

> Imagine looking upon, say, Canterbury Cathedral or Westminster Abbey piled up in heaps – heaps of stone and mortar and wood, and saints and angels and stained glass and tombs and curtains and pictures and chairs and candles and prayer books – the old and the new, the venerable stones of the year 1400 and the forgotten umbrellas of 1914 – all in one headlong humble!

> That awful sight struck me cold … The city, so silent and empty and waste, might have been unpeopled by a plague, shattered by a mad god. You looked, and still looking, could hardly believe.

He walked into the cathedral through a hole in the wall and looked up to see jagged patches of sky through the broken roof. As he made his way around the cathedral, climbing over fallen crosses and candlesticks and taking care to avoid the holes in the floor, he saw shattered tombstones and part of a charred painting by Rubens that had come away from the wall.

He went outside and in the rubble saw a brass drum that had been part of the famous carillon of Ypres and the remains of another Rubens. He also found a smouldering book that had been part of a marriage register. He opened it at random and saw records of marriages that had been held there 200 years ago.

He then walked through the streets of Ypres, passing houses without roofs and with large holes in the walls. In some cases, beds or wardrobes were protruding from the holes, threatening to fall out onto the street at any moment.[5]

Clarke realised that what he had seen would make an extraordinary account of one of the key events of the first few months of the war. But he worried that publicly admitting to having been in Ypres might give the authorities a clue to his location and put him at risk of arrest.

So when the *Daily Mail* published his account on 28 November 1914, it presented it not as Clarke's own but one he had been told by a resident of Ypres, whom it described as 'of more than average ability, a keen observer, and had literary tastes'. The *Daily Mail* went on to explain how Clarke had persuaded the resident to write down what he had seen and then translated it and sent it back to London.[6]

The deceit may have been necessary to avoid detection, but Clarke later admitted it meant a 'toning down and loss of visual quality' and this diminished the sense of achievement he felt at seeing it in print. It was not the only time he took less credit for articles than he was due. 'I can confess now to having many times, in those early outlaw days of war reporting, adopted similar little literary ruses to disguise the fact that I had been in prohibited areas,' he later wrote.[7]

★★★

The tone of Clarke's articles in the *Daily Mail* became increasingly positive as the end of 1914 approached, and this reflected his genuine belief that the Allies now had the upper hand. On 16 December, for example, he reported that the Allies were finally beginning to focus on attack. 'The change of tactics to offence after so many weeks of plodding and weary defence is wonderfully heartening to the men,' he wrote. 'A new spirit and zest are manifest in all the troops one meets.'[8]

The next day brought more good news. 'The task of pushing the Germans out of Belgium has begun,' he reported, explaining how British, French and Belgian forces had launched a 'vigorous offensive'.[9] The following day he was even more optimistic about the Allies' prospects:

The turning point in the long-drawn struggle for Flanders and Northern France has come. The Allies, working both by land and sea, have opened an offensive which has started so well and which promises so well that hopes are now at a higher pitch ... than ever since the war began.

One hesitates even to repeat the exuberant prophecies that are hazarded as to the date by which the German yoke, which has weighed so heavily on this part of the war area of late, will have been lifted ... [but] the Allies know they are winning ... If to pull a game out of the fire is one of the greatest joys of sports, as it is, how fierce a joy there must be in pulling out of the fire a warfaring such as Ypres and the Yser has seen! And that is what is being done now.

The Germans had their day on the Yser – those days when every man of the Allies was holding up four of the enemy. Now it is the Allies' turn. And they are taking it.[10]

Clarke's reports on the fighting were eagerly read by those in Britain who wanted news about the war, but a mixture of censorship and his partial view of the conflict meant that in reality his work was of only limited use as a source of information about the progress of the war. But from a modern perspective, his attempts to give a sense of which side was in the ascendency are much less interesting than those articles that gave a glimpse of the human experiences of life in Flanders.

He wrote one article, for example, about a pig that wandered into 'the strip of land between the trenches' – it seems 'no man's land' had yet to enter common usage – and was shot by soldiers from both sides who were eager to supplement their usual rations with roast pig. He reported how five soldiers were killed trying to get the pig back to their trench, before a German soldier eventually managed to creep out under the cover of darkness and tie a rope to the pig's leg. The Germans waited until morning before pulling the pig into their trench so that the British would be forced to witness their victory.[11]

Another article told of the amusement of the Belgians and French at the inclusion of toothbrushes in British kit bags, while he also gave a detailed description of how British soldiers enjoyed a warm bath despite the freezing weather by using a large rain tub as a bath and then heating bricks on their campfire and using bayonets as tongs to put the bricks in the bath. 'In time the water becomes pleasantly hot,' Clarke wrote, before going on to explain how the men would take it in turns to strip in a nearby barn, run naked into the yard to take the bath, and then run back to the barn to dress.[12]

In another article, he took the unpromising material of a mother and child walking through a village and turned it into a poignant pen portrait of life in the war zone:

> The woman never looks up. With eyes on the ground, intent on avoiding the mud-puddles, she plods on, and the child splashes cheerfully alongside – three steps to her one. The grip of his tiny fingers on hers may be tight. One cannot say. But there is nothing to show fear. They are just walking briskly along the road, these two. The shells are whizzing or whining overhead as they come or go. There is no concern, the one with the other. These shells might be mere birds. Even the child's interest in them (no doubt he had one a month ago) has waned and ebbed out. You must be well war-worn to become like that.[13]

Writing about the mother and child, it would not be surprising if Clarke was reminded of his own family, who regularly occupied his thoughts. A letter home in which he expressed his preference for George going to the same school as his brothers, for example, showed that he took a keen interest in his family's relocation to London even while he was at the centre of one of the biggest news stories in history. In the same letter, in which he addressed Alice as 'My dear old lass', he told her how much he was missing her. 'I'd like to be sitting with you opposite to me, in a big chair by the fire in our own little breakfast room having a good old gas with you,' he wrote.[14]

He did not have to wait as long as he might have expected to be reunited with her because, in a display of bravery that bordered on recklessness, Alice decided to visit him in Dunkirk. She obtained permission to travel to Paris and then at Calais crossed town to catch a train to Dunkirk and, as Clarke had done before her, entered the station by the restaurant, walked out onto the station platform and boarded a train. Clarke had told her about a spot at Dunkirk's station where by climbing a few feet and jumping down it was possible to leave the station without having to pass the ticket guards or the police. When she jumped down, Clarke was waiting to take her hand to help her. She was 'bubbling with merriment and the spirit of adventure,' he later remembered, as he hugged her and welcomed her to the war zone.[15] They would later look back with fondness on the time they spent together in Dunkirk and Clarke bought her two rings at a local jeweller as a souvenir of her trip.[16]

★★★

One of the most enduring stories of the First World War is the Christmas truce of 1914, when soldiers from both sides met in no man's land to play football and sing songs. But Clarke's experience of Christmas 1914 could hardly have been more different from the impression that has passed into folk memory.

He and Christopher Lumby, a reporter for *The Times*, were walking on the road between Dunkirk and Furnes as midnight approached on Christmas Eve. It was a clear night with a frost on the ground and the stars and moonlight illuminated the cottages they walked past.

'I suppose if you were at home you would be playing Santa Claus,' said Lumby.[17]

'No doubt,' Clarke replied.

In the distance, they heard Dunkirk Cathedral play the Hymn of Jean Bart and then the bell tolled to mark the start of Christmas Day.

'Happy Christmas to you and yours,' said Lumby.

'And to you and yours,' Clarke replied.

'And a quiet one to us both and to our lads yonder,' added Lumby. But just as he finished speaking there was a booming sound that shook the earth and the sky was lit up by the white flashes of guns, the pink flashes of howitzers and the red-yellow of exploding shells.

'Thud, boom, and boom again, we could feel the shock of them in our feet as well as hear them,' Clarke later wrote. 'Christmas Day was being ushered in by guns!'

In the *Daily Mail* he described how the noise of the guns had precipitated a gruelling and bloody Christmas Day:

> The Germans came down upon the countryside east of Nieuport in a fury of hate. Their fiercest onslaught of the week they reserved for Christmas Day. The frost had hardened the marshy fields. They came on now with a clatter instead of a squelch. And the whole afternoon the Allies were busy beating them off. The guns thumped, the machine guns tapped, and the rifles cracked. That was the music of Christmas about Nieuport.[18]

From Clarke's report, readers of the *Daily Mail* would have thought Christmas Day 1914 had been much like any other day of the war. It was not until 8 January that they learned about the other side to Christmas 1914, when the *Daily Mail* published a grainy photograph of British and German troops standing and talking together on Christmas Day. Despite the poor quality of the photograph, the newspaper immediately recognised its significance, describing it as 'one of the most interesting pictures of the war'.[19]

★★★

After various round-ups and deportations of reporters, by January 1915 Clarke and Christopher Lumby of *The Times* were reportedly the only British journalists left in Flanders, which meant Clarke's articles were by now almost unique in giving an independent — if heavily censored — account of the fighting.

On 4 January, he reported on the bombing of Metz and described how German aeroplanes had approached Dunkirk but been forced to turn back after being fired on.[20] Then two days later the *Daily Mail* published an article by him about an extraordinary duel between two armoured trains. It was a form of combat, Clarke suggested, that was 'without precedent, even in this war of many novelties' and involved two trains exchanging fire for an hour before the Allies won the duel by landing a shell in the middle of the German train.[21]

This report also included an early account of what would become known as shell shock:

> They brought in a poor fellow the other day for whose body life had been too much. He was not hurt, but was temporarily dazed and tottering in the limbs and numbed in the brain with weeks in the cellars and the cold of the trenches.

They sat him in a chair in the little hostelry and gave him hot coffee, rubbed his hands and warmed his body at the stove. And for minutes and minutes, though he seemed quite conscious, his eyes were wandering round the little mirrored room as though his mind were unable to take in all that he was seeing; as though he were trying to realise where he was and what strange things he was looking at.[22]

The day this article was published, Clarke sent another report back to London about aeroplane raids on Dunkirk.[23] It was to be his last article as a 'journalistic outlaw' in Flanders as, after avoiding capture for almost three months, his luck finally ran out.

When Clarke received an urgent message from the Commissaire of Police telling him to visit before 8.00 a.m. the following morning, he felt he had no choice but to attend.[24] When he arrived, the Commissaire greeted him with a handshake and asked him to sit down. He told Clarke he had received a message from England demanding that Clarke and Lumby be hunted down and expelled. The Commissaire said that while he was sorry, he had no choice but to arrest him and planned to do so at 4.00 p.m. that day. He pointedly asked Clarke if this time would suit him, which Clarke took to mean that this was how long he had to leave the country.

Clarke asked if the decision was irreversible and was told that it was. He bowed, thanked the Commissaire, and told him that 4.00 p.m. would be fine. The two men shook hands and the Commissaire again told Clarke how sorry he was.

Within a couple of hours, he had made arrangements with friends in the British Admiralty to take a boat back to Britain, and by 4.00 p.m. he was already at sea, 'being tossed to and fro in the cabin of the tiniest, grimmest little craft that ever hoisted the British Admiralty flag'. After 16 hours of the 'roughest and vilest' sailing he had ever experienced, he landed at Dover.

There was no one there to ask questions; just a man who assisted him by carrying his suitcase. Clarke was still wearing the same bowler hat as when he had left Britain the previous October. 'It had proved my best disguise in the War Zone,' he wrote. 'For whoever thought of looking for a newspaper man under a bowler hat?'[25]

Clarke's return to Britain meant that the *Daily Mail* no longer had access to independent reports from the Front. Instead, in the sort term, it published articles without bylines that were presumably based on official reports and then relied on George Curnock in Paris and James Dunn in Rotterdam to fill in the gaps.

The *Daily Mail* published almost no independent news from the Front for the next two weeks until Beach Thomas, a former classics master at Dulwich College and writer of countryside features, wired a report from 'Northern France' on 22 January.

While Clarke's departure disrupted the *Daily Mail's* ability to report on the war and brought the greatest adventure of his life to an end, he could at least console himself that being one of the last two reporters left at the Front had cemented his professional reputation. When he later wrote about how those early days of the war had made and broken the reputations of journalists, he must have felt great pride in the knowledge that he had been one of those who had benefited from it the most:

> Reporting the Great European War presented problems utterly different from anything in the history of war reporting. Some experienced war correspondents, men with great reputations, failed, in some cases utterly, while men of whom nothing had been heard, some of them quite young in journalism, succeeded. "Form" was no guide, as a racing expert expressed it.[26]

While he would spend many more months as a war correspondent, Clarke would always look back on the last few months of 1914 with special nostalgia. Remembering those days some twenty years later, he wrote:

> Somehow distance, and the years, soften for us the jagged edges of discomforts outlived. The wind and the rain; the interminable mud; the torment of being chivvied and badgered about by soldiers, sailors, police and civilians alike ...

> Flanders seems afar now; its worries and discomforts all faded and remote. There remains supreme over all other things, that exulting thing, the quest for which made reporters of us and will continue throughout time to make reporters – that feeling of life lived; life sought out and faced; life hot, strong and undiluted; the Male animal's conception of romance.[27]

Notes

1   Ian F.W. Beckett, *Ypres: The First Battle 1914*, Harlow, 2006, p.7.
2   *Daily Mail*, 9 December, p.7.
3   Basil Clarke, *My Round of the War*, London 1917, pp.50–1.
4   *World's Press News*, 15 November 1934, p.2.
5   Basil Clarke, *My Round of the War*, London 1917, pp.51–6.
6   *Daily Mail*, 28 November 1914, p.5.
7   Basil Clarke, *My Round of the War*, London 1917, p.51.
8   *Daily Mail*, 16 December 1914, p.5.
9   *Daily Mail*, 17 December 1914, p.7.
10 *Daily Mail*, 18 December 1914, p.6.

11 *Daily Mail*, 23 December 1914, p.4.
12 Ibid.
13 *Daily Mail*, 2 December 1914, p.4.
14 Clarke to Alice, Dunkirk, 22 November 1914. The property of the Hartley family, its contents are being published here for the first time.
15 Basil Clarke, *My Round of the War*, London 1917, p.76.
16 Clarke to Alice, from France, undated, but near the end of 1916. The property of the Hartley family, its contents are being published here for the first time.
17 *The War Illustrated*, 22 December 1917, p.377.
18 *Daily Mail*, 28 December 1914, p.6.
19 *Daily Mail*, 8 January 1915, p.7.
20 *Daily Mail*, 4 January 1915, p.5.
21 *Daily Mail*, 6 January 1915, p.5.
22 Ibid.
23 *Daily Mail*, 7 January 1915, p.5.
24 Basil Clarke, *My Round of the War*, London 1917, p.77.
25 Ibid., pp.77–8.
26 *World's Press News*, 15 November 1934, p.2.
27 Ibid.

8

Eastern Front

During the first few months of the war, British newspapers were over-whelmingly preoccupied by events in France and Belgium, but, by early 1915, the *Daily Mail* had come to believe in the importance of taking a broader view of the conflict. This meant focusing more on Eastern Europe.

'Each one of the Allies, realising what is at stake and therefore absorbed in his own particular role, is apt to take too close a view of the almighty struggle, which can only be properly overlooked from a height enabling all its wider prospects to be brought into the field of vision,' it explained in an editorial.[1]

The timing of the *Daily Mail*'s newfound interest in the east coincided almost exactly with Clarke's return from Flanders and, presumably having impressed with what he had achieved there, within days of arriving home he was given a new 'roving commission' to travel to Greece, Bulgaria and Romania – all of which had so far stayed out of the war – to try to discover their intentions.

He spent a few days securing passes and letters of introduction from diplomats in London and then the night before he was due to leave he received an unexpected phone call from a Romanian prince who told him he had enjoyed his articles about Canada.

'If you could call on me tomorrow before you leave England I can be of great help to you in Romania,' the Prince told him. 'I hope you will write some articles about that country [Romania] such as you wrote about Canada.'

The next morning the Prince arranged letters of introduction for Clarke to statesmen and royalty in Romania.[2]

★★★

With his papers in order, Clarke travelled to Marseilles, where he boarded a steamer bound for Thessaloniki, the second-largest city in Greece.[3]

On the first night of the voyage, he stood by himself on deck as it approached midnight, looking out onto the calm sea and reflecting on how far it felt from the Western Front. As he was about to go to bed, something caught his eye. It was another boat. As it got nearer, Clarke saw it was a French destroyer that was racing towards them at full speed and before long it came so close that Clarke could see the pattern on the sleeve of the officer on the bridge and the badges on the caps of the sailors. They watched Clarke's ship silently and then, when they were satisfied it did not pose a threat, sped away.

'Thus in mid-sea did war not fail to keep touch with us, and throughout our voyage I doubt whether we ever really escaped it,' Clarke wrote. 'From barren, rocky heights of Corsica, Sardinia, and Sicily, by day and night, came mysterious signals and we answered them. Little black-grey crafts of war lay almost invisible against the rocks below, ready to pounce on us should we fail in the answering.'[4]

During the journey he became friendly with a 'very pretty, very cheerful and very chatty' young woman who said she was from Serbia and had been studying in Paris. She seemed eager to spend time with Clarke, telling him her mother had told her she could safely talk to any Englishman. While he enjoyed her company, he soon began to suspect she was a spy, a belief that was reinforced when he noticed she had a Bulgarian passport despite having said she was Serbian.

After a journey that was so bumpy that half the ship's crockery was smashed, they arrived in Greece to find it 'virtually in a state of war'. They were met at the quay at Thessaloniki by soldiers instead of customs officials and Clarke's fellow passengers were searched and questioned, though a letter Clarke carried from a Greek Minister meant he was spared this ordeal.[5]

He and the young woman stayed in the same hotel and even though he thought she was a spy, he spent time with her because Thessaloniki was 'no place for a woman alone'. He did, though, take the precaution of leaving her at the hotel when he went out to make his enquiries.

★★★

The political situation in Greece in early 1915 was extremely tense. At the outbreak of war the Prime Minister, Eleftherios Venizelos, had wanted Greece to fight on the side of the Allies but the pro-German King Constantine I insisted that it remain neutral.

With such intractably opposed views at the top of government, Clarke spent time in cafés to try to gauge local opinion. They were full of talk of the war but there was little consensus about what part, if any, Greece would play in it. Clarke detected 'a very solid pro-Ally feeling, but a curious and elusive undercurrent in favour of Germany', though despite this sense of ambivalence he eventually concluded that Greece could be relied on to join the war on the side of the Allies.[6]

While Clarke was correct about which side Greece would fight on, he was wrong to think it would join the war any time soon. The disagreement between Venizelos and Constantine would become so fractious that it became known as the National Schism and Constantine forced his Prime Minister's resignation twice over the following year, before Venizelos returned as Prime Minister for a third time in June 1917 and forced Constantine into exile and declared war on the Central Powers (the collective name for Germany and its Allies) the following month. It was a decision that gained Greece territory from Bulgaria as one of the victors in the war, though the National Schism would continue to be a source of social division for decades to come.

★★★

After finishing his investigations in Thessaloniki, Clarke decided to travel to Serbia, which had suffered huge casualties since its dispute with Austria-Hungary had started the conflict six months earlier. He took a train to its temporary capital of Niš, with the girl from the boat accompanying him to the station and helping him choose a carriage on the train. She waved goodbye as the train started moving and was still waving as the track curved and she disappeared out of sight. Clarke never saw her again.

The journey to Niš was long and with numerous interruptions. But not all of them were unpleasant, as during a lengthy stop at Gevgelija in present-day Macedonia, an American Red Cross doctor invited him back to the unfurnished attic of a cottage where he and another doctor lived, and the three men enjoyed a lunch of roasted pig trimmed with hot chillies and served with rye bread, local red wine and schnapps.

The two doctors were in Gevgelija to look after a factory full of wounded Serbian soldiers and over lunch they told Clarke about the horrific nature of their work and of their deep admiration for their patients.

'You've not seen bravery till you've seen these men suffer,' one of them said. 'I'll take off a hand, an arm, a leg – without anaesthetics, mind you – and will the fellow budge? Not an eyelid ... Where this race of soldiers sprang from I don't pretend to know, but I'll tell you now they're God's own men.'[7]

When they had finished their meal, Clarke thanked the two doctors for their hospitality and returned to his train to continue on to Niš. He was impressed by their dedication and when he passed through Gevgelija again some weeks later he asked after them. He was shocked to learn they had both died of typhus.[8]

Soon after the train left Gevgelija, darkness fell and Clarke and a fellow passenger ate cold chicken and sardines by candlelight. His travelling companion's tattoos made Clarke think he was a Royal Navy warrant office. He carried a black box that he was very careful should not be knocked and Clarke could see the shape of a revolver bulging from under his coat.[9]

After dinner, they slept on the seats of the carriage and when they woke at 8.00 a.m. the next morning they had arrived in Niš. The platform was covered in snow and in the sheltered part of the station there were so many soldiers lying on the floor that Clarke had to step over them as he tried to find something to eat and drink.

After buying a coffee and some bread, he struck up a conversation with a man next to him while he waited for his coffee to cool, commenting in French that the soldiers looked tired.

'Tired?' said the man. 'No, it is not that, monsieur. They are ill. Some have enteric, others typhus.'

The man went on to tell him that Niš was so overloaded with sick soldiers that they had to lie wherever they could find space on the ground. At being told why the soldiers were lying on the floor, Clarke put his bread and coffee down on the counter and walked out of the station. 'Such little medical knowledge as I have told me that food bought in such surroundings was the likeliest vehicle for conveying the disease,' he later wrote. 'Shell fire, bullets and bombs I like no better than most people; though with these things you at least know when they have "got you". But the thoughts of disease by contagion or infection, that may not manifest itself till days later, make one "creepy".'[10]

Clarke walked into the centre of Niš but found that it, too, was full of sick people. Though he did not know it, he was in the middle of one of the worst typhus outbreaks in world history, an epidemic that resulted in about 120,000 deaths.[11] Clarke did not eat or drink anything that whole day and decided to leave the city as soon as possible, taking a train that evening to Sofia in Bulgaria.

It was snowing when he arrived in the Bulgarian capital and the last leg of the journey from the station to the hotel was made on a sleigh pulled by two ponies and driven by a man who would wave his arms and shout to clear the traffic in front of them.[12]

Almost as soon as he had arrived at the Hotel Splendide Palace, the manager, who Clarke later discovered was German, insisted on introducing him to a 'countryman' who Clarke was immediately suspicious of. 'He spoke a sort of German-English, adorned at intervals, when he thought of it, by a strong American accent to go along with his story that he was an American of British descent,' Clarke wrote.

His initial suspicions that the man was a spy seemed to be confirmed when he mentioned that Clarke had just come from Niš, something he could only have known from seeing the passport that Clarke had left with the hotel manager.

The man asked him about the condition of the Serbian Army and, having seen that the Serbians were struggling badly, Clarke told him the exact opposite.

'I am afraid that I pitched him such a yarn about Serbia as must have turned the German Intelligence Staff's hair grey,' Clarke wrote. 'Imaginative as it was, he swallowed it all, and he apparently thought it news of importance, because no sooner had I told it to him than his haste to get away became positively indecent. He might have been wanting to "scoop" all the other busy German spies with whom Sofia abounded.'[13]

★★★

Clarke spent a week in Sofia, trying to get an idea of what role Bulgaria was likely to play in the war. Its strong military meant it was seen by both the Allies and the Central Powers as an attractive Ally, but at the start of the war it had still been recovering from the economic impact of the Balkan Wars of 1912 and 1913 and so announced its neutrality.

This was followed by a period of intense diplomatic activity, as both sides competed to convince Bulgaria to join the war on their side. But the policy of neutrality was still holding firm when Clarke arrived and, despite meeting a number of diplomats and politicians in Sofia, including the pro-German Prime Minister Vasil Radoslavov,[14] Clarke did not discover anything useful during the few days he spent there.

Perhaps the most noteworthy thing to happen to Clarke in Bulgaria was an argument he had in the dining car of a train. Three men he suspected of being undercover German soldiers irritated him with what he saw as their boorish behaviour, which included one of them throwing a bottle of wine out of the train window because it was too warm and rolling his shirt sleeves up to the shoulder to eat. So Clarke tried to rile them by asking if they were soldiers and then, when they denied it, proceeding to make derogatory comments about what he had seen of the German Army in Flanders. After a tense conversation the three men left the dining car but later one of them confronted Clarke as he stood in the corridor watching the sun set over the passing countryside. The man admitted he was a soldier and told Clarke he had fought in Belgium and been wounded by a British bullet, showing him the scar it had made across the back of his hand.

Rather than backing down, Clarke called the man a 'loathsome beast' and told him it was 'a pity it did not blow your ugly head off'. The man stepped back and Clarke moved towards him with his fists clenched but just then one of the soldier's companions appeared. Clarke thought the confrontation was about to turn violent but after a tense standoff the two Germans, presumably not wanting to draw attention to their presence in Bulgaria, backed away. They changed trains later that night.[15]

★★★

From Bulgaria, Clarke took a 22-hour journey to Bucharest,[16] a city whose architecture he found disappointing and which he thought was 'symptomatic of a certain showiness of character noticeable about the life as about the buildings'.[17] He also found the Romanian capital to be very expensive, with a hedonistic atmosphere that meant the mornings were quiet and the 'night hours were late and the habits were not athletic'.[18]

The King of Romania had wanted to join the war on the side of the Central Powers but the political parties had wanted to support the Allies and so Romania had remained neutral. Because Romania was thought to have the potential to have a decisive impact on the war, its allegiance was seen as a huge prize and Clarke found Bucharest to be 'a centre of diplomatic intrigue and plotting without equal, perhaps, in all Europe'.[19] He discovered Germany was spending large sums of money on buying newspapers and bribing journalists in an attempt to influence public opinion. Clarke met one journalist who had been offered £10 a month (about £450 today) not to send news of Austrian atrocities, and when he declined the offer it was increased to £18 a month.[20]

As a foreign correspondent, Clarke attracted the attention of spies. He would see the same people wherever he went and they appeared to be trying to hear what he was saying. 'Even my order for afternoon tea at the Café Caspa … was listened to as though it might shed some light on some great diplomatic secret,' he wrote.[21] He also suspected his hotel room was being searched while he was out, so he began leaving notes with false information in the pockets of his clothes in the hope of misinforming the enemy.[22]

But any spies who followed Clarke in Bucharest were wasting their time. While he did meet politicians and statesmen – he got on particularly well with the future Prime Minister, Take Ionescu[23] – they did not tell him anything particularly useful. He soon concluded that Romania's intentions were so closely guarded that he was unlikely to discover anything of note.[24]

Like the rest of his Eastern European commission up to that point, his time in Bucharest may have broadened his horizons but it had not offered much in the way of news. It was by now mid-February and his roving commission, which must have been costing the *Daily Mail* a lot of money, had not produced any articles significant enough to carry Clarke's byline.

Frustrated by his failure to find news about diplomacy, Clarke decided to turn his focus back to war reporting. From Bucharest, he travelled to the border village of Marmornitza, which he thought would be well-positioned for reporting on the fighting between the Russians and the Austrians because it was still part of Romania but was very close to the Austrian border in one direction and the Russian border in the other.[25]

From Dorohoi in northern Romania, he took an open carriage pulled by four horses and driven by a man who had once worked as a tailor's presser in East London and so spoke English with a cockney accent. Clarke had been advised to buy furs for the journey but had ignored the advice in his haste to get to Marmornitza. It was a decision he quickly came to regret as the snow became steadily deeper and Clarke felt his cheeks and ears begin to go numb. By the time they had travelled 20 kilometres he could no longer feel his feet or move his fingers and, after 40 kilometres, he was so disorientated that the horses' bells sounded as if they were far off in the distance.[26]

It was evening when they arrived at Marmornitza's only hotel and Clarke, by now in a 'coma of cold', had to be helped out of the carriage and to the door of the hotel, where he was greeted by a man who had a beard and flowing hair and who reeked of garlic. He showed Clarke the only available bed in the hotel, which was in a room with four other men who also all smelled of garlic. 'At some recent hour there must have been celebrated in that primitive little inn a high feast of garlic,' Clarke wrote. 'And I loathe garlic.'

Despite his driver telling him there was nowhere else to stay, Clarke was so repulsed by the smell that he insisted on trying to find somewhere else. So they went back into the cold night and wandered the village until, after taking a wrong turn into someone's garden and on another occasion stumbling into a hog, they eventually met a Romanian journalist called Dobias who had a spare bed in his room.

After Clarke spent the night at Dobias's house, the next morning the two men went to try to cross the bridge over a small stream 100 yards away that served as the frontier. But the local chief of police told them they would need official permission before being allowed to cross and so Clarke telegraphed the Romanian Minister of the Interior, who he had met in Bucharest, to ask for clearance.

Until he received a reply, there was little for Clarke to do but wait. It was from here, on 13 February 1915, that he telegraphed what became the first bylined article of his 'roving commission', about how the Russians were fortifying the nearby city of Chernivtsi to protect it against the Austrians. The story was published in the *Daily Mail* two days later[27] and was followed on 18 February by an article about how the Austrians had advanced towards Chernivtsi but were driven back after a bayonet fight in a nearby village.[28]

One evening during his wait for the Minister of the Interior's reply, Clarke, Dobias and some other villagers went for a midnight picnic in the snow.

As they drank coffee and hot wine from thermos flasks, they saw a mounted Cossack on the Austrian side of the border and he told them that the 8 miles between the frontier and Chernivtsi was almost free of Austrians. This meant that if Clarke could get across the border then he would be able to get to the city, so it was a great relief when he received a message from the Minister of the Interior the next day granting him permission to cross.

He hired Dobias as his assistant and interpreter and they set off towards Chernivtsi on a rudimentary sleigh pulled by an ox. When they arrived in Chernivtsi, they found a mood of 'suppressed excitement' because of the rumour that the Russians were preparing to withdraw and leave the city to be taken by the Austrians. The Romanians who lived there were fearful of the return of the Austrians, while the Austrians among the population were 'supressing an elation they could barely conceal'.[29]

After a Russian official assured them they would not be left behind, Clarke and Dobias went to the hotel where some hours later Clarke would be woken by the night porter who had fallen asleep and so failed to notice the Russian withdrawal. It was this that led them to make their escape back to the safety of Marmornitza in the middle of the night, arriving at the frontier just before the Austrian Army.

★★★

On his first evening back in Marmornitza, Clarke dined at an inn opposite the house where he was staying. As he unenthusiastically ate the local speciality of stewed chicken with olives and maize pudding, an Austrian officer entered the restaurant. Wearing his uniform but not carrying his sword or revolver, the officer wished Clarke a good evening and Clarke reacted with surprise.

'We can chat – or associate – together, can't we?' said the Austrian, smiling uncomfortably.

'But perhaps I should tell you that I am English,' said Clarke.

'So?' the Austrian replied. 'We are on neutral territory. What does it matter?'

Clarke was worried that being seen talking to an Austrian officer might be misinterpreted by local people.

'Don't you think it would be better if we kept apart?' he said. 'Our association here might be misunderstood both in your own case as well as mine.'

The Austrian officer paused, laughed to himself and turned away, calling to the landlady to bring another table and more wine. Then a few minutes later he was joined by another Austrian. Clarke only saw the newcomer from the back but he noticed the 'livid scarlet' colour of his neck. The two Austrians sat together talking in whispers and at one point Clarke heard the first man mention a 'cursed Englishman', which he assumed was a reference to him.

Clarke was still eating when three Romanians he knew arrived at the inn. They told him that the Austrian with the red neck was a notorious lieutenant called Klappa. It was a name Clarke already knew well. 'Of all the names most hated in Romania at that time, that of Klappa came an easy first,' he later wrote. 'The simple peasant soldiers spat when they repeated it.'

Klappa was loathed because of the zeal with which he had apparently denounced Romanians as spies and then presided over their executions. Some people were reportedly killed for as little as giving beer to Russian soldiers.

Klappa heard Clarke's companions whispering about him and turned to face them. Clarke was shocked by the sight of his face, which he thought was one of the ugliest he had ever seen. 'Search among all the gargoyles of Europe and you will hardly find so hideous a face,' he later wrote.

'Yes, I am Lieutenant Klappa,' the Austrian said. 'I came over the frontier to buy a few cigarettes and a drink, and this is what I get. Why can't you come over here and have a drink together?'

'With you?' said one of Clarke's companions. 'My God, I can't even sit in the same room as you.'

With that, Clarke's companion picked up his hat and walked out. Klappa shrugged his shoulders and turned back to his table but then a moment later got to his feet, his face twitching with rage.

'If you Romanian swine think …'

His voice trailed off as he looked towards the door. Clarke looked over and saw that the doorway to the adjoining peasants' dining room was filled with faces all staring at Klappa, who sat back down but continued to look anxiously at the doorway and the window, where more faces were appearing.

'Klappa the butcher!' the peasants muttered to each other. 'We've got him in here!'

Before long the next room became so crowded with peasants jostling to get a glimpse of the notorious Austrian that two of them were pushed through the door and into the room where Klappa and Clarke were dining, which Clarke thought was exceptional because the 'timid modesty and deference' of Romanian peasants meant they would never normally step outside their section of the restaurant.

Klappa suddenly got to his feet and strode across the room and into an adjoining bedroom. Clarke heard the bang of a window being opened and followed Klappa into the bedroom but he was already gone. Clarke was later told that the peasants chased Klappa into the maize fields behind the inn but he managed to escape back across the frontier by running through fields and then wading across the stream separating Austria and Romania.[30]

★★★

On 18 February 1915, the servant in the house where Clarke was staying was making him coffee when the quiet was shattered by a loud boom. She spilt the coffee and stood paralysed with fear but Clarke, displaying the instincts of a natural war reporter, hurriedly put on his coat and boots and rushed out to see what was going on.[31]

The booming sound signalled the start of a new battle between the Austrians and Russians. And while it may have been unremarkable from a military perspective, its location meant Clarke was able to get an exceptionally good view of the fighting.

'It took place almost in my back garden – only a hundred yards or so away,' he later wrote. 'To see it I only had to go down the back veranda steps, climb a little hill, and look on. And for telegraph office – one was most conveniently established on the other side of the hill about 200 yards away … Nothing could have been more handy or more safe.'

As the battle unfolded in front of him, Clarke began to write his report about it for the *Daily Mail*:

> I am now watching the opening of a battle from a hill at Marmornitza. The Cossack cavalry is exchanging shots with Austrian infantry on the Czernovitz road. The artillery is getting into position. I can see more troops advancing. Young Russians are replacing older reserves.[32]

Half the population of Marmornitza gathered on the hill to watch the fighting and Clarke passed his field glasses around to give the local people a better view. He later recalled the extraordinary level of detail he had been able to see:

> We could see the men working the guns and hear their talk and the orders to fire. The Russian shells, on the other hand, exploded right under our gaze not a hundred yards away. We could watch each shell drop, see the upheaval it made, what havoc was caused, and the ensuing commotion among the Austrians among whom it fell.

Sometimes Russian infantry crept up close to the river bank and tried to pick off Austrian infantry who were lying on the northern bank of the high road from Marmornitza to Czernovitz. 'Through a glass I could watch their eager faces as they crept among the high grass and brush near the river or lay flat, with eye along rifle barrel, waiting greedily for a favourable chance to shoot,' he said.

His excellent view meant Clarke's dispatches read at times more like sports reports than war correspondence, such as an article he wrote about an exchange of fire between the two sides:

The Austrians opened the attack from batteries about a hundred yards from the house where I am staying, just across the frontier stream, and fired 30 rounds before the Russians replied. Then the first Russian shrapnel whistled overhead, followed quickly by others. Their shooting was excellent.[33]

Soon after the battle began, the Russian Army invited Clarke to visit its forces in a nearby village and he had lunch with twenty Russian soldiers. They were generally able to overcome the language barrier by communicating in a mixture of Russian, French, English and German and Clarke described it as 'one of the jolliest of lunches'. Tsar Nicholas II had recently banned the drinking of alcohol in the Russian Army so they had mineral water. But during dessert Clarke's host gave in to temptation and port and liqueurs were produced to toast the success of the Allies.[34]

After lunch, Clarke took a train to the Front, a journey that made him nervous because he had watched the Austrians firing at the same train from the safety of his hilltop in Marmornitza. He mentioned this to the commander of the train.

'Possibly the Austrians will have another try at us today,' the Russian replied laconically. 'Then you will have seen both sides of the show.'[35]

But the Austrians did not fire on the train and after a relatively uneventful journey Clarke got the chance to see the Russian Army in the field at close quarters for the first time. He was impressed, noting how they had endured great hardship and a lack of food but after only a few days rest 'were as happy and fit as sandboys again'.

At the Russian headquarters, a general told Clarke he had read translations of his articles about Flanders in Russian newspapers and the two men drank tea with lemon and ate bread and biscuits and bon bons as they discussed the Western Front. Then as Clarke was leaving, he recognised one of the soldiers as the man who had promised to warn him before any Russian withdrawal from Czernovitz. The soldier apologised profusely, telling Clarke he had completely forgotten about his promise until it was too late and he had been worried about it ever since.

'He looked so genuinely concerned, and wrung my hand so warmly, that I felt sure he was not exaggerating,' Clarke wrote. 'I assured him and the General, who had drawn near to listen to our talk, that my midnight escape through the snow from Czernovitz had occasioned me no greater discomfort than a prodigious appetite for breakfast on arrival in Romania.'[36]

After the months Clarke had spent evading the attention of the authorities in Dunkirk, the accommodating treatment he received from the Russians was a new experience. And while it was a welcome one, he found part of him missed the 'subtle spice of mischief which the breaking of regulations and the invention of makeshifts' had given his time as a fugitive in Dunkirk. 'I suppose it is this queer lust for appetising adventure that leads one into these restless callings,' he wrote.[37]

★★★

On 21 February, Clarke was on top of the hill at Marmornitza and watching about 100 Austrian soldiers shelter from Russian shellfire behind a customs house. The Russians began to direct their fire towards the building and despite by now being used to the sights of war, Clarke found it disturbing to have such a clear view of men who were facing death:

> A whining whirr in the air, and they, as well as we, knew a shell was coming. In that horrible moment of waiting for the fall some never moved, but went on smoking their cigarettes. Others, you could see, were racked by the pains of fear – by the vision of sudden death. They tried to draw their bodies still closer to the white walls; they hunched up their shoulders as though trying to bury their heads; you could see their shoulders working under their greatcoats. Their gaze went upwards, as though they were trying to foresee the danger coming to them. At the moment of the explosion of a shell some gave up all attempt at composure, but clapped hands to ears or round their heads in a paroxysm of terror.

> It was a startling thing to see one's enemy in this way – to watch every face, every finger-twitch, so to speak, so intimately, and yet to be safe oneself. For to see shell-fire's effects so closely before I have had to be under it and in it; and then perhaps one's vision is liable to be less clear, one's conclusions less coherent …

> I wondered whether gunners would aim as well if they could watch at close quarters, as I was watching, the fall of their shells; if they could see the bodies and the faces, and could read in the eyes the very hearts, almost, of the men they sought to kill. It is doubtful whether they would. To kill a man at a mile or two is quite impersonal – an easy matter. And the soldier fighting at close quarters has the heat of battle and the need to defend his own life to help him to kill and to wish to kill. But here on my safe hillside I had none of these aids. It needed a little buffeting of mind to keep steadfast to this; that for my nation's sake and my own these men on the steps must be killed, the more the better.[38]

The Austrians eventually retreated from the customs house to an orchard across the road but the Russian guns soon began to reach them there as well.

So it must have been a relief to the Austrians when the arrival of darkness meant the day's fighting was at an end.

At daylight the next morning Clarke climbed the hill to see the resumption of battle, only to discover that the Austrians had retreated during the night.[39] He sent the news back to London that day and it was published in the *Daily Mail* two days later.[40]

The Austrian retreat meant Clarke no longer had the opportunity to write first-hand descriptions of battle, but during the next two weeks he at least managed to produce regular articles. One of these was about how two Romanian priests were rumoured to have been hanged as part of a 'reign of terror' the Austrians had imposed in Chernivtsi,[41] while in others he reported that the Russians were in 'fine spirit and confident of a decisive victory'[42] and were threatening to retake Chernivtsi.[43] As well as his news articles, he also produced a dramatic account of his escape from Chernivtsi.

At this point Clarke decided to leave for Bucharest and so he left Dobias with a 'watching brief' in Marmornitza. By the next day he was already in Bucharest and reporting back to London that King Constantine of Greece's unwillingness to enter the war on the side of the Allies was the reason for Prime Minister Eleftherios Venizelos's resignation and that 'violent demonstrations are already taking place in favour of war'.[44]

In finding news in Romania itself, though, Clarke was no more successful than during his previous stay in Bucharest. 'The amount of hard war news that was worth telegraphing to England was not very considerable in quantity, nor important in quality,' he later admitted, 'and for news other than war news the papers at home had no great keenness just then.'[45]

He spent his mornings in Bucharest visiting diplomats and statesmen and even had afternoon tea with Princess Bibesco at Castle Mogoshoia,[46] but these visits failed to elicit anything particularly newsworthy. With little else to occupy his time, Clarke discovered that horse riding was one of the few pursuits there that was relatively inexpensive and so he spent his afternoons taking 'happy jaunts' over the open countryside outside Bucharest.

Following Clarke's report about Venizelos's resignation, the *Daily Mail* did not publish another bylined article by Clarke for over two weeks, when he reported on discussions between the Bulgarian King and Prime Minister about the prospect of a coalition government in the event of Bulgaria entering the war.[47] Then six days later the *Daily Mail* published an article about his visit to the Russian Army, which he followed a few days later with another article in which he predicted Romania would join the war within the month. 'As one counts on the ultimate success of the Allies, so faithfully may one count on Romanian participation in that victory,' he wrote.

After one more story, about how Austrian and German food supplies were being affected by the closure for repair of four key supply roads,[48] he decided to leave Bucharest for the Romanian port of Constanta. Clarke hoped its position on the Black Sea would give him access to news from the Dardanelles and Constantinople, an area that was moving to the centre stage of the war following the Allied attack on the Dardanelles that preceded the disastrous Gallipoli landings.[49]

★★★

On Easter Monday 1915, Clarke took a train to Constanta,[50] whose warm weather made a welcome change from the cold of Marmornitza. It was, he wrote, a place where 'all the youth and beauty of Romania hurries as soon as it gets a weekend off and some money to spend'.[51] He would later compare it to Blackpool because of the way 'youngsters toil with bucket and spade on those sands, and somewhat older youngsters toil in foxtrot and jazz and native Romanian dances on the pier that points out its blunted nose seawards'.[52]

He made the most of Constanta's warm weather by hiring the captain of a small boat to take him out in it. Once they were away from the shore, Clarke took his clothes off and dived in for a swim, though he was later told that Romanians waited until the Black Sea was much warmer before swimming in it. In fact, the captain of the boat was so surprised that an article appeared in a local newspaper shortly afterwards about 'the Englishman who bathed at Easter'.[53]

In Constanta, Clarke met a sailor who was about to visit Constantinople and who agreed to report back what was happening there in exchange for some gold coins. As the two men negotiated the deal in a café over a bottle of Romanian wine, Clarke noticed a 'solid-looking' Turkish man who seemed 'much more interested in us than he cared to appear'.

Then on the day the sailor was due to arrive back in Constanta, Clarke was alarmed to see the same Turkish man waiting alongside him at the quay. So Clarke spent much of the rest of the day trying to shake him off – he tired out his overweight pursuer by going on a brisk but aimless 10 mile walk in the heat – and once he had lost him he met the sailor in his hotel.

The sailor told him his ship had been stopped by a Turkish warship as it had left Constanta and his clothes were searched. The ship was searched again on reaching the Bosphorus and a third time on arriving at Constantinople. The sailor was followed during his three days in the city and then as his ship was preparing to leave it was searched again and he was subjected to a full body search.

Clarke's class at Manchester Grammar School poses for a photograph in 1890. Clarke, at this time either 10 or 11, is on the far right on the back row. His school cap is askew and he has a defiant expression on his face, reflecting the fact that he spent his time there railing against authority.

A portrait of Clarke. The date is unknown, but was probably from his time as a journalist before the First World War. (*Courtesy of the Hartley family*)

Clarke as a young man. The date is unknown. (*Courtesy of the Hartley family*)

A drawing of Clarke by one of his
friends, September 1917. The helmet
shows that even though he was now
an accredited reporter at the Somme,
covering the war was not without its
danger. (*Courtesy of the Hartley family*)

Clarke sits with officers of the Queen's Royal West Surrey Regiment in a captured German dug-out in
Beaumont Hamel in November 1916. He is on the right. (*Courtesy of Gerald Gliddon*)

After living as a fugitive in Dunkirk in late 1914, when Clarke returned to the Western Front in 1916 he looked like he was part of the military, rather than just reporting on it. (*Courtesy of Annie Bibbings*)

Clarke relaxes in military uniform. This was probably taken in late 1916. (*Courtesy of the Hartley family*)

Clarke the accredited war correspondent poses for photographs, probably in late 1916. (*Courtesy of the Hartley family*)

'My dear old lass': A portrait of Lady Alice Clarke, whom Clarke married in 1904 and who was his close companion for the rest of his life. Date unknown. (*Courtesy of the Hartley family*)

Alice Clarke with six of her and Basil's seven children. 'What married people get, in return for not having kiddies I don't know,' Clarke once wrote to her, 'but whatever it is, whether fame or position or pleasure or merely wealth, it is jolly well not worth it.' This was taken in the late 1910s or in 1920. (*Courtesy of the Hartley family*)

Above: A painting by a friend of Clarke's of him playing the piano, probably at his 'charming little house' in Dulwich village. It was completed in 1918, just after he joined the Ministry of Reconstruction and in doing so became Britain's first public relations officer. (*Courtesy of the Hartley family*)

A professional portrait of Clarke. The date is unknown. (*Courtesy of Annie Bibbings*)

Clarke, back row on the far left, poses with fellow civil servants at Dublin Castle during the Irish War of Independence. They lived in the castle grounds for their own safety. Clarke is on the back row on the far left. Sir John Anderson, the Under-Secretary for Ireland who later became Chancellor of the Exchequer during the Second World War, is seated second from the right on the front row. This was probably taken in 1920 or 1921. (*Courtesy of Annie Bibbings*)

The large house Clarke and Alice shared in Eton, at a point on the River Thames where Izaac Walton, the author of the *Compleat Angler*, had spent time fishing in the seventeenth century. (*Courtesy of Annie Bibbings*)

Clarke poses for a photograph at the Thames near his home in Eton. It was near here that he fought with a former colleague, leading to a court appearance that was covered prominently in the press. (*Courtesy of Annie Bibbings*)

Clarke (far left) and Alice relaxing. The date is unknown. (*Courtesy of the Hartley family*)

Clarke poses for a photograph on a rickshaw during his trip to South Africa after his stroke in 1935. He hoped the trip would herald the beginning of a return to health, but it was not to be. (*Courtesy of the Hartley family*)

Clarke poses for a photograph in his later years. 'He bore his heavy physical troubles with high humour and never lost his humour and hope,' according to the *Manchester Guardian*. (*Courtesy of the Hartley family*)

C.P. Scott: the legendary editor and owner of the *Manchester Guardian*. Clarke found him 'a formidable and rather terrifying' figure but he gave him his first real job in journalism, as a sub-editor, in 1903. (*Author's collection*)

Charles Rolls' fatal crash. Clarke was among those present at Bournemouth when Charles Rolls, the co-founder of Rolls-Royce and aviation pioneer, became the first person to be killed in an aeroplane accident in the UK. Clarke's eyewitness account of the disaster was praised by C.P. Scott when Clarke later left the newspaper. (*Author's collection*)

Above: Lord Northcliffe: the newspaper proprietor (seated, right) had a huge influence on early twentieth-century Britain. He brought Clarke to the *Daily Mail* in 1910 and told him to 'go about with a bomb in your fist, my boy'. Though a controversial figure, Clarke developed a good relationship with him and would later remember that he 'was always good to me'. (*Author's collection*)

Lord Kitchener may have been a military hero, but when Clarke met Kitchener he found him 'rather stupid' and he was also opposed to Kitchener's ban on reporters near the front line. (*Author's collection*)

Dr Christopher Addison, the UK's first Minister for Health, took a keen interest in propaganda and was responsible for making Clarke the UK's first real public relations officer in 1917. (*Author's collection*)

General Nevil Macready, the head of the British Army in Ireland. Macready and Clarke had very different ideas on propaganda, with Macready complaining that 'Clarke has not the foggiest idea of how to set about propaganda from the point of view of a military operation'. (*Author's collection*)

Despite the close attention, the sailor had managed to see wounded Turkish and German soldiers being brought from the Dardenelles and Clarke thought his information would make an interesting article. But he was worried about how to send it back to London without it being intercepted by spies. So he wrote two articles, one an innocuous piece about shipping on the Black Sea and the other describing what the sailor had seen.

He took the first article to the wire room at the post office, noticing on the way that the Turkish man from the previous day was following him again. He left the article there and returned 5 minutes later to find the Turkish man looking through some papers behind the counter. His decoy seemed to have worked. He then sent the real article by registered post to a friend in Dorohoi in northern Romania, who sent it on to London.[54]

Soon afterwards, Clarke received an urgent telegram from Dobias telling him to return north and so he left the sunshine and travelled to meet him in Dorohoi, from where they took a coach back to Marmornitza. During the journey, Dobias explained that he had called him back because the Russians were planning to retake Chernivtsi.[55] It was, though, a false alarm and for reasons Clarke never discovered, the expected Russian offensive never materialised. He stayed in Marmornitza for just over a week and then returned to Bucharest.

A month had now passed since his prediction that Romania was about to join the war, but it had yet to declare its intentions. On arriving in Bucharest, Clarke wrote another article insisting a decision was imminent and that 'everyone is saying that Romania's moment is at hand'.[56] He sent another report a few days later repeating the claim, adding that 'it is regarded as inevitable that Romania will now take to the field'.[57]

Apart from this, Clarke found Bucharest to be 'just as dead as far as news for England was concerned' and so he decided to head home. After a journey that took two weeks and involved passing through Niš, Athens, Messina, Rome and Paris, he arrived in Britain and so ended his Eastern European commission.[58]

He is likely to have been disappointed by how little newsworthy material it had produced, certainly compared to his time in Flanders. While he had been reporting on the intricacies of Eastern European politics and idling away his afternoons riding horses and swimming in the sea, his *Daily Mail* colleagues had been covering events of great historical significance such as the sinking of the *Lusitania* and Italy's entry into the war.

But with his final article about Eastern Europe, Clarke at least fulfilled the wish of the Romanian Prince who had asked him to write about his country in the same way as he had done about Canada. Published on 13 June 1915, Clarke's article about Bucharest was more travel writing than news. He called Romania the 'gayest country in Europe' and suggested that Bucharest was the continent's 'capital of luxury and pleasure'.

There are those who call it the 'Pocket Paris', and not a few there who will tell you quite seriously that it 'out-parises' Paris. In the less innocent forms of giddiness this is perhaps true. For though Bucharest's fashions are the fashions of Paris, its pleasures and social forms those of Paris, the mind behind these things is something different from the mind of Paris – something more Eastern, more reckless, and abandoned, and extravagant than the Parisian mind at its giddiest.[59]

Clarke also explained how Bucharest's inhabitants differed from the British in their attitude to romance. 'The man who smiles at a lady he does not know is considered not so much as a "bounder" to be kicked as we in the West think,' he wrote. 'The most strait-laced critic would offer some excuses for him, and by the majority he might even be regarded as a commendably dashing and gallant fellow.'

Clarke may not have approved of men smiling at women they did not know, but he was happy to apply the critical eye he had used to appraise the attractiveness of women in British cities to their counterparts in Bucharest. 'The Bucharest women are distinctly pretty,' he concluded. 'They have big, bright eyes, brown or black, pretty hair, and faces delicately shaped. Yet, quite unnecessarily, they adorn nature by heels of three or four inches, by face powders pink and white, and by lip-salve of the most telling vermilion.'

His article about life in Bucharest gave an interesting insight into an exotic foreign capital and meant his Eastern European commission at least ended on a high note. But while his writing may have been as compelling as ever, as the months passed it became clear that he had been incorrect in his prediction that Romania was on the brink of joining the war.

It would be over a year before it finally declared its hand, joining on the side of the Allies in August 1916. And the commonly held belief that its participation might be decisive would also prove to be wrong. Left isolated by Russia's withdrawal from the war following the October Revolution, it negotiated an armistice with the Central Powers in December 1917 before re-joining the war on 10 November 1918, the day before the fighting ended in the west.

Notes

1   *Daily Mail*, 15 January 1915, p.5.
2   Basil Clarke, *My Round of the War*, London 1917, pp.81–2.
3   Ibid., p.83.
4   *Daily Mail*, 23 February 1914, p.5.

5   *Daily Mail*, 23 February 1914, p.5.
6   Basil Clarke, *My Round of the War*, London 1917, p.87.
7   *Daily Mail*, 23 February 1915, p.6.
8   Basil Clarke, *My Round of the War*, London 1917, pp.90–1.
9   *Daily Mail*, 23 February 1915, p.6.
10 Basil Clarke, *My Round of the War*, London 1917, pp.93–4.
11 Matthew Smallman-Raynor and Andrew David Cliff, Oxford, 2004, *War Epidemics: an Historical Geography of Infectious Diseases in Military Conflict and Civil Strife, 1850–2000*, pp.657–60.
12 Basil Clarke, *My Round of the War*, London 1917, p.95.
13 Ibid., pp.96–7.
14 *The War Illustrated*, 9 December 1916, p.386.
15 Basil Clarke, *My Round of the War*, London 1917, pp.99–104.
16 Ibid., p.105.
17 Ibid., p.105.
18 Ibid.7, p.107.
19 Ibid., p.109.
20 Ibid., p.110.
21 *The War Illustrated*, 21 October 1916, p.234.
22 Ibid., p.234.
23 Basil Clarke, *My Round of the War*, London 1917, p.114.
24 Ibid., p.116.
25 *The War Illustrated*, 22 July 1916, p.531.
26 Basil Clarke, *My Round of the War*, London 1917, pp.116–7
27 *Daily Mail*, 15 February 1915, p.5.
28 *Daily Mail*, 18 February 1915, p.5.
29 Basil Clarke, *My Round of the War*, London, 1917, p.124.
30 Ibid., pp.131–8. The version of this incident is different to the account Clarke wrote in the *Daily Mail* (8 March 1915, p.4), which ends simply with the detail that Klappa put down his money and slipped out into the darkness. It is not clear whether the account in *My Round of the War* is an exaggeration or whether the account in the *Daily Mail* had to be reduced for length. The only factual difference is that in the *Daily Mail* he states that he went to the restaurant specifically to see Klappa, while in *My Round of the War* the meeting was an accident. I have included the latter version. This also tallies with the version of the story Clarke told in *The War Illustrated* (28 October 1916, pp.242–4).
31 Basil Clarke, *My Round of the War*, London 1917, pp.139–40.
32 *Daily Mail*, 20 February 1915, p.5.
33 *Daily Mail*, 23 February 1915, p.6.
34 Basil Clarke, *My Round of the War*, London 1917, p.148.
35 *The War Illustrated*, 22 July 1916, p.531.
36 Basil Clarke, *My Round of the War*, London 1917, pp.148–52.
37 *The War Illustrated*, 18 November, 1916, p.316.
38 Basil Clarke, *My Round of the War*, London 1917, pp.140–3.
39 Ibid., pp.143–4.
40 *Daily Mail*, 24 February 1915, p.5.
41 *Daily Mail*, 3 March 1915, p.5.
42 *Daily Mail*, 1 March 1915, p.6.
43 *Daily Mail*, 8 March 1915, p.5.

44 *Daily Mail,* 9 March 1915, p.5.
45 Basil Clarke, *My Round of the War*, London 1917, p.153.
46 Ibid., p.153.
47 *Daily Mail*, 24 March 1915, p.5.
48 *Daily Mail*, 5 April 1915, p.6.
49 Basil Clarke, *My Round of the War*, London, 1917, p.154.
50 Ibid., p.156.
51 *Manchester Guardian*, 5 February 1940, p.10.
52 Ibid.
53 Ibid.
54 Basil Clarke, *My Round of the War*, London, 1917, pp.160–5. This story was also related in *The War Illustrated*, 21 October 1916, pp.234–6.
55 Ibid., p.165.
56 *Daily Mail*, 4 May 1915, p.5.
57 *Daily Mail*, 13 May 1915, p.6.
58 Basil Clarke, *My Round of the War*, London, 1917, p.165.
59 *Daily Mail*, 13 June 1915, p.4.

9

Home Front

Whether it was a consequence of the underwhelming output from his Eastern European commission or because of a desire to finally spend an uninterrupted period of time with his family, on Clarke's return to Britain he began to focus on the effect the war was having at home.

Settling back into family life in the 'charming little house' in Dulwich village where they now lived, he was surprised by how closely he felt the impact of the war despite being many miles from the fighting. He would later write about the difficulty of getting his sons to make their daily rations last much beyond breakfast and of getting them out of their beds and into their dressing gowns during air-raids.[1]

One of his first articles after returning to Britain examined how the large number of Belgian refugees were integrating into British society and his starting point was to visit a Belgian woman he had met in Flanders. Her home had been destroyed by a German shell and the last time Clarke had seen her she was preparing to leave for Britain despite never having been there before and not even being able to pronounce her destination of Folkestone. But when Clarke arrived at her home, he got an immediate indication of how well she had adapted when she offered him tea from a Queen Anne teapot.

'You take two pieces of sugar, monsieur?'[2]

She saw Clarke was amused to find her acting in such a typically English way. 'Ah, yes, you find us quite Engleesh now,' she laughed.

'You are indeed English,' he replied.

She introduced him to her two sons, who seemed to have settled equally well into their new surroundings. Dressed in cricket flannels and dark blue blazers, they had just finished playing cricket and one of them told Clarke how he had 'swiped a yorker and missed it'.

'It was odd to hear the old cricketing phrases from lips that had still a difficulty in pronouncing them,' Clarke wrote in his article about the visit.

His first impression that Belgian refugees were integrating well into British life was supported by visits to other Belgians around the country. He found Belgian girls playing tennis in suburbs and country towns, and Belgian families rowing and punting at Richmond, and was so impressed that in his *Daily Mail* article he made the case for them being allowed to stay in Britain after the war.

'There must be some subtle quality about British soil that makes it specially suitable for the transplanting of homes,' he wrote, expressing a tolerance that was notable given the *Daily Mail*'s reputation for hard-line views on immigration. 'Hugnenots, Italians, Portuguese, and others whose home roots were torn up and lacerated at different troublous times in history, came here and in time renewed those roots, becoming a thriving and flowering part of us. No one will grudge our plucky Belgian guests a little room if, after the war, they are loath to leave our shores.'

Having looked at the integration of refugees, Clarke then began to examine the economic impact of the war on prices and wages.

The issue has first been raised by the *Daily Mail* in February 1915, when Clarke had still been in Eastern Europe. It had welcomed the smaller than expected rise in food prices and interpreted the fact that 'the purchasing power of the average working man has not apparently diminished' as 'wonderful proof of the strength of our financial and industrial fabric'.[3] But though initially positive about the lack of economic hardship, four months later it had come to a more pessimistic view. The high level of expenditure on the war had created an illusion of extreme prosperity, it argued, but the extra income had been spent too freely and so had 'vanished as a five-pound note vanishes when it is burnt'.

'We are now approaching the second year of the war, when money will not be so plentiful or so easily obtained,' it warned. 'Everything that can be spared during the war should be spared … The individual German thinks of economy all day long and economises for his or her country. Can we not all of us show the same earnest thoughtfulness for the sake of our Motherland?'

Clarke was sent on a tour of the country to try to find evidence to support the *Daily Mail*'s belief that the free-spending of the British public was undermining the war effort.

His first stop was Bermondsey in South London, chosen because it was not obviously supplying equipment for the armed forces and so, Clarke reasoned, was likely to be representative of the country as a whole. It did not take him long to find a caretaker of a tenement block who seemed to confirm the *Daily Mail*'s fears.

'There's more money coming into Bermondsey than I've known in my 20 years here,' he said. 'And I tell you, they're having the time of their lives and no mistake.'

The caretaker claimed the separation allowance the Government paid to the families of men in the armed forces meant they were better off than before the war, while the large number of men who had gone to fight meant there was plenty of work for those left behind.

'Some who have never handled a hammer or a paint-brush before, or for years and years, have turned to joinering, painting, and such,' the caretaker told Clarke. 'All the women can get work, and there are very few of them who are not adding to their separation allowance in one way or another … With their separation allowances, I tell you, they're getting more, besides earning more, than ever in their lives.'

Clarke visited some of the occupants of the flats and among them found two sisters whose silk dresses and matching hats had been paid for with the extra money their mother earned from sewing coats for the Army. Another woman whose sons were in the Army had recently bought a sideboard and some ornaments, Clarke noted disapprovingly. He was also told that Bermondsey's newfound affluence had made people greedier; one local man had apparently eaten three dozen oysters on his way home to dinner.

Clarke's article about his visit was judgemental of those he met and it set the tone for a series of articles about what he called 'war prosperity'. 'One hates to blacken and belabour people whom life has already quite lustily belaboured,' he wrote, before going on to do just that. 'Money is going, relatively, very freely into even the poorest homes just now,' he reported, 'and … it is being very freely spent … spent without any real thought of the morrow and the hard times which are certain as night follows day to follow this war … Thriftlessness is more of a danger than any Zeppelins down Bermondsey way.'[4]

After Bermondsey, he visited an English village – he did not name it because this might give information to the enemy – where 2,000 soldiers were billeted. Despite having a population of just a few thousand, Clarke estimated the village was getting at least £700 extra (the equivalent of over £30,000 today) a week through payments to families who housed the soldiers; the separation allowance; the money soldiers spent in local shops; and the rations soldiers gave their host families. Clarke claimed soldiers were given so much food that some families did not have to buy any beef, bread, bacon or cheese and even had leftovers to give relatives in neighbouring villages.

Clarke reported that the extra money was being spent as freely as in Bermondsey, with lace curtains going up in the windows of the village's houses and the sounds of new pianos and organs being heard in the evenings. He also took a train to a market town 7 miles away to investigate the effect of the village's newfound prosperity on the surrounding area. Shopkeepers there told him they 'could not grumble', while some said business was considerably better than it had been in peacetime.[5]

After the village, Clarke's next stop on his tour of the country was Manchester and he arrived there to find the factories and mills working flat out to produce supplies for the trenches. 'The nights are alive with the lights and rumble and the hammerings of it,' he wrote, and yet still the signs in the windows of the labour-exchanges appealed for more workers.[6]

Clarke found that the plentiful supply of work meant people were earning more than ever before; one labourer he met had been paid 18s a week before the war but was now making over 17s a night. He spoke to girls who had never worked before but were now making shells for over 20s a week. Again, he did not believe the extra earnings were being saved in anything like the quantities needed to prepare for the 'hard times that must come' after the war.

From Manchester, he crossed the country to Tyneside, where along the river banks he saw workshops, factories, shipyards and gunshops that all had many more workers than usual.[7] He stood at the gates of a Tyneside factory on a warm evening and watched the workers leaving. Some had new bicycles or motorbikes and he also concluded that the fact that a number of workers had shiny new watch chains and new boots was further evidence of 'war prosperity'.

He spent the rest of the evening in Newcastle city centre and thought the people there seemed better dressed than on his previous visits to the city. Local shopkeepers he spoke to seemed to agree that people were buying more clothes and at higher prices, while the manager of a jeweller's shop told him he was selling more watches, chains and £5 rings than ever before. In the city centre he witnessed organised 'fuddling cruises', which were pub crawls with the purpose of getting drunk, and 'sobering parties' where people had lobsters, oysters and mineral water to try to undo the effects of the alcohol.

In his article about Tyneside, Clarke once again made the point that the working classes were not saving enough money for the hard times that would follow the war. 'It is quite evident that the workers of Tyneside regard the future with no apprehensions and are making all they can of the present,' he wrote. 'If they could see ahead and see the aftermath of scanty years that must follow this war their spending just now could hardly fail to follow very different lines.'

After Newcastle, the last stop in his tour was Paisley in Scotland, where he found unemployment to be almost non-existent and he witnessed what he judged to be the most 'needless luxuriousness' he had seen, with much of the extra money being spent on clothes. One man he met had been told he would have to wait six weeks for a new suit, which Clarke took as evidence that tailors were struggling to keep up with demand. Clarke also noted that Paisley had more sweet and cake shops than most towns of its size and saw the fact that they seemed to be doing well as further proof of extravagance.[8]

Having now visited a number of places, Clarke seemed confident in his judgement that the working classes were experiencing unprecedented prosperity but were squandering the extra income. His 'war prosperity' articles put forward his case:

Of thought for the morrow there is in many cases little; in most cases none. The poorer working families who in the past have suffered hardship, who have "gone short" for the mere lack of money to buy, will naturally provide for their wants at once now that times are so good.

Provision is not improvidence; and for the poor soul who found Paradise in a separation allowance of £1 a week for herself and three children and "no husband to keep" one can find sympathy and the wish of a longer prospective tenure of her simple happiness ... But the spending of Great Britain's huge industrial and "war income" just now is with thousands of richer workers more than a "provision", more than a filling of needs ...

It is improvidence as wanton and as wicked as it is unwise. These workers, too, would seem to regard the present time of prosperity as a Paradise. Brief as this time must be, is it not rather, for all of us that are thriftless, a fool's Paradise?'[9]

While Clarke's conclusions were based on what he had seen with his own eyes, they still relied on anecdote. Given that he seems to have set out with the intention of proving the existence of war prosperity, it is not surprising he was able to find people and places to support his argument. But it seems that virtually all of his conclusions were flawed.

According to the economic historian Peter Howlett, it is true that wages increased during the war, but so did prices. By mid-1915, as Clarke toured the country, prices had actually increased by more than wages. And while the separation allowance did make some people better off, Clarke failed to recognise that many families fell into poverty because it did not increase with inflation. Far from the UK being in the grip of reckless spending across the board, consumption as a percentage of Gross Domestic Product actually fell during the first year of the war. So while some people did become better off as a result of the war, this prosperity was by no means universal.

One of the few things Clarke got right was that the war would be followed by hard times. But he was wrong to suggest that economic downturn is an inevitable consequence of large wars; the Second World War, for example, was followed by economic growth and full employment.[10]

In his defence, his war prosperity articles are likely to have been the idea of his employers and, certainly, the *Daily Mail* was covering the supposed problem long after Clarke stopped writing about it. But even so, their lack of basis in fact meant they were as ill-conceived as they were mean-spirited. Just as the warmth and humanity in his articles about Belgian refugees showed Clarke at his best, his willingness to make sweeping generalisations about complex economic issues showed him at his worst.

While Clarke's first draft of the war's economic history has not stood the test of time, he was more prescient in his reporting on the new role it had given women in the workforce. In response to the shortage of men, thousands of women were employed in munitions factories across the country. These 'munitionettes' are today seen as having played an important role in the movement towards gender equality because the tough and dangerous nature of their jobs challenged the view that women were only capable of doing certain types of work.

Clarke witnessed this landmark social change first-hand when he took part in a tour of a weapons factory in Birmingham that employed 2,000 women. His article about the visit gave a sense of how attitudes towards women workers were beginning to change:

> Where were these girls a year ago? No works manager can tell you. They have just sprung into being—a new genus. Watch them as they feed piece after piece of metal into a machine with one hand, pull a lever with another, and push a third with a foot—all at a rate that makes one giddy.

> Girls acquire soon a quickness and deftness and aptitude for this kind of work that few men can attain. And one great qualification they have that few men ever learn—namely, patience. That the girls are cheerful and happy is shown by their quickness to smile at you, by their chatter, and by little things like the flags which ornament the shops. [11]

This positive impression was reinforced by an expert in weapons manufacture who, in extremely patronising terms, told Clarke he thought women might even be better at munitions work than men.

'A man will say "Can't you give me a new job? I'm fed up on this",' the expert explained. 'Whereas keep a girl on that job and say you're going to change her and she begs you to let her stay, and weeps if you don't.'

Clarke's article on munitions offers an insight into a key point in the history of women's rights in Britain, but Clarke produced little else of note during the second half of 1915. And the year came to a disappointing end when he had to travel to Denmark and so missed spending Christmas with his family for a second year running.

He sailed to Copenhagen in 'the horriblest, nastiest, beastliest little boat I ever sailed in'. It spent a day travelling along the British coast while it waited for permission to set sail, and then, when permission was finally granted, the crossing was rough and windy and included the terrifying experience of passing within 20 feet of a mine.

The unpleasantness of the crossing did not, though, destroy the Christmas spirit entirely. A group of the younger passengers dragged the saloon piano onto the deck and played Danish songs and then Clarke took over the piano and played while people danced on the tarpaulin covers. Then another passenger took over the piano playing and Clarke joined in the dancing until 3.00 a.m.[12]

He made enough of an impression on his fellow passengers to be invited to spend Christmas Day with a group of them and he enjoyed their festive hospitality. Then the following day he turned his attention to his assignment. He was in Denmark to investigate a story that would cause a global scandal and set him on a collision course with the British Government.

Notes

1 Basil Clarke, *Unfinished Autobiography*, p.200.
2 *Daily Mail*, 2 July 1915, p.4.
3 *Daily Mail*, 15 February 1915, p.4.
4 *Daily Mail*, 9 July 1915, p.4.
5 *Daily Mail*, 10 July 1015, p.3.
6 *Daily Mail*, 12 July 1915, p.3.
7 *Daily Mail*, 13 July 1915, p.3.
8 *Daily Mail*, 14 July 1915, p.6.
9 *Daily Mail*, 8 July 1915, p.4.
10 These judgements are based on correspondence between the author and Dr Peter Howlett, of the London School of Economics.
11 *Daily Mirror*, 10 November 1915, p.13. It is not clear why this article was published in the *Daily Mirror*, given that Clarke was still working for the *Daily Mail*. The most likely explanation is the close ties that existed between the *Daily Mail* and the *Daily Mirror*. While the *Daily Mirror* was no longer owned by Lord Northcliffe in 1915, it was by then the property of his brother, Lord Rothermere.
12 *The War Illustrated*, 22 December 1917, p.377.

10

'We Are Feeding the Germans'

For the first few weeks of the First World War, censorship prevented newspapers from giving the British public the full picture of how perilous the situation in Western Europe had become. But this suddenly changed at the end of August 1914 when *The Times* and the *Weekly Despatch*, both owned by Lord Northcliffe, published articles about the British retreat from Mons that included graphic descriptions of the 'sheer unconquerable mass of numbers' of the enemy and the 'broken bits of many [British] regiments'.[1]

After the anaesthetised reporting that went before it, what became known as the 'Amiens Dispatches' shocked Britain by laying bare the scale of the challenge that lay ahead. They also caused a national scandal; F.E. Smith had to resign as head of the Press Bureau and much of the blame for their publication fell at the door of Northcliffe.

Clarke was among those who believed their publication was justified. 'Hard things were said by people … but that message was correct in its tenor and general significance,' he later wrote. 'That despatch was the first thing to shake the silly "cocksureness" of the British nation and to awaken it to some sense of the gravity of things.'[2]

The two articles may have set Northcliffe in opposition to the Government, but the public's willingness to give the Government the benefit of the doubt at the start of the war meant he initially felt limited in how critical he could be. '[My newspapers are] dealing very gently with the Government now, because the public, who know nothing about the war, will not tolerate criticism of our public men,' he wrote in January 1915. 'But, believe me, we shall not be patient much longer.'[3]

Northcliffe was true to his word. In April 1915, the *Daily Mail* claimed there were problems with the type of ammunition being sent to the Front, and then the following month Northcliffe personally wrote an excoriating editorial about Lord Kitchener in which he claimed that his incompetence had directly led to the deaths of thousands of British soldiers.[4]

Criticising the Government in such strong terms at a time of war was shocking enough, but the fact that the broadside was aimed at a national hero made it particularly incendiary. There was a huge overnight drop in the *Daily Mail*'s circulation and advertising sales, while copies of the newspaper were burned in the street, and a placard accusing those who worked there of being 'Allies of the Hun' was hung outside its city office.[5] But while it may have been unpopular, the resulting scandal was one of the reasons, along with the failure of the Gallipoli landings, that the Liberal Government fell and was replaced by a coalition.

The coverage of the shells issue was the most extreme example of Northcliffe's willingness to criticise the Government, but it was by no means an isolated case. In fact, the Northcliffe press was so antagonistic that a Cabinet paper was prepared about how the Germans were using its coverage for propaganda. It cited, for example, how the *Daily Mail*'s description of members of the Government as 'incompetent bunglers' had been 'given special prominence in all German newspapers' and highlighted a 'specially violent' leader column in the *Daily Mail* that had been circulated by a German news agency throughout Scandinavia.[6]

It was against this backdrop that Northcliffe became, as Clarke put it, 'all het up' about the apparent lack of effectiveness of the British naval blockade of Germany.[7]

***

The aim of the British blockade was to prevent Germany from importing food and other supplies and so make it more difficult for it to continue to fight. But while its objective may have been straightforward, its implementation was complicated by the fact that Germany had land borders with neutral countries such as Denmark and the Netherlands. This meant that for the blockade to be truly effective, the British also had to stop goods being imported to neutral countries and then being sent on to Germany.

Traders proved adept at finding loopholes in any restrictions that were imposed. When the Swedish Government banned the export of copper to Germany but allowed an exception for works of art, for example, traders simply turned the copper it wanted to export into statues of the German military hero Paul von Hindenburg.[8] It was not just neutral countries that were making money from the situation; goods from Britain itself were being exported to neutral countries and then sent on to Germany.

As well as the practical difficulties, the British feared that restricting the trade of neutral countries might alienate them and Foreign Secretary Sir Edward Grey was particularly concerned about the rights of neutrals.

Publicly, the Government insisted the blockade was robust and effective, but privately its officials knew it was not working.[9] Concerns began to enter the public domain towards the end of 1915, with opposition MPs questioning its effectiveness in the House of Commons, and the *Daily Mirror* calling it 'our slipshod blockade'. Yet despite the failure of the Government to mount a convincing defence, this criticism did not seriously damage the Government because there was no strong evidence to support it.[10] And so Clarke arrived in Copenhagen at the end of 1915 to try to find that evidence.

★★★

Clarke started his investigation into the blockade by trying to get import statistics from the Danish Government, only to be told it had stopped issuing them and had banned their publication. He did, though, manage to find a Danish trade newspaper called the *Borsen* that listed imports to Copenhagen. While these figures did not include imports to other Danish ports, Clarke thought they might at least give an indication of whether more goods were being imported than before the war. So he hired an out-of-work Danish journalist to undertake the laborious task of taking the totals for each merchant and each ship for every day in 1915 and adding them together to give totals for all the imports into Copenhagen for the whole year.[11]

The results were staggering. In 1913, the whole of Denmark had imported 2,860 tons of rice, but according to Clarke's figures Copenhagen alone had imported 16,625 tons in 1915. In 1913, Denmark had imported 4,000 tons of lard, but the 1915 total for Copenhagen was 15,000 tons. Pork imports followed a similar pattern, with 950 tons imported to Denmark in 1913 rising to 12,500 tons for Copenhagen in 1915.

Clarke immediately realised the figures compiled from this obscure Danish journal would be a major international story. He thought that some of the increase could be explained by reductions in imports from Germany and an increase in exports to Sweden and Russia, but he did not believe these explanations could account for the scale of the increase, which meant he had uncovered apparently incontrovertible evidence that goods were being shipped to Denmark and then being sent on to Germany.

While the Danish journalist had been compiling the import data, Clarke had spent time at the docks at Copenhagen and seen sacks, boxes and barrels being loaded onto German-bound boats. He heard orders being given in German and even saw some boats flying the German flag. Clarke managed to get on board one of these boats and travelled in it to Malmo in Sweden with a cargo of oils, fats and iron. Once they arrived at Malmo, the cargo was unloaded onto the quay to wait for a German steamer.[12]

With his observations supporting the *Borsen's* statistics, he was confident that he had strong evidence that the blockade was being routinely flouted and so he returned to England. When Northcliffe heard the results of his investigation, he was so pleased that he invited Clarke to his house for lunch. As Clarke sat down at the table with the other guests, the waitress asked him if he would prefer white or red wine with his meal and he asked for a glass of the white.

'No you don't, my boy,' Northcliffe said, snatching the newly poured wine away. 'You've got that blockade article to write this afternoon.'

Northcliffe was so keen for the article to be given Clarke's full attention that after lunch he personally took him back to the *Daily Mail* and installed him in the directors' room so he could write without being disturbed.[13]

As he sat down to begin working, Clarke must have had many pages of notes in front of him. But he was able to summarise his findings in a five-word introduction that was as devastating as it was succinct: 'We are feeding the Germans'.

His article, published in the *Daily Mail* on 12 January 1916, made the shocking allegation that 'ship after ship and train after train, as I have seen for myself, are still pouring the world's goods into Germany'. 'In setting out the facts on which these deplorable conclusions are based,' he wrote, 'I will try to keep from my presentation of them any distortion due to the disgust and burning anger that they evoke in me, as they must do any patriot of this Empire.'[14]

He went on to set out the statistics for how greatly imports to Denmark seemed to have increased since the start of the war, explaining how the *Borsen* figures represented a 375 per cent increase in imports of lard and a 1,300 per cent increase for pork. After setting out similar increases for cocoa and coffee, he argued that the only possible explanation was that the extra goods were going to Germany. '[Denmark's] 2,900,000 population could not use so much cocoa and coffee, for instance, if they drank nothing else night and day,' he wrote. 'To argue that Denmark is using these commodities herself is mere foolishness. She is exporting, of course.'

The article was accompanied by a scathing editorial. Headlined 'Deplorable, Pernicious, and Dangerous', it lambasted the Government for letting down 'the young men who form the flower of this nation' by failing to take 'proper steps to cut off the supply of food which sustains the Germans of the material for making ammunition with which the Germans are to kill our men'.[15]

'The mothers and fathers, the sisters and sweethearts, of the young men now enrolling should bestir themselves,' it continued. 'They should bring the matter to the attention of members of Parliament. For the war, with its toll of killed and wounded, will last indefinitely if, for the sake of being gentle to Germany and conferring benefits on a few neutral traders, food and other supplies are delivered with clockwork regularity to the enemy.'

The publication of Clarke's article caused an immediate worldwide sensation. Newspapers around the world, including influential American newspapers such as the *Washington Post*[16] and the *New York Times*,[17] repeated the *Daily Mail's* claim that the Government's failure to impose an adequate blockade was a betrayal of the men who were fighting and dying at the Front. Yet despite the seriousness of the allegation and the fact that it struck at the heart of the Government's competence to run the war, there does not initially seem to have been any real attempt to rebut it.

The lack of a government response did not mean Clarke and the *Daily Mail* were about to let the story drop. Over the next few days there were two follow-up articles, one by Clarke claiming British tyres were being used on German cars[18] and the other a leader column accusing the Government of running a 'sham blockade'. The editorial demanded that the Admiralty be put in charge of it and warned ominously that Britain 'is going to insist on a real blockade of Germany and it will make short work of its Ministers if they do not convert their sham blockade into a real strangle-hold'.[19]

The allegations shocked the country. Five days after Clarke's initial article, he wrote another piece headlined 'Sham Blockade'[20] and in the same edition it was reported that Parliament was planning to debate the issue.[21] Then the following day the conservative *Morning Post* joined the *Daily Mail* in criticising the blockade. One of its reporters had uncovered separate statistics suggesting Germany had imported 4 million pairs of boots from the United States in 1915, which it used as evidence that 'Germany has been permitted by the British Government to import through neutral countries essential supplies to an amount exceeding the amount imported by her in time of peace'.[22]

The *Daily Mail* welcomed the *Morning Post* article with an editorial that demanded that control of the blockade be taken from the Foreign Office and given to the Admiralty, which consisted of seamen who it believed were the only ones in government with 'the requisite knowledge to conduct it'.[23] Then it maintained the pressure with another article by Clarke about how workers at Dunlop's Birmingham plant had demanded assurances before agreeing to work on a consignment of tyres for Copenhagen, telling the company's management they were 'not going to make tyres for the Germans'.[24] The protest was only settled, Clarke reported, when managers were able to prove the tyres would not be sent on to Germany.

Because of the controversy, the MP Sir Henry Dalziel placed a motion on the House of Commons' order paper for a select committee to investigate the blockade, while a separate motion was put before Parliament that called for the blockade to be enforced as effectively as possible.[25]

By now, almost a week had passed since Clarke's first article and, if anything, interest in the story appeared to be increasing. It was around this time that the Government began to fight back. The *Westminster Gazette*, which was generally considered to be a mouthpiece for the Government, published an editorial on 18 January defending the blockade:

> Whatever else it may be, the blockade is not a sham ... whether it can be made more effective still is a question which concerns us all, but we are not at the beginning of wisdom on that subject until we understand the very real difficulties which surround this question. It alarms us to see these very difficult and delicate questions ... discussed without, apparently, any understanding of the necessary conditions.[26]

In the same edition, the *Westminster Gazette* reported that the Government had recently sent 'a business man of eminence' to Scandinavia, and he had concluded the blockade was working well. 'Such a man would have very much better means of examining the situation from within than any correspondent sent out to make a case against the Government,' it suggested.[27]

Clarke responded to this claim a week later, writing that an attempt to 'discredit my figures has been made by a vague allusion to a visit of enquiry by "an eminent man of business"' that he understood to be a reference to the financier and politician Sir Alexander Henderson. 'Sir Alexander, if he reported "all well" with our blockade, was wrong,' wrote Clarke.[28]

The day after its claim about the 'business man of eminence', the *Westminster Gazette* urged its readers not to 'be led away by mere clamour',[29] and then the following day rubbished Clarke's articles as 'only a phase of the conspiracy to bring the Government down' that was being orchestrated by Northcliffe.[30] It quoted an anonymous MP who claimed to detect a sinister motive behind the articles:

> If the Daily Mail would study the German papers, instead of talking about statistics which it does not understand, it would get a little nearer the truth of the effects of our blockade. But it does not want to do this, because it is out not to beat Germany, but to destroy the Coalition Government at home, by the continual process of sapping and undermining its prestige and authority ... The country believes the stories about our feeding Germany, and the Government must do everything in its power to make the truth known, and rebut these calumnies, or it may find it difficult to exert its authority in the administration of the law.[31]

As dismissive as the anonymous MP may have been about their substance, his acknowledgment that they posed a serious threat to the Government showed just how much impact Clarke's allegations had made, and also how high the stakes had become.

For all the difficulties Clarke may have experienced during his eight years as a journalist, his work had never been subjected to anything like the level of scrutiny now being applied to it. By this stage, he was expending as much energy responding to criticism of his articles as he was to making the case against the Government. On 20 January, for example, he described the suggestion that the extra imports to Copenhagen were being sent on to Russia rather than Germany as ranking 'among the very poorest of all the bad arguments that have been put forward to defend our sham blockade,' before going on to claim that Russia had 'almost negligible' trade with Denmark.[32]

The story had by now been running for nearly two weeks and still the *Daily Mirror* reported that businessmen in the City of London were 'discussing nothing else but the inefficiency of the blockade' and that 'a great popular demand for freedom of action for our Fleet is growing in force every hour', with the 'man in the street ... crying out for a check to be put upon this abuse of privilege'.[33] It was not just in London that Clarke sparked debate, with the *Livingstone Mail* in Northern Rhodesia calling the blockade's effectiveness 'one of the questions of the hour'.[34] So when a scheduled statement to the House of Commons about the blockade was delayed for a week, it must have added to the impression that the Government was in crisis. After the Foreign Secretary Sir Edward Grey announced the postponement, the MP Rowland Hunt asked him how much longer the Navy was to be crippled by the Foreign Office, prolonging the war and unnecessarily sacrificing British lives.

'The statement made in the question is grossly unfair and entirely misrepresents the facts,' Grey replied. But any further explanation would have to wait.

★★★

On 21 January, the *Westminster Gazette* continued its defence of the Government. 'It is quite untrue to suggest there is widespread alarm in the House in consequence of the recent attacks that have been made on the Government,' it reported. 'The object of these attacks is well understood, and the authority of the paper that made them counts for very little in the House of Commons.'[35] But even as the *Westminster Gazette* tried to diminish the significance of the story, it acknowledged that MPs 'realise that these articles have shaken public confidence to some extent'.[36]

On the same day, the *New York Times* reported that public discussion of the blockade 'continues bitterly'[37] and its claim that 'Germany is far better supplied than the official British statements permit Englishmen to believe' suggests it accepted at least some of Clarke's arguments as fact.

With almost every day that passed, the *Daily Mail* published a new article. On 22 January, for example, Clarke reported that a Viennese newspaper had recently published an advert for 40 tons of prime beef from the Netherlands, and a weekly supply of a wagon full of cement and linseed oil from Denmark.[38] 'It is not easy to imagine what burst of confidence prompted the advertiser to disclose the origin of his supplies,' he wrote. 'No doubt it was to help to assure clients of their excellence. It will also help to assure Great Britain of the existence of this feeding of our enemy by neutrals through us … Forty tons of beef from Holland! It is just possible that this beef is Dutch, though it might just as easily be American or South American. But she would not sell it, or nearly so much of it as she does sell, unless she could get imported meat-stuffs to replace it, and these she gets in vast quantities from America and elsewhere through the kindness of our Foreign Office with its "paper blockade".'

On 24 January, at the start of the week when the blockade was scheduled to be discussed in the House of Commons, one Danish newspaper reported that 'every capital in Europe is full of the sensational rumours used by Mr Clarke'.[39] The *Daily Mail* began the week with an editorial that, after dismissing the *Westminster Gazette*'s criticism as that of a 'party hack newspaper', once again set out the case against the Government and tried to rally the public to put pressure on their elected representatives:

It is beyond possibility to repudiate the figures published by the Morning Post and the facts revealed by the able Daily Mail Special Commissioner, Mr Basil Clarke, clearly showing that the Germans are getting vast stores through neutral countries.

It is absurd to contend that this food is not reaching and strengthening the German people and the German Army. That very elastic and much discredited political dodge, the "official denial", will not again satisfy the wives, mothers, and sisters of those whose lives are at stake …

If you have near and dear ones in any of our fighting forces, you cannot do better this Monday morning than by bringing some pressure – postal, telephonic, or verbal – upon any member of Parliament to get him to stop the food and explosive supplies we are permitting to pass into Germany. By so doing you can shorten the war and save lives.[40]

In the same edition, Clarke wrote an article defending himself yet another argument used by those defending the blockade – that the extra goods arriving into the ports were replacing goods that had previously been imported from Germany.[41] His article was accompanied by a review of how German newspapers had covered the story, which claimed their tone was one of 'undisguised fear and trembling over the prospective tightening up of the British blockade'. 'Judging by whining headlines, Berlin cherishes the hope that the worst may yet be staved off for Germany by protests over "violation of neutral rights",' it concluded.

But while the *Daily Mail* may have been justified in accusing the *Westminster Gazette* of being biased towards the Government, criticism of its coverage was also beginning to emerge from more credible sources. *The Economist* magazine, for example, questioned whether Clarke and his colleagues at the *Daily Mail* were capable of grasping the complexity of the issue. 'Whether our so-called blockade really contributes to the difficulties of the German Government is a scientific problem which the leader-writer of a half-penny dreadful is quite incapable of solving,' it suggested rather dismissively.[42]

★★★

On the Tuesday, the day before the Parliamentary debate, the *Daily Mail* published yet another article by Clarke, this time addressing claims that a tighter blockade would threaten relations with neutral countries.

'It has about as much reality as our "blockade of Germany",' he wrote. 'My experience of neutrals and neutral countries during this war is pretty extensive, and it is that they are amazed at the extent of the trade powers we leave in the hands of neutrals.'[43]

As Clarke wrote these words, he would have expected that the day after they were published the Government would finally give its official reply. Actually, he did not even have to wait that long. On the same day, 25 January, the Government unexpectedly issued a lengthy memorandum responding both to Clarke's articles and those in the *Morning Post*.[44]

The memorandum was forensic in its detail. And while it lacked the hyperbole of Clarke's articles, it rebutted the allegations in a way that was quietly devastating and showed that the *Daily Mail's* confidence that it was 'beyond possibility'[45] for Clarke's story to be repudiated had been badly misplaced.

The memorandum showed that the Government had spent the previous two weeks carefully preparing its defence. It had tracked down copies of the *Borsen* and discovered its figures included consignments bound for other countries. The memorandum gave the example of a cargo of rice and pineapples that were included in the *Borsen* figures but were actually being shipped to Norway.

It also revealed that some goods were only allowed to continue to Denmark if the British were guaranteed that they would either be returned to Britain or stored in Denmark until the end of the war. This was because some goods covered by the blockade were stored near the bottom of the ship, which meant removing them would involve unloading the whole ship and lead to delays and congestion in ports. Yet the *Borsen* had listed the contents of the whole cargo, even when much of it was to be returned to Britain or stored in Denmark. The memorandum argued that this had significantly inflated the *Daily Mail*'s figures for 1915.

Having pointed out two general problems with Clarke's conclusions, it then systematically went through each type of goods mentioned in the original *Daily Mail* article. With rice, for example, it accused Clarke of failing to compare like with like, because the 1913 total had only included rice meal or ground rice, while the 1915 total included whole rice, rice groats and rice meal. It also suggested that any increase to rice imports could be explained by the fact that the price of rice had increased by much less than the price of pearl barley or oatmeal.

While these arguments were in themselves enough to raise serious doubts about Clarke's figures, the memorandum's final point was perhaps most effective in undermining the credibility of both the story and also of Clarke himself. Clarke had got his maths wrong.

In his original article, he had reported that the increase in lard imports from 4,000 tons to 15,000 tons had represented a 375 per cent rise. In fact, this is a 275 per cent increase. Similarly, he claimed the increase in pork imports from 950 tons to 12,500 tons was a 1,300 per cent increase. It should have been 1,216 per cent. There were similar mistakes in other calculations.

Considering how obvious it must have been that his article would be highly contentious, it is extraordinary both that Clarke made such basic mistakes in the first place but also that nobody at the *Daily Mail* seems to have bothered checking the percentages before publishing them. The error made a mockery of the *Daily Mail*'s claim in the editorial accompanying the first article that Clarke was 'an able man, with great experience in sifting and analysing facts and figures'.[46]

Perhaps the most frustrating thing for Clarke was that the correct percentages still represented huge increases and there is little difference, from the point of view of constructing an argument, between an increase of 375 per cent and 275 per cent, or between 1,300 per cent and 1,216 per cent. This was a point Clarke made in his response to the memorandum in the following day's *Daily Mail*, as he tried to defend what he must have known was a serious error by accusing the Government of splitting hairs:

> My percentages, Alas! were wrong in some cases. The increase in rice imports, for instance, should have been only a tiny 480 per cent, not 580; lard a mere

275 per cent, not 375 per cent, pork only 1,216 per cent, not 1,300 per cent; and so on. To have reduced each of these totals by 100 may give the War Trade Arithmetic Department much joy, but it does not show that extra food in colossal quantities is not going into Germany – as it undoubtedly is.'[47]

Clarke also accepted that the Government's point about goods being stored in Denmark or being sent back to the UK might be 'partly true', but he questioned whether this really had a significant effect on the totals. He also expressed his frustration at the fact that the Government response had dealt only with the *Borsen* statistics, whereas he saw these figures as only part of a wider investigation. 'Let me say at once that had the Borsen figures alone been the evidence on which I asserted that Denmark is acting as a food-getter for Germany I might too have been doubtful,' he wrote. 'But these figures were but a fraction of the sum total evidence I collected and wrote.'

Clarke's response was accompanied by an editorial that weakly tried to excuse the errors in the percentages – 'No doubt these statistics contained inaccuracies. Most statistics do' – and then wrongly attributed the errors to a Danish Government statistician. Then, like Clarke's own article, it attempted to put the Government back on the defensive by highlighting the fact that it had not made 'the slightest attempt to dispute any of Mr Clarke's own statements concerning what he saw and heard with his own eyes and ears about the vast volume of supplies pouring through the Danish ports into Germany'.[48]

As part of the Northcliffe press's response, *The Times* published a letter by Clarke in which he reasserted his claim that the blockade was leaking:

> There is still an ample margin of truth left in those Danish returns, even accepting the contention that they are not absolutely accurate, to justify the deduction I drew from them, which was, that foodstuffs in most unusual quantities are being imported by Denmark. The War Trade Department makes no attempt to dispute the large mass of other evidence which I collected from personal observation and inquiry on the spot regarding the great quantity of these extra supplies which is going through Danish ports into Germany.[49]

The Times's editorial adopted a more measured tone, but it also thought the Government still had a case to answer. It acknowledged that the memorandum 'points out a serious error ... but it leaves the broad fact unchanged and unquestioned that, in spite of all precautions, goods in considerable amounts continue to reach the enemy through these neutral channels'.

It was, though, in a minority, as most of the next day's press considered the memorandum to have been a masterstroke.

'While the *Daily Mail* and the *Morning Post* stick to their ground and declare that the Government's statement deals mostly with side issues, other newspapers assert that the Government's reply is absolutely convincing and unanswerable,' the *New York Times* reported,[50] while the *Sydney Morning Herald* described the memorandum as 'a very effective answer to figures and criticisms'[51] and the *Livingstone Mail* in Northern Rhodesia thought 'the official reply reduces very materially the value of the attack made upon the Government'.[52] In London, the *Evening Standard* reported that the memorandum contained strong evidence that 'our strangle hold on German trade has been increased in firmness every week',[53] while the *Westminster Gazette* suggested that the use of statistics by both the *Daily Mail* and the *Morning Post* 'are now proved to contain nearly every kind of error which haste or irresponsibility could devise – errors of carelessness, errors of arithmetic'. An editorial in that day's *Daily News* argued that the memorandum exonerated the Government and called Clarke's professionalism into question:

> There has rarely been a more crushing exposure than that issued by the War Department of the latest Northcliffe scandal ... Nearly every fact on which the case is built up is found to be either an ignorant misapprehension or a garbled half-statement ... It is found in nearly every case that the allegation of the scare-mongers is a gross and fatuous alarm.[54]

If the decision to release the memorandum the day before the Parliamentary debate was intended to take the sting out of the story, then it succeeded. *The Times* may have still believed that 'today's debate is anxiously awaited throughout the civilized world', but much of that day's press coverage gave the impression the Government had won the argument even before Edward Grey stood up in Parliament that evening to defend the blockade.

We do not know whether Clarke was in the House of Commons to watch Grey's statement, or if he was at the *Daily Mail* office, anxiously waiting for news to come through. But as the debate preceding it progressed, it became clear that while MPs may have been concerned about the blockade, they were generally willing to accept that the issue was more complex than Clarke had allowed for. In fact, perhaps the most severe criticism during the debate was Conservative MP Leslie Scott's accusation that the Government had showed 'great discourtesy' in issuing its response to the press before giving it to Parliament. It was also Scott who best summed up the constructive spirit in which the debate was conducted. 'Let us discuss this question in order to see what more can be done,' he said, 'rather than to see whether the Government are to blame for not having done enough hitherto.'[55]

After several MPs had had their say, Grey got to his feet just after 6.00 p.m. to give his statement to a packed House of Commons. Watched by Ministers from Denmark and Sweden in the public gallery and to the cheers of Arthur Balfour, the First Lord of the Admiralty whose navy his policies were accused of restricting, Grey began his response:

> I must deal with some of the figures scattered broadcast lately in some organs of the press, which have created a grotesque and quite untrue impression of the amount of leakage through neutral countries – figures which will not bear examination, but the conclusions founded upon which have undoubtedly done great harm.[56]

Grey went through the figures released in the memorandum and argued they showed the Government was already doing all that could reasonably be expected, given its obligation to respect the rights of neutrals. He also called for an end to newspaper attacks on the blockade because of the dispiriting effect they were having on the Navy.

His statement was well-received by his fellow MPs, with the *New York Times* reporting that it left 'the position exactly as before the debate, except that Parliament seemed more converted to the Government policy'.[57]

The *Daily Mail*'s response the following morning was still critical, though perhaps less truculent than might have been expected. But any doubts the editorial's relatively measured tone may have raised about its stomach for continuing its fight with the Government were dispelled by the response by Clarke that was published alongside it. Dripping with vitriol, he made no attempt to hide his anger as he railed against what he viewed as the underhand tactics of the Government:

> Such is their guilt and knowledge of it that a last-minute reply had certain attractions for them. They take a fraction of the twenty or more columns of evidence that I adduced, showing how we are feeding Germany, and they point out in what direction that fraction of evidence may have been misleading to me and others. They deal, in short, solely with statistics I quoted from the Danish trade paper Borsen and assume (quite wrongly) that I omitted to take notice of certain considerations which might qualify these statistics.

He went on to challenge the Government to prove its claim that large quantities of goods had been sent back to Britain or were being stored in Denmark until the end of the war, and he argued that the effort the Government had put into discrediting his articles would have been better used combating German propaganda in neutral countries than in 'seeking minor journalistic victories at home'.

Given the scandal caused by his allegations, the idea that the Government should not have bothered to investigate them was so obviously weak that it suggests Clarke was beginning to feel the effect of day after day of biting criticism.

He was on firmer ground with his claim that by focusing exclusively on the figures from the *Borsen*, the Government had ignored everything else in his articles. It was, perhaps, an early example of the now established public relations tactic of identifying a single flaw in an opponent's argument and focusing on it disproportionately in the hope of undermining their overall credibility. Clarke finished his article with an accusation:

> The British Government ... know of it [the leaks in the blockade]; or are deliberately shutting their eyes and discrediting the evidence of their own agents.

> If they would say, "Our blockade is not perfect; we are sorry; it cannot be made more perfect without incurring disadvantages greater than the advantages we should reap through perfecting it" – if they would say this one would at least sympathise with their point of view even if one did not share it.

> But in solemn, full, round phrases they insist for the benefit of a trusting people (and of the Allied nations who fight with us) that our blockade is real and sound and true; and they take laborious means to discredit all those who on the evidence of their own eyes and common sense would show that it is not. This may be politics, but it is not cricket. Nor is it war.

As bombastic as his article was, there was something in its tone that hinted that, having staked his reputation on his fight with the Government, he realised the initiative was slipping away. Certainly, most of the next day's newspapers were fulsome in their praise of Grey's statement.

The *New York Times* reported that 'Sir Edward Grey's effective speech appeared to finish the work thus begun' by the memorandum the previous day,[58] while the *Manchester Guardian* judged that 'the statistical case against the Government's blockade policy has been almost completely demolished'[59] and the *Daily Mirror*, which had itself previously questioned the effectiveness of the blockade, reported that Grey's statement had fully addressed 'some grotesque figures which had been published and which were quite untrue, but the conclusions founded upon which had done great harm'.

The potentially damaging effect of the *Daily Mail*'s coverage was also highlighted by *The Economist*. After congratulating Grey for his speech, it chastised the Government's critics for the 'amazing carelessness in their use of statistics' and claimed 'it is also sufficiently clear that it has brought us to the verge of collision with neutral countries'.[60]

Of all the coverage of Grey's speech, perhaps the most extreme in its criticism of Clarke's argument was the *Daily News*. 'Dragged into the light it is found to be an impudent invention, based on grotesque figures and falsified deductions,' it concluded. 'Its aim has been, not to enlighten the public, but to bewilder it.'[61]

The combination of the memorandum and Grey's speech seemed to have won the Government a decisive victory but, as battered as their reputations may have been, neither Clarke nor the *Daily Mail* were about to give up. Clarke followed his response to Grey's speech with a defiant article the following day headlined 'Leaks in the blockade' and the next day he wrote yet another piece, this time with the headline 'Leaky blockade'. Yet despite Clarke's determination not to be beaten and the *Daily Mail*'s willingness to let him continue criticising the Government, his articles were beginning to give the impression that the story was running out of steam.

In another article on 31 January, Clarke turned his attention to the newspapers that had been so critical of him, describing them as the 'Hide-The-Truth press' for having defended the Government. German traders, he wrote, 'must be delighted to find the impression spreads … that the Foreign Office has proved that no food or supplies, or only negligible quantities, are going to Germany'.[62]

Clarke argued that this would reinforce the idea that Britain tolerated traders who sold goods illegally to Germany. 'Till now these traders have been like people dodging the policeman,' he wrote. 'Now they have been seen by the policeman, and he has given them, instead of a shaking up, merely a nod.'

But even as he criticised other newspapers, his acknowledgement of a consensus that the blockade was working could be read as an implicit acceptance of defeat.

The next day, another article by Clarke rebutted the claim that the extra tea arriving in Denmark was being sent on to Russia rather than Germany,[62] and then three days later he wrote about a Danish trader who had advertised 200,000 pairs of military horseshoes in a German newspaper.[64] The following day he claimed iron ore was getting through the blockade.[65]

And then there was silence. The article about iron ore was the last one Clarke wrote about the blockade.

★★★

It is unclear why his articles stopped so suddenly. It may be that the *Daily Mail* felt his credibility had been too badly damaged, or perhaps he had simply run out of things to say. Clarke's last article about the blockade, did not though, mean the end of the *Daily Mail*'s interest in it.

After just over a week of not covering the subject, it published an article by the reporter Robert Segar about problems with the blockade in the Netherlands. Under the headline 'The blockade failure; how we are still feeding the Germans', Segar continued in the same vein as Clarke as he claimed the Netherlands was 'being used by the Germans as a vast storehouse'.[66]

The next day, on 15 February, the *Daily Mail* published another article by Segar that described how the blockade was 'leaking at every seam'[67] and over the course of nine days, between 14 February and 22 February, the *Daily Mail* published six articles criticising it. Neither Clarke nor his investigation were mentioned once.

Then on 23 February, the Government announced the establishment of a Ministry of Blockade. The *Daily Mail* may have been calling for responsibility for the blockade to be given to the Admiralty, but it could justifiably count the announcement of the new ministry as a victory. Over the previous month it had printed thousands of words criticising the blockade, and now the Government was changing the way it was managed.

That is not to say newspaper coverage was the only reason the Ministry of Blockade was established. Grey was not the kind of politician to change course just because journalists were telling him to; in fact, he had such little interest in newspapers that he apparently only learned the detail of Clarke's allegations when he read about them in the *Westminster Gazette*.[68]

Nor was Grey desperate to keep control of the blockade. He had actually written to the Prime Minister Herbert Asquith to suggest it would be difficult for him to effectively monitor the blockade at the same time as carrying out his other duties as Foreign Secretary.[69] And as well as the press, both the Navy and Parliament put pressure on the Government to improve the blockade. But even with these caveats, it still seems certain that newspaper coverage and the resulting public anger was one of the main reasons for the change.

In his biography of Grey, the historian Keith Robbins wrote: 'Changes in administration of blockade policy were only in part for administrative convenience. They were also the result of attacks made on the Foreign Secretary's policy … [and the] vigorous public clamour for an intensification of the economic campaign was not without its effect.'[70]

While Clarke cannot take all the credit for the pressure exerted by the press – Segar and the *Morning Post* also played their part, and Northcliffe must get some of the credit for becoming 'het up' about it in the first place – his articles were by far the most controversial, and towards the end of his life Clarke himself certainly believed it had an impact. Referring to his original piece in the *Daily Mail*, he wrote: 'That article of mine did some good.'[71]

★★★

The establishment of the Ministry of Blockade was not just a cosmetic change. The new Minister of Blockade, Sir Robert Cecil, was less sympathetic to the rights of neutral countries than Grey, and the historian Eric W. Osborne has suggested the creation of the ministry heralded a 'change for the better'.[72] It was not, though, a single decisive turning point. The blockade would be strengthened still further after Lloyd George became Prime Minister at the end of 1916[73] and it was only when the United States entered the war in April 1917 that it became a truly effective weapon.[74]

There is also the question of how important the blockade was in the final defeat of Germany. Osborne has described it as 'the greatest factor behind the Allied victory'[75] but the historian Niall Ferguson has argued that although its effect was 'undoubtedly severe',[76] it never achieved its aim of starving Germany into submission because its victims were mainly those who were not vital to its war effort.[77]

What does seem clear is that despite the flaws in his articles, Clarke was right about the ineffectiveness of the blockade. In fact, a confidential Foreign Office memo from the previous December had admitted that 'goods may and do reach our enemies'.[78] But the errors in his reporting of it, of which the working out of percentages was only the most glaring, ultimately made it all too easy for the Government to undermine his credibility.

Clarke had many strengths as a journalist. His descriptive writing was often excellent and he had shown great resourcefulness and tenacity in lasting for so long in Dunkirk during the early months of the war. But he also had weaknesses and there had already been signs that he might not be ideally suited to a story that relied on statistical analysis.

His 'war prosperity' articles six months earlier had contained flawed conclusions about extra income being squandered on needless luxuries. But because those articles had criticised the working class, they went unchallenged.

The same was never likely to be the case with his allegations about the blockade, which were played out under the glare of the world's media and at one point threatened to do the Government serious damage. This meant that even though he was right that goods were being shipped to neutral countries and then being sent on to Germany, the lack of rigour with which he conducted his investigation meant that his decision to spoil for a public fight with the Government was always likely to lead to a bruising experience.

Notes

1 J. Lee Thompson, *Northcliffe: Press Baron in Politics 1865–1922*, London, 2000, p.227.
2 *The War Illustrated*, 30 June 1917, p.428.
3 J. Lee Thompson, *Northcliffe: Press Baron in Politics 1865–1922*, London, 2000, p.233.
4 Ibid., p.241.
5 Tom Clarke, *My Northcliffe Diary*, London, 1931, p.78.
6 National Archives, Kew, CAB 37/137/9 Cabinet paper about the use of the Northcliffe press as German propaganda, 1 November 1915.
7 Basil Clarke, *Unfinished Autobiography*, p.204.
8 Sir Edward Grey, *Twenty-Five Years 1892–1916*, Vol.2, London, 1925, p.109.
9 Eric W Osborne, Britain's Economic Blockade of Germany 1914-1919, London, 2004, p.107.
10 Ibid.
11 Basil Clarke, *Unfinished Autobiography*, p.205.
12 *Daily Mail*, 12 January 1916, p.5.
13 Basil Clarke, *Unfinished Autobiography*, p.205.
14 *Daily Mail*, 12 January 1916, p.5.
15 *Daily Mail*, 12 January 1916, p.4.
16 *Washington Post*, 12 January 1916, p.3.
17 *New York Times*, 13 January 1916, p.1.
18 *Daily Mail*, 14 January 1916, p.5.
19 *Daily Mail*, 15 January 1916, p.4.
20 *Daily Mail*, 17 January 1916, p.5.
21 *Daily Mail*, 17 January, p.6.
22 *Morning Post*, 18 January 1916, p.6.
23 *Daily Mail*, 18 January 1916, p.4.
24 *Daily Mail*, 19 January 1916, p.5.
25 *Westminster Gazette*, 19 January 1916, p.9.
26 *Westminster Gazette*, 18 January 1916, p.1.
27 *Westminster Gazette*, 18 January 1916, p.5.
28 *Daily Mail*, 19 January 1916, p.5.
29 *Westminster Gazette*, 19 January 1916, p.1.
30 *Westminster Gazette*, 20 January 1916, p.5.
31 *Westminster Gazette*, 20 January 1916, p.5.
32 *Daily Mail*, 20 January 1916, p.7.
33 *Daily Mirror*, 20 January 1916, p.4.
34 *Livingstone Mail*, Northern Rhodesia (present-day Zambia), 25 February 1916, p.7.
35 *Westminster Gazette*, 21 January 1916, p.4.
36 Ibid., p.4.
37 *New York Times*, 21 January 1916, p.2.
38 *Daily Mail*, 22 January 1916, p.6.
39 *Manchester Guardian*, 26 January 1916, p.12, quoting the National Tidende.
40 *Daily Mail*, 24 January 1916, p.4.
41 *Daily Mail*, 24 January 1916, p.7.
42 *The Economist*, 22 January 1916, p.123.
43 *Daily Mail*, 25 January 1916, p.5.

44 National Archives, Kew, CO 323/716 492 284-6, Memorandum from War Office (this version dated 27 January 1916). The entire memorandum was published in *The Scotsman* (26 January 1916, p.8) and there was also a detailed report on the contents in the *New York Times*, 26 January 1916, pp.1–2.

45 *Daily Mail*, 24 January 1916, p.4.

46 *Daily Mail*, 12 January 1916, p.4.

47 *Daily Mail*, 26 January 1916, p.6.

48 *Daily Mail*, 26 January 1916, p.4.

49 *The Times*, 26 January 1916, p.9.

50 *New York Times*, 26 January 1916, p.2.

51 *Sydney Morning Herald*, 27 January 1916, p.8.

52 *Livingstone Mail*, Northern Rhodesia (present-day Zambia), 25 February 1916, p.7.

53 *New York Times*, 26 January 1916, p.2, quoting from that day's *Evening Standard*.

54 *Daily News*, 26 January 1916, p.1.

55 Hansard, House of Commons, 26 January 1916, John Leslie, British Blockade.

56 Hansard, House of Commons, 26 January 1916, Edward Grey, British Blockade.

57 *New York Times*, 27 January 1916, p.1.

58 *New York Times*, 27 January 1916, p.1.

59 *Manchester Guardian*, 27 January 1916, p.6.

60 *The Economist*, 29 January 1916, p.166.

61 *Daily News*, 27 January 1916, p.4.

62 *Daily Mail*, 31 January 1916, p.7.

63 *Daily Mail*, 1 February 1916, p.7.

64 *Daily Mail*, 4 February 1916, p.2.

65 *Daily Mail*, 5 February 1916, p.2.

66 *Daily Mail*, 14 February 1916, p.5.

67 *Daily Mail*, 15 February 1916, p.5.

68 F.H. Hinsley ed., *British Foreign Policy Under Sir Edward Grey*, Cambridge, 1977, pp.544–5, under K.G. Robbins, 'Foreign Policy, Government Structure and Public Opinion'.

69 George Macaulay Trevelyan, *Grey of Falloden*, London, 1937, p.308.

70 Keith Robbins, *Sir Edward Grey*, London 1971, p.333.

71 Basil Clarke, *Unfinished Autobiography*, p.205.

72 Eric W. Osborne, *Britain's Economic Blockade of Germany 1914–1919*, London, 2004, p.194.

73 Ibid.

74 Ibid., p.193.

75 Eric W. Osborne, *Britain's Economic Blockade of Germany 1914–1919*, London, 2004, p.4.

76 Niall Ferguson, *The Pity of War*, Penguin, 2006, p.252.

77 Ibid., p.291.

78 National Archives, Kew, CAB 1/15/1, Confidential memo from the Foreign Office to the Cabinet Office, 28 December 1915.

11

Leaving the Mail

The weeks after the blockade articles were quiet ones for Clarke professionally, but the lull did not last long and two months later, in April 1916, he once again found himself at the centre of a story of huge historical significance. This time it was not about the war with Germany but instead centred on events in Ireland.

The British had passed legislation granting Irish Home Rule, a limited form of self-government, in 1914, but its implementation had been delayed because of the outbreak of the war. While a large proportion of Irish people were prepared to wait for Home Rule – and many Irish even fought and died in the war on the side of the Allies – there were also those who wanted the end of British rule to be both immediate and absolute.

So on Easter Monday 1916, 1,000 members of the Irish Republican Brotherhood (IRB) seized control of a number of buildings in Dublin, and in what became known as the Easter Rising they declared the General Post Office to be the seat of a new provisional government.

Britain was deeply shocked by the rebellion, as the threat of nationalists attempting to take control of Ireland by force had not been taken particularly seriously. But despite having the advantage of surprise, a small group of freedom fighters was never likely to be successful in an open fight against one of the world's great military powers, even one that was preoccupied by a battle for its own survival against Germany, and the Easter Rising hardly spread outside Dublin. The IRB, whose number included future President of Ireland Éamon de Valera and the legendary Republican Michael Collins, did, though, fight bravely, and it took the arrival of reinforcements and several days before they were finally beaten.

As big a story as the Easter Rising was, the English press had great difficulty in reporting it. The military blocked lines of communication between Dublin and London, which meant newspapers were extremely limited in their access to information. The *Daily Mail*, in particular, was furious about how the news was effectively being suppressed, complaining that 'whatever news the Cabinet have had from Dublin, there are countless other people with relatives in the centre of rebellion who have had no intelligence for almost a week of anxiety'.

To try to break the news blackout, the *Daily Mail* dispatched several reporters to find out what was happening. One of them was Clarke, who again showed his resourcefulness by managing to get to Ireland and get eye-witness accounts of the rebellion. He then faced the challenge of getting the story back to England, though his time in Flanders meant he was by now adept at dealing with obstructive officials. On his way back to the coast from Dublin he was questioned by soldiers but, rather than admitting he was trying to get back to England, he told them he wanted to get to Dublin. The soldiers told him this would not be allowed and the more he protested that he must be allowed to proceed to Dublin, the more insistent the soldiers became that he should return to England.[1] He was soon on a mail boat back to Holyhead, from where he telephoned his story to London. His description of the devastation in Dublin was apparently the first independent report of what had happened there:

> There will ever be the picture in the mind's eye of Sackville-street torn up and ramparted with overturned vehicles of every kind; of the Four Courts [the Irish Law Courts] invested and turned, so to speak, inside out with the rebels entrenching themselves behind great piles of ancient and historic tomes and records, and of machine guns whirring from the front windows of the aristocratic and elegant Shelbourne Hotel. And all through the popular shopping centre, loot, loot, and once again – loot![2]

While he had seen little of the Easter Rising himself, Clarke was given information by a source who 'has been behind the scenes a good deal in this business' and also from a 'prominent Dublin citizen' who had been in Cork when the fighting started but who kept in contact with his wife in Dublin via his private telephone line.

Clarke set out what he had been told in great detail: how the civil servants in the post office had used the counters as barricades and brandished bayonets; how trams had been pushed onto their sides to be used as barricades and the clubs in St Stephen's Green turned into sniper posts; and how the city had been plunged into darkness on the Monday night because all the street lights were either not working or had been smashed.[3] Clarke may not have seen much of this with his own eyes but, after almost a week of limited news, his dramatic description delighted his employers at the *Daily Mail*. Not only did it represent a significant exclusive, but it was a fitting response to the Government's efforts to suppress news of the rebellion.

'In publishing these first independent messages from Ireland after six days of secrecy, we protest against the suppression of news, and point out the evils of the suggested control of newspapers by Government,' one of Clarke's colleagues recorded in his diary. Lord Northcliffe was equally pleased and he offered his personal congratulations to everyone involved.[4]

★★★

The Easter Rising was Clarke's last big story for the *Daily Mail*. In September 1916 his time there came to an abrupt end as a result of his inability to control his temper.

Clarke's news editor was Walter G. Fish, whom he respected for having been a 'first-rate reporter himself in his day' and who would later become editor of the *Daily Mail* and gain a degree of notoriety for threatening to sue Northcliffe for libel.[5] Clarke was disappointed when Fish sent him to Leicester to investigate a story. The trip failed to yield anything newsworthy, and when Clarke arrived back in London that night he went straight home rather than reporting back to the office.

He arrived at work the following morning to be accused by Fish of 'slacking'. Clarke responded furiously and spoke to Fish in such strong terms that it was immediately obvious to him that 'further work under W.G. was impossible'.[6]

When Clarke explained his reasons for leaving to C.P. Scott at the *Manchester Guardian*, he blamed his departure on the 'minor Napoleons' at the *Daily Mail*, while one of his colleagues wrote that Clarke 'felt aggrieved at what he called the "Prussian methods" of some of the higher-ups' and described his departure as 'a burst of personal independence rivalled only by that of Northcliffe'.[7] But while he may have initially believed himself to be the wronged party, when he looked back on the incident years later he did so with a sense of regret. 'I ... said to him things of which I have been ashamed and sorry ever since,' he wrote. 'If the man thought I had been slack he was perfectly right to say so and I was a cad.'[8]

It might be tempting to attribute his outburst against Fish to the pressure of the blockade story or the trauma of what he had seen in Flanders and Eastern Europe. In reality, though, Clarke's combustible temper pre-dated the war and perhaps the most surprising thing about his outburst at Fish is that it took twelve years of working in journalism for this kind of incident to occur.

The timing of his departure was not ideal. Alice was pregnant again and so, with five children to support and another one on the way, Clarke was out of work for the first time since joining the *Manchester Guardian* as a sub-editor. His acrimonious departure did not, at least, lessen his respect for Lord Northcliffe. Immediately after leaving, he still described the press baron as a 'good and kindly chief'[9] and the feeling seems to have been mutual, as Northcliffe continued to admire Clarke's courage and independence. He made it known that he would be welcomed back at the *Daily Mail* at any time[10] and three years later he publicly referred to Clarke as his 'friend'.[11]

For many years, one of Clarke's most treasured possessions would be a signed photograph of Northcliffe. Its message read: 'With best wishes for sincere and simple work – Northcliffe.'[12]

Notes

1   *Advertising World*, July 1931.
2   *Daily Mail*, 29 April 1916, p.5.
3   *Daily Mail*, 29 April 1916, p.5. The piece does not carry Basil Clarke's byline, but Tom Clarke, *My Northcliffe Diary*, London, 1931, p.96 states that Basil Clarke was the author.
4   Tom Clarke, *My Northcliffe Diary*, London, 1931, pp.95–9.
5   *New York Times*, 16 June 1922, p.1.
6   Basil Clarke, *Unfinished Autobiography*, p.206.
7   Tom Clarke, *Northcliffe in History, An Intimate Study of Press Power*, London, 1950, pp.165–6.
8   Basil Clarke, *Unfinished Autobiography*, p.206.
9   Manchester University: John Rylands Library, A/C55/8, Letter from Clarke to CP Scott, 11 October 1916.
10 Tom Clarke, *Northcliffe in History, An Intimate Study of Press Power*, London, 1950, p.166.
11 *Sheffield Independent*, 17 December 1919, p.4.
12 *The Times*, 13 December 1947, p.7.

The Somme

By the time Clarke left the *Daily Mail*, the life of reporters on the Western Front had changed immeasurably since his fugitive days there almost two years earlier.

Even as Clarke had been evading arrest at the end of 1914, Lord Northcliffe had been applying private pressure in addition to the *Daily Mail's* public calls for an end to the ban on journalists in the war zone. An example of this is a letter he wrote to Lord Riddell, the managing director of the *News of the World* who acted as a liaison between the Government and the press during the war. 'I realise ... that a newspaper man with an army is just as much of a nuisance as a soldier would be in a newspaper office,' he wrote, before going on to make the case that, despite the inconvenience, the potential of press coverage to get the nation behind the war effort meant the Government should 'strain every nerve to get really distinguished writers to make the war what it is – a matter of life and death for the nation'.[1]

What was perhaps the decisive intervention came from the unlikely source of Theodore Roosevelt. In January 1915, the same month Clarke was forced to return to Britain, the former American President wrote to Sir Edward Grey to warn that the ban meant 'the only real war news, written by Americans who are known and trusted by the American public, comes from the German side'.[2]

Eventually, the Government agreed for three groups of journalists to make short visits to France in March and April 1915.[3] Then in May it allowed six accredited journalists to stay at General Headquarters in France. Lord Kitchener, whose idea it had been to ban reporters in the first place, never officially recognised their position, but neither did he try to have them removed and they remained there until the end of the war.[4]

Both the ease with which these accredited reporters could find and send back news and the comfort of their living quarters must have seemed like luxury compared to what Clarke had endured during the early months of the war. And so although Clarke initially toyed with the idea of emigrating to America, when he was offered the chance to become an accredited war reporter as a temporary joint representative for Reuters and the Press Association, he decided to take it.

He had got to Dunkirk in 1914 by being smuggled onto a train, but this time he presented himself at the War Office in London and was given a license, a book of rules for press correspondents and a typewriter. He then took a boat to France and was met coming off the boat by a car that took him first to a British base at Boulogne-sur-Mer and then on to Amiens, a city 75 miles north of Paris.[5]

He was based in a chateau off the main street that he shared with a group of four other accredited journalists that included Beach Thomas, his former *Daily Mail* colleague whom he described as 'one of the finest and most loveable of men'.[6] The other occupants of the chateau were a press officer, assistants, typists, orderlies and servants.

This is an early example of what is now known as embedded war reporting. As Clarke discovered, it enables the journalist to build relationships with soldiers and also offers relatively safe and easy access to the fighting. It is not, though, without its downside.

The assistant press officers who accompanied the journalists as they looked for stories served, as Clarke put it, 'in the curious dual capacity as friend and monitor' and they were not afraid to 'pass a quiet veto' if the journalist wanted to do something that was considered unacceptable. However, while embedded war reporting has become controversial for the way it tends to lead to coverage that is favourable towards the host army, this was less of an issue in the First World War because the strict censorship meant newspaper coverage was never likely to be objective anyway.

Clarke enjoyed working with these assistant press officers, who were usually soldiers no longer able to fight because of injury. While some historians have focused on how they frustrated the efforts of journalists,[7] Clarke would later remember them as 'excellent fellows' who exercised the 'more unpleasant part of their function sparingly and kindly'. He appreciated their willingness to put themselves in great danger just to satisfy what he called 'that insatiable curiosity and lust for experience which characterises every good journalist'.[8]

While Beach Thomas would later feel guilty for having allowed his coverage to be manipulated by the authorities,[9] Clarke's only real problem with the embedded system was that it was less exciting than his previous experience on the Western Front. Though he was as effusive in his praise for the 'excellent press arrangements' he enjoyed in 1916 as he had been critical of the decision to ban reporters in 1914, his nostalgia for those 'journalistic outlaw' days meant he felt a twinge of regret at how having almost his every need catered for diminished the 'spirit of personal adventure' of war reporting.[10]

★★★

For Clarke and his fellow accredited reporters, the daily routine at the chateau would begin with eating breakfast together while the colonel who acted as press officer briefed them about what had happened overnight. Based on this, they would then decide which of them would go where to find out more information, and then after breakfast a driver would be waiting to take each of them to the scene of whichever story he had been allotted.

On a typical day, Clarke and the other journalists met back at the chateau late in the afternoon and shared the day's news over tea. This form of debriefing meant he quickly learned the art of what he called 'taking notes and munching bread and butter simultaneously'. Clarke would then go to his room to write up his news, where a fire of birch logs would be burning; from his desk he could hear the never-ceasing sound of guns in the distance as he typed by the light of a paraffin lamp.

When he had finished writing, he would give his work to a press officer for it to be censored and then it would be either telegraphed to London if it was short, or given to a messenger if not. The messenger would take these longer articles to the coast so that a boat could take them back to England, and this meant the journalists had to finish their articles by dinner time to ensure they reached the evening boat. Clarke's writing speed may have improved since his time at the *Manchester Guardian*, when he had spent up to 10 hours on a single story, but he still found the tight deadlines challenging.

'It is amazing in such circumstances how long you can sit at a typewriter with brain quite numb, bereft of all ideas,' he wrote. 'Then the idea comes at last, and how your fingers fly! Line after line – the warning bell at the end of each recurs with almost continuous tinkle, and at a minute to the hour you clutch a dishevelled sheaf of fluttering pages and dash downstairs, arranging them as you go, to dump them down on the table as the censor with a weary smile and a look at the clock, says, "just on the dot, my boy".'[11]

He and the other journalists – 'more loyal, more unselfish colleagues one could not hope to meet' – usually spent their evenings relaxing in the salon, smoking pipes as they sat in easy chairs in front of the fire and read their mail. They would then read the latest newspapers, their friendly conversation giving way to silence as they scrutinised their own work. It was a quiet that was only interrupted by the occasional 'damn' as one of them spotted what Clarke described as 'the sins of sub-editors and printers super-added to one's own'.

They would often be joined in the salon by the press officers or officer friends who were stationed nearby and they would help themselves to drinks, and on nights when German aeroplanes were active would sometimes go through the French windows and into the garden to watch the anti-aircraft fire against the night sky.[12]

While the life of an accredited reporter was a comfortable one, its relative luxury did not, though, insulate them from the horrific reality of war. On one of Clarke's outings, for example, he saw the uniformed bodies of German soldiers whose heads had been eaten by rats so that only the skulls remained. 'To walk ... over desolate mud and waste, past grim remains such as these, with the moon dodging in and out of flying scud overhead, and rats scooting about my very boots, was an experience to make one shudder,' he wrote.[13]

On another occasion, he noticed a group of soldiers who were standing at the bottom of a slope and seemed to be thrusting out their bayonets as if fending off an attack by an invisible enemy. Clarke watched them for a while and saw that they did not move.

'Are they drilling?' he asked his guide. 'They have been standing there without moving for ever so long. Their instructor seems to be keeping them at it.'

'No, they are not drilling,' his guide replied. 'Walk down and look.'

Clarke did as he was told, making his way down the slope towards the men. As he got nearer he realised they were all dead. They had been shot as they had run down the slope and were now being held up by wire.[14]

★★★

Clarke was in France during the latter stages of the Battle of the Somme, a battle so deeply engrained in the British psyche that even a century later the name of the River Somme is still synonymous with senseless slaughter in horrifically muddy conditions. About 131,000 British soldiers died in the battle between July and December 1916, a total that accounted for over 10 per cent of British Empire deaths in the entire war.

About 19,000 of these deaths happened around the villages of Beaucort and Beaumont Hamel on the first day of the battle, in what was one of the worst military disasters of the war.[15] But by the time Clarke came to report on it, the Battle of the Somme was entering its final stages and it was the Germans who were now being driven back.

When the British finally recaptured the villages in mid-November, Clarke was taken there to see them for himself. Even though the British were now in control, his visit gave him a sense of the horror the soldiers had endured.

Arriving by car, he had to continue on foot because the enemy were still firing and a car would be too visible a target, so he slowly began to trudge towards Beaucort and Beaumont Hamel, trying to avoid German shellfire by sticking where possible to abandoned trenches. As he made his way, his guide shouted a warning at the same time as Clarke heard a familiar whining sound and jumped into a nearby trench, where he was relieved to find that the mud at the bottom of it made for a relatively soft landing. The shell exploded 80 yards away.[16]

He eventually came to a patch of land that until a few days before had been the no man's land separating the British and German trenches. As he walked over it, he saw that it was littered with shell fragments, rifles, helmets and other debris that hinted at the ferocity of the fighting that had occurred there. Clarke paid particular attention to those items that alluded to a human story: a handkerchief with the initials 'J.B' and a pack of cards scattered over the mud and rock with a bullet hole through the seven of diamonds.

The first village he came to was also covered with the evidence of destruction; it was just the type of debris that changed. He saw a scorched chair leg, a piece of a clock and a child's drinking mug, and then he made the grisly discovery of a woman's black silk cape folded around a German boot that still had part of a leg inside.[17]

Clarke joined British officers for lunch in the hillside cave in Beaumont Hamel that served as regimental headquarters. They ate at a table made of loose boards and used a wine bottle as a candlestick holder as they dined on preserved shrimps followed by beef, and then milk pudding and fruit for dessert. Clarke was disturbed by how the cave shook as shells landed outside, though he found it interesting that none of his companions seemed to notice. Then after lunch he was given a tour of the cave's passageways, which had until recently been occupied by the Germans. During the tour his guide found a box of German grenades and Clarke noted how casually he picked one up, unscrewed it and absent-mindedly threw it up and down as they talked. Clarke kept one of the grenades as a souvenir.

As he toured the tunnels, he would occasionally emerge into daylight and make his way across muddy ground, walking past bits of shells and dead bodies as he did so. But it was not until he reached the centre of Beaumont Hamel that he grasped just how complete the destruction had been. He could not even see the road that had ran through the village, and the only clue to the location of the high street was some white powdered stone where the church had stood.[18]

He had planned to go from Beaumont Hamel to the Front but the muddy conditions meant progress was slow and he could see shells exploding some 200 yards ahead of him.

'Hard going here after the rain, isn't it?' a nearby soldier shouted to him.

Clarke thought of the dangers that lay ahead from snipers and bombs and also of the dead bodies he would have to climb over to get there. And with the cold wind blowing against him, he decided to turn back.[19]

★★★

By the end of 1916, many thousands of injured British soldiers had been sent home but it occurred to Clarke that the public knew little of how they travelled back to Britain. He decided it would be an interesting subject for an article and so he made arrangements to accompany an injured soldier on his journey right from the point of being injured all the way through to his arrival back in Britain. Clarke also had a personal reason for wanting to return to England, as Alice was due to give birth in just a few weeks, and it would also mean he could spend Christmas with his family after being overseas for the previous two years.

So one day in December he said goodbye to his fellow journalists and left the chateau to travel to Beaumont Hamel, where he had arranged to wait at a dug-out for news of an injured soldier who might be a suitable subject for his article.

When the call came for the stretcher-bearers, Clarke followed them over an open piece of ground, though he found it difficult to keep up and later admitted that he arrived 'a "very bad last" – as the racing reporters might express it' to find them finishing dressing a wound on a soldier's leg. The soldier was called John Oldham and Clarke was told he had been shot in the thigh by a sniper who he had shot at earlier in the day but had then forgotten about until it was too late.

'Beats me why some o' you lads comes 'ere without your mothers,' said the corporal who was tending to him. One of the other stretcher-bearers lit a cigarette and put it in Oldham's mouth.

Once Oldham was loaded onto the stretcher, the stretcher-bearers lifted him and began to carry him across the rough terrain. Clarke followed them but again found it difficult to keep up, despite the fact that they were now carrying a man and he was carrying just a stick and a gas mask. They eventually stopped 100 yards from the German trench and decided to wait until the light faded to avoid being shot at. It was so cold that Clarke's teeth chattered and his feet were 'as painful as if they had been squashed under a cart wheel' but, showing the compassion that made as great an impression on Clarke as the speed with which the stretcher-bearers could carry heavy loads quickly over muddy ground, the corporal took off his own coat and put it over Oldham to keep him warm.

When it was finally dark enough to risk finishing their journey, the corporal ran into the open and stood upright facing the enemy. No bullet came.

'We can get a move on,' he said. 'The snipe-shop's shut up for the day.'

Once Oldham had been carried to the first aid post and his wound had been looked at, he was to be taken by ambulance to an Advanced Dressing Station a few miles away in the ruined village of Mailly-Maillet. The stretcher-bearers had to carry him part of the way because the road was not good enough for the ambulance to drive down and, as they walked along the track, Clarke was alarmed to notice shell-holes that had not been there half an hour before.[20]

They walked half a mile until they came to the waiting ambulance, which they saw ahead of them in the darkness by the light of the drivers' cigarettes. Oldham was lifted into the back and Clarke and the captain accompanying him agreed to continue on foot and meet the ambulance again in Mailly-Maillet. As he and his companion began walking, Clarke commented that it felt good to be away from the dangers of the Front.

'Depends on what your idea of danger is,' the captain replied. 'You are not likely to be sniped here or mined or blown to bits with a hand bomb as you were in Beaumont Hamel trenches – that's true enough. But there are quite enough dirty roads to death to be found in this area to suit my appetite any day. In fact about this time of day I should feel safer in the trenches than where we are at this moment. They usually begin their evening strafe about this time … and you never know quite which district they'll pick upon. They might begin any minute to drop them on this road.'

Clarke found himself nervously readjusting his helmet to make sure it was covering his neck as he dwelt on the captain's words. Sure enough, the shelling began shortly afterwards and Clarke heard shells pass overhead towards their destination of Mailly-Maillet and then explode in and around the village. He later admitted that 'as the shells came over, one after another, I am afraid I loitered just a little on the road to Mailly'.

The British soon began to return fire and Clarke later gave a memorable description of the surreal feeling of walking through the countryside as war raged around him:

> To stand thus in a dark country lane, hearing the amazing barks of many different guns and the whine of many different shells, and to see the gnarled and shattered trees jump out at you, black and still, against momentary backgrounds of livid flame, struck me as the most unreal thing I have ever watched. But for one's ever conscious knowledge of its deadly seriousness, one might have thought it all a product of stage-craft rather than of war.[21]

When they finally reached Mailly-Maillet, Clarke was reunited with Oldham in a small house with broken windows that was being used as an Advanced Dressing Station, and then later that night they travelled by ambulance to a

Main Dressing Station, where Clarke was greeted by two orderlies who assumed he was a wounded soldier and so grabbed him under the arms and carefully lowered him down from the ambulance.

'Take it gently,' one of them said. 'You might happen to do yourself harm if you don't go gently.'

It was the first but not the only time Clarke was mistaken for an injured solider during his journey with Oldham. 'Men of all grades showed the same inclination to treat me as an invalid,' he later wrote. 'I had to explain to them that I was neither wounded nor ill, but even then they would sometimes look me over carefully for a casualty card … Some of them seemed disappointed that they could do nothing for me.'[22]

From the Main Dressing Station, Oldham was sent to a Casualty Clearing House beyond the village of Puchevillers. This was good news because it meant he was likely to be sent back to Britain and it was also notable in that some of the staff there were female. Clarke, always a keen observer of people, was fascinated by how Oldham's eyes 'opened with a jump' as he heard the voice of one of the nurses for the first time after not having seen a woman for months. Clarke also noticed that the only patients there who 'did not become agog with interest at the sound of an Englishwoman's voice' were the ones who were asleep.

Later, Clarke spoke to a nurse about the reaction and she told him wounded men would often think of questions just to keep them talking. 'Perhaps it is the sight of women again that makes them think of home and makes them forget for a time the dreadful things they have been seeing and feeling out yonder,' she said.

After his conversation with the nurse, Clarke went back to see Oldham.

'It looks a bit more like civilisation to see an English woman again, doesn't it?' Clarke said.

Oldham began to answer but his words trailed off as his lip began to tremble and tears started to roll down his cheek.

★★★

After a few days of Oldham being treated in the Casualty Clearing House, on a cold and misty morning, he and Clarke boarded a train for Boulogne-sur-Mer, the port that represented the last stop before Britain. They stopped at another Casualty Clearing Station at Varennes to pick up some more injured soldiers, and Clarke volunteered to act as a stretcher bearer so he could see what it was like. But the 13-stone Irish soldier he was asked to carry was too heavy for him and he gave up after 50 yards.

Once the wounded were aboard, the train started moving again, and as they headed towards the coast Clarke noticed the sound of the guns becoming fainter as they got further from the Front. Eventually, the sound disappeared, and after many weeks of it being a constant presence in the background, he felt a sense of relief at its sudden absence. He remembered how staff at the various clearing houses for injured men had told him the most common complaint they heard from soldiers was that they could still hear the guns in the distance.

Clarke spent much of the train journey speaking to wounded officers and even met a pilot who, by remarkable coincidence, he had seen being shot down. He also acted as a translator for the eleven German prisoners on board, which gave him the chance to see how they interacted with British soldiers. As he facilitated conversations, he was impressed by the respect with which they treated each other, which he thought could act as 'something of a lesson perhaps for less tolerant people'. Some of the men even exchanged souvenirs and one of the prisoners showed the British soldiers a bullet that had been removed from his lungs. A British soldier held it in his hand and turned to one of his friends.

'It would be a damn funny thing now if it was me as shot that bullet, wouldn't it?' he said. 'But who knows I didn't?'

Clarke translated what the British soldier had said and the German shrugged his shoulders and laughed. 'Perhaps I shot him,' the German replied.

That afternoon, Clarke was drinking a cup of tea when he heard the sound of singing coming from a nearby carriage. He got up and walked to where the song was coming from and there he saw men, some of them with appalling injuries, laughing as they sang: 'Oh my, I'm too young to die, I just want to go 'ome.'

Clarke found it unsettling to watch badly injured soldiers making light of death in this way and one man, who Clarke described as a 'poor wreck of humanity whose face, peeping from a mass of bandages, was almost whiter than his wrappings', made a particular impression. Though he grinned happily as he sang 'I'm too young to die' and used his one remaining hand to beat time, Clarke noticed he had a red and white ticket to denote he was considered a 'dangerous case'.

'He'll do well if he gets his wish,' a surgeon who was standing near Clarke whispered as they listened to the song.

'Shouldn't they stop him?' Clarke asked.

'Not a bit,' the surgeon replied. 'That's the spirit that may help him dodge death after all.'

Later that night, Clarke was given a tour of the train and he noticed the strange positions the wounded men slept in. Arms and legs extended out of the beds and blocked the passageway, which meant Clarke had to move carefully to avoiding disturbing them.

During his tour, he saw one patient who was having his pulse checked by a man while a nurse put a hot-water bottle at his feet. 'He's very bad,' he heard one of them whisper. Clarke looked at the patient's face and saw it was the same man who had been singing so defiantly earlier in the day about being too young to die.

★★★

The train arrived at Boulogne-sur-Mer in the middle of the night and Clarke accompanied Oldham to hospital and then left him to try to find somewhere to stay. All the hotels were full so he ended up sleeping in an office at the railway station, using a pile of railway guides as a pillow.

As the medical staff prepared Oldham for the boat home, Clarke spent several days browsing Boulogne's shops and buying Christmas presents for his family.[23] But as the days passed with still no confirmation of when they would travel, Clarke began to doubt that he would get home in time for Christmas after all.

Finally, though, Oldham was given clearance to travel and Clarke joined him as his stretcher was carried onto a boat bound for Britain. After a night voyage, it was just getting light on Christmas Eve when word began to spread among the wounded men that England was in sight. All those who were able to get out of bed went to look out of the port holes and Clarke watched the soldiers' eyes sparkle as, through the rain and mist, they got their first glimpse of home.

Once they were off the boat, Clarke went with Oldham to a London hospital, said goodbye to him and then went home to his five sons and pregnant wife.

'Alice was radiant, the little fellows swarmed around me, an avalanche of excited humanity,' he later wrote. 'And they hung up their stockings that night, and Santa Claus put in them unusual little presents, some of them marked "Boulogne-sur-Mer".'[24]

Notes

1   Lord Riddell's War Diary, London, 1933, p.22.
2   Phillip Knightley, The First Casualty: The War Correspondent as Hero, Propagandist, and Myth-Maker, London, 1978, p.94.
3   Lord Riddell's War Diary, London, 1933, p.17.
4   Ibid., p.23.
5   Basil Clarke, My Round of the War, London, 1917, pp.170–1.
6   Ibid., p.177.
7   Philip Knightley, The First Casualty: The War Correspondent as Hero and Propagandist from the Crimea to Kosovo, London, 2000, pp.101–2.
8   Basil Clarke, My Round of the War, London, 1917, pp.172–3.

9 Adam Hochschild, T*o End All Wars: A Story of Loyalty and Rebellion, 1914–1918*, New York, 2011, p.223.
10 Basil Clarke, *My Round of the War*, London, 1917, p.169.
11 Ibid., pp.172–5.
12 Ibid., pp.175–80.
13 Ibid., pp.207–8.
14 Ibid., p.238.
15 Peter Hart, *The Somme*, London, 2006, p.528.
16 Basil Clarke, *My Round of the War*, London, 1917, p.225.
17 Ibid., p.226.
18 Ibid., pp.227–32.
19 Ibid., p.231–2.
20 Ibid., p.257.
21 Ibid., pp.258–61.
22 Ibid., p.270.
23 *The War Illustrated*, 22 December 1917, p.377.
24 Ibid., p.377.

13

Into Government

After three difficult years packed with extreme experiences, Clarke's arrival back in England marked the end of his time as a war correspondent and the beginning of a period when he was able to give more attention to his family. His eldest son, Arthur, was now thirteen and just days after Clarke returned home, on New Year's Eve 1916, Alice gave birth to their sixth child. It was yet another baby boy and they called him Ian.

During 1917, Clarke pursued a 'very agreeable, if not very remunerative'[1] freelance career that included contributing regularly to *The War Illustrated*. He wrote, for example, a series of articles evaluating the merits of soldiers from different countries, and another article about what he called the 'queer yarns the Germans believe'.[2] These included the German belief that a secret tunnel had been built under the Channel connecting Britain and France specifically to wage war on Germany. It was an idea Clarke may have thought belonged to the realms of science fiction, but it would actually be in operation less than eighty years later.

Perhaps his most memorable article in 1917 was one about British diplomacy that he wrote for the *Evening Standard*. Showing the blockade controversy had not dulled his pugnacity, it criticised the Foreign Office for having continued to see the kings of Romania and Greece as Allies long after the British people had 'seen through the roguery of the first and the even more despicable treachery of the second'.[3] He was clear that the blame lay at the door of British diplomats and put this down to the fact that they lacked intuition, observational skills, 'ability to read men' and any conception of their own limitations.

'This seems a harsh reading, perhaps, but it is sadly substantiated in many cases where our diplomacy has been really hard-tested during the war,' he wrote.

He argued that while British diplomats were more dignified and honest than their French and Russian counterparts, they were inferior in all other ways and, using a rather odd comparison, he wrote that the British diplomat 'is a laughing stock among diplomats, just as the simpleton at a race meeting is a laughing stock'.

Perhaps thinking of the less rigid class system that had so impressed him in Canada, he argued that the solution to Britain's ineffective diplomacy was an end to the insistence on diplomats having a 'distinguished appearance and an Eton manner' and instead giving a chance to 'men of the big world – not of the tiny world that our diplomats have made their own'.

Clarke also spent 1917 working on a memoir of his experiences of the war. Based on articles he had written for the *Daily Mail*, *The War Illustrated* and other publications, *My Round of the War* was published at the beginning of 1918.[4]

'What I have done is to winnow sheaves of memories and of war writings, the outcrop and gleanings of 30 crowded months of work as a war correspondent ... and to garner in one binding things, thoughts and happenings that impressed me,' he explained in the preface. 'Some of these things were important, some trivial, but the test I applied in the choosing was neither importance nor triviality, but just that of "humanness".'[5]

The book comprised four parts. The first part was about his time in Flanders in late 1914 and its inclusion of his full eyewitness account of the destruction of Ypres must have gone some way towards rectifying the fact that it had been presented as someone else's work when it had originally appeared in the *Daily Mail*.[6]

The second part of the book dealt with his Eastern European commission; the third section covered his time as an accredited reporter in France; and the fourth told the story of John Oldman's trip back to Britain. It was this last section Clarke thought was the best and the reviewers agreed, with the *Manchester Guardian* describing it as 'a memorable finish'.[7]

The reviews of *My Round of the War* were generally positive. The *Manchester Guardian* praised its former reporter's 'valuable gift of seeing things always from the point of view of the man in the street' and described his work as never failing to 'touch the sentimental element of human nature'. But it also concluded that, with the exception of his description of Oldham's journey home, the book did 'not really rise above the best newspaper level'. *The War Illustrated* called it 'an admirable book, and one that may be commended to the notice of those on the look-out for good war reading',[8] while the *Irish Times* thought it was 'excellently well put together' and that 'it abounds in those touches of human sentiment that make the whole world kin'.[9]

One aspect of Clarke's war experiences not included in *My Round of the War* was his coverage of the blockade. He may have decided the blockade did not fit with the theme of the book because it had been more to do with global politics and diplomacy than 'humanness', but another possible explanation is that its inclusion would have reminded members of the Government just how critical he had been. This might have caused problems for Clarke because, having failed to beat them, he was preparing to join them.

★★★

It is clear that Dr Christopher Addison, who was appointed Minister of Reconstruction in early 1917, saw the value of public relations. He had advised Lloyd George to use 'vigorously prosecuted propaganda' in enemy countries[10] and he later recommended that the Government should 'have a large central propaganda section under a good director' to help it cope with a 'very hostile press'.[11] There are also suggestions that Addison's interest in propaganda may have extended to unauthorised briefings to journalists, as he was twice forced to deny to Lloyd George that he was the source of a leak.[12]

Given Addison's record, it is not surprising that the Ministry of Reconstruction, which had the role of preparing for normal industrial, trading and social conditions to be restored at the end of the war, was interested in recruiting a propagandist. So in late 1917, just before *My Round of the War* was published, Clarke was offered the role of Director of the Special Intelligence Section on a salary of £600 a year,[13] the equivalent of about £30,000 today. The offer was put to him by the businessman Sir Alexander Roger and while Clarke never found out who had suggested him for the job, he suspected Lord Northcliffe may have had a hand in it and in more fanciful moments even imagined it might have been Lloyd George who recommended him.[14]

Clarke would later claim that joining the Civil Service was his way of contributing to the war effort after being declared unfit for active service,[15] presumably on account of only having one eye. But while joining the Ministry of Reconstruction may have been Clarke's second choice, his appointment was enormously significant in the history of public relations because in accepting the role he is generally regarded to have become Britain's first fully fledged public relations officer and in doing so started what has since grown into a multi-billion pound industry that has had a profound impact both on society generally and the news media in particular.[16]

His appointment marked the beginning of a period of exponential growth in government spending on publicity. Three years later, the Government would be spending about £21,000 a year on public relations[17] (the equivalent of about £500,000 today) and by 2008 the spend for advertising, marketing and public relations had reached a staggering £391 million a year.[18]

Official minutes from May 1918 set out Clarke's new duties as 'getting matters connected with this ministry inserted in the daily Press, interviewing journalists, discussing the matter of the work of the Ministry of Reconstruction with distinguished foreigners ... and in keeping in touch with what is being done in foreign countries with regard to Reconstruction'.[19]

It is unclear how much newspaper coverage Clarke actually secured for the ministry and he later admitted that his biggest impact there was some advice he gave Addison on the national building programme that would come to symbolise the mixture of idealism and profligacy both of Addison personally and the post-war Coalition Government more generally. Clarke made the suggestion that there should be an investigation into women's views on housing because he thought it was important to take into account the views of those who, as he put it, had to 'run the blessed place'. His initiative earned him a rebuke of 'considerable length and with no little heat under the collar' from the head of the ministry's women's section, who thought Clarke had undermined her by taking his idea directly to Addison.[20]

If Clarke did struggle to secure newspaper coverage for the work of the ministry, one of the reasons may have been that it was difficult to get journalists interested in what post-war society might look like at a time when the outcome of the war was still very much in the balance. The Germans launched a major offensive in early 1918 to try to knock the Allies out of the war before American soldiers started arriving in Europe in greater numbers. The Spring Offensive resulted in large German advances, but the Allies managed to cling on and, by July, the German momentum had been lost and they were being pushed back by an Allied counter-offensive.

After this, the outcome of the war began to seem inevitable and, by October, Germany was seeking a negotiated peace. But while the approaching end of four long years of conflict may have filled the country at large with euphoria, Clarke was unable to share in the jubilation. Just two weeks before the Armistice was signed, on October 28, Clarke suffered a crushing personal tragedy when his 10-year-old son, George, died of scarlet fever. Clarke was at his bedside when he died and was devastated by his loss. Years later, he would describe his memories of this 'terrible affair':

It remains photographed in my mind's eye in a series of vivid and searing snapshots: first his hearty waving of arms and legs and his brave, full-throated shout of "toodle-oo" and "goodbye" as the ambulance man carried him in arms, like a baby, through our garden gate; later: myself staggering to hold a heavy cylinder of oxygen gas while the ward sister pluckily tried to direct its sizzling nozzle on to his punctured and tube laden throat.

Clarke wrote the inscription for George's gravestone, describing him as 'a little boy of singular beauty, affection and courage', and a family friend painted a pastel portrait of George almost entirely from memory. It became one of Clarke's most treasured possessions.[21]

Clarke is likely to have still been stricken by grief when he secured what was probably the biggest achievement of the early part of his public relations career. A month after George's death and just a fortnight after the end of the war, *The War Illustrated* published the first of a series of six articles by Clarke called 'When the Boys Come Home'.

The first article in the series, which was little more than promotion of the work of the ministry, set out the logistical challenge of demobilising the Army, explaining how military personnel would be grouped by their trade and where they lived. This would mean the Government could ensure workers who were needed for an essential part of the economy were brought home first.[22] Clarke described how the men would be kept in 'great concentration camps' while they waited to be sent home, which suggests the term did not then have the negative connotations it acquired following the use of concentration camps by the Nazis.

The second article in the 'When the Boys Come Home' series looked at the future of the Army and his explanation of why every soldier leaving the Army would have to give basic personal information such as age, rank and medical condition showed that the hope that it had been a 'war to end all wars' was not being taken for granted:

> Everyone hopes, of course and expects that no such cataclysm as has upheaved the nation for the past four years will ever occur again, but it would be folly for the authorities to assume definitely that it cannot.[23]

The series of articles also included an analysis of the economic situation that was considerably more optimistic than Clarke's 'war prosperity' articles two years earlier.[24] 'The world and its markets are crying out for goods,' he wrote. And while he acknowledged that shipping enough raw materials to meet this demand would be difficult, he insisted that 'there seems no need for brooding'.

As well as promising a plentiful supply of jobs, Clarke's articles also set out a future where Joint Industrial Councils of managers and union representatives would lead to workers getting 'a much fuller share of the pleasures and advantages of life than they had in the past', and this would mean that 'the relation will become more and more of a partnership'. Reflecting the Government's fear of Communism following the Russian Revolution in October the previous year, Clarke promised an end to workers being treated as 'cogs in the machine'. But this idea proved hopelessly optimistic, and the end of the war marked the start of a period of industrial turmoil that culminated in the General Strike seven years later.

From an interesting beginning, the 'When the Boys Come Home' series became progressively duller, eventually drifting off the subject of the war completely. The last two articles, which set out the finer points of the Government's rural development policy in turgid detail,[25] must have seemed odd to those readers who remembered Clarke's earlier articles. And as well as much of the material being of limited interest, there was also the ethical problem that they did not make it clear that Clarke was now working for the Government. Nevertheless, his employers at the Ministry of Reconstruction must have been delighted at securing thousands of words of what amounted to free advertising.

They are likely to have been less pleased, though, with another piece of writing he produced around the same time that was perhaps the most significant thing he wrote while at the Ministry of Reconstruction and was a work of satire rather than news. Published at the beginning of 1919, the *Cow Cake Papers* lampooned the bureaucracy and inertia of Whitehall by telling the story, though a fictional folio of Civil Service memos, of a farmer who had written to the Government to ask for permission to give his cows a special type of feed. As the story unfolds through correspondence between civil servants with humorous names such as Sir Tainley Passiton, Mr Dallymore and a Minister called Taiman Yielding, the farmer's cows gradually starve to death while the farmer waits for a decision. In the end, the civil servants are still debating whether the farmer really wants the cow feed and whether there should be a Royal Commission into the benefits of fattening cattle when they are informed that all the cows have died. It is Mr Dallymore who closes the file. 'The admitted death of his alleged cattle now disposes of the whole case satisfactorily,' he concludes.

The humour of the *Cow Cake Papers* may have dated slightly, but it displayed a keen sense of wit and made many of the same satirical points as 'Yes, Minister' would many years later. Certainly, it met with positive reviews. It 'tickled the nation's funny bone', according to the *Daily Express*, while the *Manchester Guardian* reported that 'the remarkable gift which is attributed to some "control" departments of doing nothing at all in the most elaborate possible way has been often satirised before, but never, perhaps, with such effectiveness as in this bundle of "official papers"'.[26]

It was published anonymously, which led to rumours about the identity of the author; the *Manchester Guardian* speculated that 'we are perhaps not far wrong in attributing the skit to a group of officials well practised in the art of writing round a subject without touching it'. Sir Robert Cecil, the former Minister for Blockade, was among those suspected of writing it. And while

Clarke's authorship of the *Cow Cake Papers* would be public knowledge by the end of the year, even today it is still unclear whether he was the sole author. There is a suggestion that Ernest Benn, who was the uncle of future Cabinet Minister Tony Benn and who worked at the ministry at the same time as Clarke, may have had a hand in it.[27]

In January 1919, the same month the *Cow Cake Papers* was published, Addison left the Ministry of Reconstruction to become President of the Local Government Board. He took with him his view on the importance of propaganda, insisting to Lloyd George that 'there should be an active Propaganda and Publicity Department [as] ... I am certain that an absolutely frank and vigorous propaganda is essential to success.'[28]

Two months later, on 14 March, Clarke joined him at the Local Government Board as the Principal of the Publicity Branch and Editor of its official journal, managing to negotiate a £200 pay rise to £800 a year into the bargain. Then three months later his role changed again, as publicity was among the functions transferred to the newly created Ministry of Health when Addison was appointed the UK's first Minister of Health.

Just as his career was in a state of upheaval, there was also change in his family life, and one that may have helped alleviate the pain of George's death eight months earlier. After six successive boys, Alice gave birth to a baby girl on 7 July 1919. They named their daughter Alice Margaret Beatrice, though she was known as Margaret. While little is known about what newspaper coverage Clarke secured for the new Ministry of Health, Margaret's birth provided proof of his ability to use creativity to attract the attention of the media. By focusing on the angle of her being the couple's seventh child and being born on the seventh day of the seventh month to Alice, who was herself a seventh child, he was able to get both *The Times* and the *Daily Express* to report the birth as a quirky news story. And in an early example of how public relations success depends as much on a willingness to repeat successful formulas as on creativity, Clarke would get similar press coverage seven years later to mark Margaret's seventh birthday.

★★★

Perhaps not surprisingly given the *Cow Cake Papers'* negative portrayal of Whitehall, Clarke did not last long at the Ministry of Health. In fact, he had hardly started working there when he was approached to become editor of the *Sheffield Independent*, a daily newspaper that was somewhat overshadowed by the better-resourced *Sheffield Telegraph*.

'The answer was, of course, in the affirmative,' Clarke later wrote. 'I say "of course" because no journalist who has left journalism can resist any adequate excuse or inducement to get back into it.'[29]

When the *Sheffield Independent* announced his appointment on 5 September 1919, it certainly gave the impression that his move into public relations had only ever been temporary: 'His friends know that his right place will always be on the alert and anxious watch towers of the world, and journalists everywhere are glad that he is going back to his first love.'[30]

While the chance to edit a newspaper would certainly have been attractive, Alice was not pleased by the prospect of having to leave their home in Dulwich. But a reported salary increase of over 50 per cent to £1,250[31] meant they were able to rent one of the finest houses in Sheffield, which came complete with a coach house, stables and a ballroom for 200 people that was used for a house-warming party for the newspaper's staff.[32]

In moving into the *Sheffield Independent*'s editor's chair, Clarke was replacing an institution. W. W. Chisholm had spent fifty-two years there and had been editor for the previous decade.[33] While the newspaper appeared delighted by Clarke's arrival, describing him as a 'journalist of the widest repute' who had 'done work not only of national but international importance',[34] the leader column introducing him also made a point of emphasising the importance of continuity. While the newspaper had 'known many men', it proclaimed, it had always stood for 'the good of the people' and 'for this principle it stands today as it has stood in many periods of world stress, and for this principle it will continue to stand'.[35]

Clarke's career had already shown that he was restless and impetuous and this, together with his introduction of a more aggressive editorial style that echoed that of the *Daily Mail*, meant he was an odd choice if the owners of the *Sheffield Independent* wanted either to preserve tradition or enjoy a quiet life.

★★★

One of Clarke's first acts as editor was to hire his friend Peter Somerville, a Scot who had worked in a factory in Massachusetts before becoming a journalist, while another of his editorial appointments gave a start in journalism to Richard Strout, a young American who had been rejected by C. P. Scott at the *Manchester Guardian* because of his lack of shorthand, but who many years later would win a Pulitzer Prize for his work as a columnist for the *Christian Science Monitor* in the United States.

Somerville became leader writer and, while Strout would later remember Somerville as a 'solemn Scot with a wide, wrinkled brow, a big head, and his left hand in a sling glove',[36] his dour exterior masked a wicked sense of humour. One of the regular features in the *Sheffield Independent* was 'Thought for the Day', which was a quotation from an historical figure, philosopher or poet. Clarke and Somerville would sometimes amuse themselves by inventing their own quotations and presenting them in the newspaper as anonymous quotes that had been passed down through history. No one ever seems to have noticed until their 'comical deceit' was revealed by Clarke's friend James Lansdale Hodson in the 1940s.[37]

If Clarke's attempts at humour were known only to him and Somerville, the stridency he brought to the *Sheffield Independent* was all too apparent in leader columns that, even from the earliest days of his editorship, criticised the Government in terms that were extraordinarily intemperate given he had just left the Civil Service.

When the *Sheffield Independent* commented on the failure of negotiations with the railway unions, for example, it blamed the Government's 'shiftiness' and suggested that 'by its acts ... reaching back right to the heart of the war period ... [it has] made itself a thing not to be trusted'. On another occasion, it accused Winston Churchill, then Secretary of State for War, of being an 'expensive luxury for the country' because of his poor judgement and adventurism. It argued that 'it is a little difficult to understand how a Minister who has committed so many mistakes should have been able to retain his place in public life' and concluded it was 'obvious that he has not retained it on merit' and that his continued membership of the Government must be due to the fact that he was 'supported by social and personal influence'.[38]

This antagonistic approach seems to have been a conscious decision by Clarke and he would greet angry letters from readers with undisguised glee. 'We're stirring them up!' he would announce as he read them. 'It was the great, stony silence of the audience that he couldn't endure,' Strout later remembered.[39]

While Churchill may now be considered by many as the greatest ever Briton, Clarke's *Sheffield Independent* did not always get it so wrong. It was an early champion of the idea of a football world cup, believing that the rise in the standard of football across Europe meant that 'nothing could be better calculated to promote international understanding and banish war'. And following the good example he had set with his war reporting, he continued to insist on referring to German people respectfully. Less than a year after the end of the war, the *Sheffield Independent* urged its readers not to use the word 'Hun', arguing it was mainly used by 'die-hards who never went to the war'[40] and that 'the man who, having knocked out his enemy and won his fight, cannot stop calling him names is about the poorest sort of "sport" we know'.

★★★

Three months into his editorship, Clarke oversaw the *Sheffield Independent*'s centenary. It was marked with a special edition, and as part of the celebrations it published congratulatory messages from prominent people in Sheffield and beyond.

Three of these came from figures from Clarke's own past. Christopher Addison wrote to offer 'congratulations and good wishes' to the newspaper for reaching the milestone, and C.P. Scott, the editor of the *Manchester Guardian*, wrote:'Under its new management – and, may I say, its most capable new editor, it is bound to go on and prosper.'[41] Then six days later it published a note from Lord Northcliffe that personally endorsed his former employee's editorship. 'I should like to add my testimony to the revived energy and enterprise of the old "Independent",' the press baron wrote. 'I remember the "Independent" under several editorships, but I do not think it has ever had a more enterprising occupant of the chair than my friend Basil Clarke.'[42]

While its newfound 'energy and enterprise' met with Northcliffe's approval, the robustness that went with it was beginning to cause tension. During a moulders' strike in late 1919, the newspaper responded forthrightly to criticism of its coverage by the workers, stating that 'it is no evidence of friendship to encourage men to persist in an unwise course'.[43] But if the *Sheffield Independent's* response to the moulders' complaints was spiky, it was nothing compared to its criticism of a lock-out by the Yorkshire Federation of Master Painters in February 1920.

The Master Painters had called a lock-out – where an employer responds to a limited strike by refusing to allow any of the workforce to work – in response to industrial action by painters in Keighley and Wakefield. Quite reasonably, the *Sheffield Independent* thought this was unfair on those workers who were losing their wages despite having nothing to do with the industrial action. But rather than simply criticising the Master Painters, it provocatively compared them to Moritz Von Bissing, the notorious German Governor General of occupied Belgium during the war. Its leader column attempted to justify what was an extraordinarily tasteless comparison:

> The punishment of the many for the delinquencies of the few we regarded as reprehensible even in the German governors of Flanders, who, to keep order among the vanquished population during war-time, had at least the excuse that their task was difficult.

> But to find a handful of "little masters" solemnly trying to impose this sort of thing upon British workmen of all Yorkshire because the painters of Keighley and Wakefield have displeased them is hardly believable. The sooner that the master painters come to their senses and back to earth – Britain this time and not Prussia – the better it will be for themselves and the community.[44]

The Master Painters were understandably furious at being compared to Von Bissing, who during the war had been described as the 'Despot of Brussels'.[45] But the following day the *Sheffield Independent* was unrepentant:

> We are glad the thrust has gone home, and repeat it. To take away the livelihood of hundreds of painters in Sheffield, Leeds, and a score more places because of the action – be it right or wrong – of a handful of painters of Wakefield and Keighley cannot by any argument be made to appear to us as either justice or humanity.

> It stands revealed as an act of tyrannous retaliation, an act of which Von Bissing might well – as we said yesterday – have been the parent.[46]

As well as angering prominent members of the local community, the comparison with Von Bissing was also the kind of polemic that had the potential to alienate advertisers and, just a month later, on 11 March 1920, relations between Clarke and the newspaper's owners were so strained that he was in negotiations to return to his old job at the Ministry of Health.

His replacement as the head of publicity there had decided to leave after being offered £1,000 a year to take a job in Manchester, and Addison believed they would be 'very fortunate' to persuade Clarke to return.[47]

Clarke told the Ministry of Health that the managing director of the *Sheffield Independent* had agreed to talk to the other directors about him returning to the Civil Service. 'I think they will let me leave,' he wrote,[48] though in reality the newspaper's owners seem to have been as keen to end his editorship as he was.[49]

It is perhaps a sign of desperation that Clarke, who was earning a reported salary of £1,250 a year at the *Sheffield Independent*, did not reject out of hand the ministry's offer of £700 a year, which was £100 less than it had paid him previously. He did, though, make his feelings plain in a letter to a contact at the ministry, in which he wrote that the Treasury were 'measly blighters' and that reducing his salary 'would be regarded as a vote of no confidence in future service and no appreciation of past'.[50]

The dispute about his salary was still unresolved when, barely six months after leaving the Ministry of Health, he re-joined it on 29 March 1920,[51] though once in post the Treasury did reluctantly agree to match his previous salary of £800.

The time he had spent away from the ministry had not diminished Addison's enthusiasm for propaganda,[52] but his belief in its potential was not shared across Whitehall. Addison admitted he was likely to face 'great difficulty' in strengthening the ministry's publicity department because the Cabinet had 'laid down quite specifically that one of the economies in public service is to be the abolition or reduction of publicity branches'.[53] To make matters worse, a conference Addison convened on health propaganda did not reveal any great enthusiasm for publicity work, with one of the civil servants present believing that the ministry should issue as little propaganda as possible.[54]

Perhaps not surprisingly given these obstacles, there is no evidence that Clarke's return to the Ministry of Health was any more productive than his previous time there. But while discussions about whether and how the Ministry of Health should be using propaganda would continue – it is something on which a consensus has never been reached – there was another area of the Government's work where the need for propaganda was both obvious and immediate.

Britain's hold on Ireland was under serious threat from an armed rebellion that commanded the support of large parts of the population. The heavy-handed British response to the rebellion had resulted in an almost constant stream of criticism of its Irish policy and, having realised it was losing the propaganda war, Clarke was identified as the man to help turn the situation around.

So just two weeks after Addison's meeting to discuss the future of health propaganda, on 9 August 1920, a letter was sent from the Irish Office to the Ministry of Health confirming that Clarke was to be 'lent' to the Chief Secretary of Ireland.[55] It marked the start of what he would later look back on as the most difficult period of his career.[56]

Notes

1 Basil Clarke, *Unfinished Autobiography*, p.206.
2 *The War Illustrated*, 15 September 1917, p.88.
3 *Evening Standard*, 12 July 1917, p.6.
4 Basil Clarke, *My Round of the War*, London, 1917 (it is listed as being published in 1917, but the reviews strongly suggest that it actually became publicly available at the beginning of 1918).
5 Ibid., Preface.
6 Ibid., p.51.
7 *Manchester Guardian*, 26 January 1918, p.6.
8 *The War Illustrated*, 16 March 1918, p.xx (back cover) It could hardly be seen as an impartial endorsement, as on page 97 of the same issue was 'Safeguarding the Soldier', an article by Clarke about Australian efforts to support soldiers after they had finished fighting.
9 *Irish Times*, 23 February 1918, p.5.
10 Parliamentary Archives, Houses of Parliament, LG/F/1/4/4, Addison to Lloyd George, 13 December 1917.
11 Parliamentary Archives, Houses of Parliament, LG/F/1/6/4, Addison to Lloyd George, 3 March 1920.

12 Parliamentary Archives, Houses of Parliament, LG/F/1/6/5, Letter to Addison, 23 March 1920. Addison's reply (LG/F/1/6/5) was dated 24 March 1920; also see LG/F/1/4/21, Lloyd George to Addison, 4 June 1918, and Addison's reply (LG/F/1/4/21) dated 15 June 1918.

13 National Archives, Kew, MH 107/23, Letter from Clarke, 4 June 1919, states that he had been at the Ministry of Reconstruction for 16 months before joining the Ministry of Health in March 1919.

14 Basil Clarke, *Unfinished Autobiography*, p.206.

15 National Archives, Kew, 20120/1, Clarke to Mr Leggett, 14 February 1919.

16 Jacquie L'Etang, *Public Relations in Britain: A History of Professional Practice in the Twentieth Century*, New Jersey, 2004, p.48.

17 National Archives, Kew, T142/62/270.

18 The Political Quarterly, Vol. 80, No. 1, January–March 2009, Ivor Gaber, 'Exploring the Paradox of Liberal Democracy: More Political Communications Equals Less Public Trust'.

19 National Archives, Kew, RECO 1/204, 3 May 1918, Minute from Mr Davies.

20 Basil Clarke, *Unfinished Autobiography*, pp.206–7.

21 Ibid., p.201.

22 *The War Illustrated*, 23 November 1918, p.237.

23 *The War Illustrated*, 7 December 1918, p.269.

24 *The War Illustrated*, 14 December 1918, p.287.

25 *The War Illustrated*, 4 January 1919, p351; and 11 January 1919, p.371.

26 *Manchester Guardian*, 17 January 1919, p.6.

27 Douglas Jerrold, Georgian Adventure, London, 1937, p.215.

28 Parliamentary Archives, Houses of Parliament, LG/F/1/5/3, Addison to Lloyd George, 22 January 1919.

29 Basil Clarke, *Unfinished Autobiography*, p.208.

30 *Sheffield Independent*, 5 September 1919, p.4.

31 National Archives, Kew, 20120/1, 11 March 1920, letter from Clarke.

32 Basil Clarke, *Unfinished Autobiography*, pp.208–9.

33 *Sheffield Independent*, 5 September 1919, p.4.

34 Ibid.

35 Ibid.

36 *Christian Science Monitor*, 1 April 1977, p.18.

37 James Lansdale Hodson, *Home Front*, London, 1944, p.119.

38 *Sheffield Independent*, 28 October 1919, p.4.

39 *Christian Science Monitor*, 1 April 1977, p.18.

40 *Sheffield Independent*, 1 November 1919, p.4.

41 *Sheffield Independent*, 11 December 1919, p.4.

42 *Sheffield Independent*, 17 December 1919, p.4.

43 *Sheffield Independent*, 23 January 1920, p.4.

44 *Sheffield Independent*, 4 February 1920, p.4.

45 *Daily Mail*, 9 February 1915, p.8.

46 *Sheffield Independent*, 5 February 1920, p.4.

47 National Archives, Kew, 20120/1, Memo dated 12 March 1920.

48 National Archives, Kew, 20120/1, 11 March 1920, letter from Clarke.

49 Alan Clarke, *The Life & Times of Sir Basil Clarke – PR Pioneer, Public Relations*, 1969, Vol. 22 (2) pp. 8–13, states that his editorship ended 'by mutual consent' after relations became strained.

50 National Archives, Kew, 20120/1, Letter dated 12 March 1920.
51 National Archives, Kew, 20120/1, 21 April 1920, Memo from Clarke.
52 National Archives, Kew, Mh 55/27, Memo, 4 May 1920.
53 National Archives, Kew, Mh 55/27, Memo, 21 July 1920.
54 Muriel Grant, *Propaganda and the Role of the State in Inter-War Britain*, Oxford, 1994, p.128
55 National Archives, Kew, MH 107/23, Letter from the Irish Office to Ministry of Health, 9 August 1920.
56 Alan Clarke, *The Life & Times of Sir Basil Clarke – PR Pioneer, Public Relations*, 1969, Vol. 22 (2) pp. 8–13.

14

Ireland

On 10 September 1919, Clarke's *Sheffield Independent* had published an editorial about the deteriorating situation in Ireland:

Our long-drawn suppression of Ireland is a thing to make any honest British citizen burn with shame. If our long-continued repression of Irish national sentiment and life evokes natural anger, even madness, and violence, are we quite fair in calling that rebellion? Sit on a man and hold him down: you may say truly that you are not hurting him, but he will struggle none the less to rise. He may even bite.

Ireland, driven mad by long suppression, has arrived at the stage where she bites. She robs officials and may even murder them; she drives cattle, shoots police, and plays the devil generally. But remember that Ireland is, or feels she is, under the weight of fat Britain's body, and that that alone is why she bites.[1]

This was only the first of several articles the *Sheffield Independent* published about Ireland during Clarke's editorship. An editorial in November 1919 highlighted what it saw as the hypocrisy of the UK's championing of the right of nations to choose their own destiny in the post-war settlement at the same time as shrinking 'with horror from the idea of giving the people of Ireland the same freedom'.[2]

The following month it accused the Government of not having the 'consent of the governed',[3] and a week later claimed that 'our government is not wanted in Ireland' and pointed to how local communities were siding with the killers of police officers as evidence that 'our government in Ireland is on completely the wrong lines and has no moral sanction'.[4]

These editorials could hardly have been stronger in their criticism of the Government's Irish policy. But in August 1920, just eight months after his newspaper accused the Government of having 'no moral sanction' in Ireland, Clarke travelled to Dublin to take charge of propaganda there.

It is unclear why he did this. It could have been because of a sense of duty or a belief that it might further his career, though perhaps the most likely explanation is that going to Ireland appealed to the adventure-seeking part of him that missed the danger of life as a war correspondent. It was certainly not the result of a sudden change of view about Britain's policy; his son Alan later wrote that the excesses of the British forces continued to appal him.

If danger-seeking was Clarke's motive, he had chosen the right place. Hostility towards the British had grown considerably since he had visited Dublin in 1916 following the Easter Rising, when public opinion had been mixed and many people had been angry at the actions of the rebels. The ruthless response of the British, who arrested more than 3,500 people alleged to be involved with the Rising and executed fifteen of them, fermented anti-British feeling, and Sinn Fein, a political party closely linked with the paramilitary Irish Republican Army (IRA), won the 1918 General Election by a landslide with around 70 per cent of Irish seats.

Instead of taking their seats at Westminster, Sinn Fein set up its own Irish Parliament, which it called the Dáil Éireann, and declared an 'existing state of war between Ireland and England'. The Dáil Éireann met for the first time on 21 January 1919, and this, together with the unrelated shooting of two police officers on the same day, marked the start of the Irish War of Independence.

★★★

The War of Independence was a difficult time to be an Irish journalist. Newspapers risked provoking violence if they criticised the British, as journalists at the *Irish Independent* discovered when members of the Royal Irish Constabulary (RIC) raided its offices and held a gun to a sub-editor's head.[5] And while the British were responsible for most of the violence against newspapers, antagonising the Republicans could also be dangerous. The offices of both the *Irish Independent* and the *Cork Examiner* were attacked and their printing machinery damaged as punishment for articles that displeased the IRA.[6]

As well as living under the threat of violence, newspapers had to contend with legal restrictions on what they could publish. The Defence of the Realm Act (DORA), which forbade the printing of 'seditious speeches, articles or other matters which might cause disaffection', had been passed in 1914 to help the war effort, but the British repeatedly used it to suppress criticism of its Irish policy.[7] Then just before Clarke arrived in Ireland, DORA was replaced by the Restoration of Order in Ireland Act, which imposed such draconian restrictions that the historian Ian Kenneally has described it as 'the end of what remained of free speech for Irish newspapers'.[8]

These difficult working conditions did not, though, neuter Ireland's press completely. In fact, it is surprising just how strong some of them were prepared to be in their criticism of the British and Clarke quickly became so irritated by Ireland's journalists that he decided they were 'about the worst reporters in the world and distort all that one says'.[9] While without the legal restrictions and the threat of violence, the mostly nationalist press would have been even stronger in its condemnation, as Clarke arrived in Ireland the fact that journalists felt constrained as to how critical they could be was just about the only propaganda advantage the British enjoyed.

Considering its relatively meagre resources, Sinn Fein proved surprisingly effective at propaganda. It had established its own newspaper, called the *Irish Bulletin*, and sent copies of it to influential people in Britain and overseas. While some propaganda newspapers fall into the trap of making wild and inaccurate claims about their enemy, the editors of the *Irish Bulletin* were shrewd enough to realise that, given the bulk of its readers were not supporters of independence, it would only be effective if it were able to establish a reputation for accuracy. The fact that it published corrections[10] and was seen as a credible source of information by English newspapers[11] suggests its commitment to providing accurate information was a strategy it was prepared to follow through.

The British propaganda effort, on the other hand, was fragmented and lacked any sense of leadership. The civil administration that Clarke joined was based at Dublin Castle and shared responsibility for propaganda with the RIC and the Army. And while all sides agreed about the importance of propaganda, they lacked Sinn Fein's clarity of vision about the best approach. So as Clarke moved into his quarters at Dublin Castle – civil servants stayed at the castle for their own safety, though Clarke insisted in a letter home to Alice that 'the danger here, so called, is vastly overstated'[12] – the challenge facing him and his team of eight in Dublin and three in London was as much to do with rallying the British around one common approach as with tackling the Sinn Fein propaganda machine.

Given the scale of the challenge, it is not surprising that Clarke was immediately inundated with work. 'You would hardly believe how I am kept going,' he wrote home to Alice, going on to describe how a typical day would involve 'ding–dong grind' from 10.00 a.m. to 8.00 p.m. with only a 40 minute break for lunch.[13]

It seems that he quickly made an impression: journalists in Ireland took to calling him the 'Black and Tan publicity man'[14] (after the notoriously violent 'Black and Tans' division of temporary constables) and a diary entry by Mark Sturgis, a fellow civil servant at Dublin Castle, suggests he was initially ambivalent about him:

> The CS [Chief Secretary Hamar Greenwood] likes Basil Clarke. Personally I am not clear as to Clarke's position. I think it a mistake he ever came to live in – he is not out half enough.[15]

There was little opportunity for Clarke to settle in, as even in his first few weeks he had to manage a story that captured the attention of the world's press.

The Lord Mayor of Cork, Terence MacSwiney, was arrested in August 1920 for possession of seditious articles and documents and a cipher key, and was on hunger strike at Brixton Prison after being sentenced to two years in prison. On 25 October, after seventy-four days without food, MacSwiney died. The Government – and presumably Clarke was involved – tried to mitigate the damage to its reputation by releasing statements claiming that MacSwiney had previously endorsed violence against a British administration he had described as 'a thing of evil incarnate'.[16]

Whether this was true, any attempts to reduce public sympathy for him were unsuccessful. Some 30,000 people paid their respects at Southwark Cathedral, while in the United States the flag at Newark's City Hall was flown at half-mast in honour of him.[17] And this was nothing compared to the anger in Ireland. Feelings ran so high that in London the Government began to worry about the risk to public order from MacSwiney's body arriving in Dublin, unsure whether it would be better to send it directly to Cork.

Clarke and his colleagues waited anxiously at Dublin Castle as the procrastination continued in London, and as it approached the evening before MacSwiney's body was due to arrive they feared that any decision might be taken too late to get the news out to the public.

'Even Shinns are entitled to be told tonight if tomorrow's circus is off,' Mark Sturgis wrote in his diary. 'To rob them of their meat at the last minute may provoke a far bigger row than the funeral itself.'[18]

As the minutes ticked by without a decision, Dublin Castle wired London to say it would announce at 8.00 p.m. that MacSwiney's body would not be landing in Dublin unless it received orders otherwise. Shortly afterwards, Dublin Castle released a statement:

> The Irish Executive has been informed that the Government has decided that the remains of the Lord Mayor of Cork are not to be conveyed by way of Dublin. This decision is owing to the risk of political demonstrations that might result in loss of innocent lives.[19]

By the time the statement was issued, many newspapers had already gone to print. Clarke had to persuade staff at the *Dublin Evening Mail* to contact its owner, whom he convinced to put out a special edition announcing that MacSwiney's body would not be arriving in Dublin the following morning after all. The first copies containing the news appeared in the city at 9.00 p.m.[20]

★★★

As well as helping to manage the British response to events, Clarke spent his first few weeks at Dublin Castle trying to implement a system of propaganda that would allow the British to seize the initiative.

He established a Press Bureau at Dublin Castle that journalists could visit twice a day and get the British version of the news. It was presumably based on the Press Bureau in London during the early days of the First World War and, just as Clarke had criticised the way the Government had tried to control the news agenda in 1914, his new bureau was far from universally popular and one newspaper later recalled that journalists had 'unpleasant recollections' of Clarke's 'obnoxious' Press Bureau.[21]

At one point journalists in Dublin even began to boycott the Press Bureau, presumably in protest at the one-sided nature of its news. But the information it issued must have had some value because the boycott eventually broke down. Then when the pro-Republican *Freeman's Journal* announced that it would no longer publish Dublin Castle statements, Clarke responded by deliberately timing the release of news to benefit its rivals and, shortly afterwards, the *Freeman's Journal* requested to be given reports from Dublin Castle again.[22]

While Clarke's bureau was controversial, not every newspaper was hostile to it. Even journalists on the *Manchester Guardian*, which was especially critical of the Government's Irish policy, saw Clarke as someone who did a 'difficult and distasteful job honourably and well'[23] and its editor and his former employer, C.P. Scott, later thanked Clarke for being 'certainly very kind to the MG men' in Dublin.[24]

The evidence of the bureau's success was the number of journalists who used it. Clarke wrote in a memo to a colleague at Dublin Castle:

> About 20 Pressmen, Irish, British and foreign, visit the Castle twice daily, take <u>our version</u> of the facts – which I take care are as favourable to us as may be, in accordance with truth and verisimilitude – and they believe all I tell them. And they can't afford to stay away.[25]

But as effective as the Press Bureau may have been, any effect it had on public opinion during Clarke's first few months in Ireland was greatly outweighed by an issue that would prove to be his greatest obstacle in presenting the British case in a sympathetic light.

As the violence escalated during 1920, the British often responded to the killings of its soldiers and police officers by rampaging through the local area, burning buildings and threatening and beating people. Whether the result of poor discipline or a deliberate tactic to discourage people from assisting the IRA, what became known as the Reprisals was a public relations disaster. As well as fuelling Irish animosity towards the British, they caused revulsion around the world and meant that, in the words of the *Manchester Guardian*, 'Sinn Fein is able to issue a list of outrages almost as grave as that which Dublin Castle daily publishes'.[26]

Reprisals were already happening when Clarke arrived but during his first few weeks there was an incident that, perhaps more than any other, focused the world's attention on them.[27]

On 20 September, Peter Burke, a Head Constable with the RIC, was shot dead by the IRA as he drank with his brother in a hotel in Balbriggan in County Dublin. The RIC responded by setting fire to the town and taking two men they suspected of involvement in Burke's murder from their homes and killing them, reportedly with bayonets.[28]

While previous Reprisals had mostly affected relatively remote areas, Balbriggan's proximity to Dublin meant it was within easy reach of journalists, who were then able to write graphic accounts of the behaviour of the British.

The *Manchester Guardian*, for example, described police officers shooting wildly and burning indiscriminately, while the *New York Times* claimed residents had run into the nearby countryside to escape the gunfire and that one woman only just managed to rescue her baby from its cot before her home was set alight. It also reported that the morning after the attack the roads to Balbriggan were filled with women and children – many with injuries caused by flying glass – trying to escape.[29]

As well as being personally appalled by the Reprisals, Clarke realised they were likely to have a disastrous effect on any remaining goodwill that existed towards the British in Ireland. He discussed the issue with Hamar Greenwood, the Chief Secretary of Ireland, and came away from their conversation with a guarantee that there would be no more Reprisals.[30] He then passed this guarantee to the *Daily Mail*, which was one of the Government's severest critics of the way the violence in Ireland was spiralling out of control.[31]

In trusting Greenwood, Clarke was making a mistake. Greenwood was already considered as something of a joke by journalists because of inaccuracies in his public statements[32] and even Nevil Macready, the head of the Army whose own views sometimes had only a loose basis in reality, complained that Greenwood's performances in the House of Commons 'often carried him beyond the boundaries of fact so that he became as one crying in the wilderness'. Macready was also critical of the tone of Greenwood's public statements, writing to a friend that his over-optimism 'does an infinity of harm'.[33]

Whether Greenwood's promise of an end to the Reprisals was due to a lack of truthfulness or an over-abundance of optimism, it did not take long for Clarke to discover how little it meant.

Just days after he was given permission to brief journalists that the Reprisals were over, on 28 September, the IRA attacked an army barracks in Mallow, County Cork, taking guns and ammunition and shooting one officer dead. The response from the British was swift and violent. The Army arrived in the town and set fire to buildings in what *The Times* called a 'mad orgy of destruction' that left Mallow with the 'appearance of having undergone a bombardment'.[34]

Under the headline 'A National Disgrace', *The Times* called the Reprisals a 'system deliberately organised' and argued that 'the name of England is being sullied throughout the Empire and throughout the world by this savagery, for which the Government can no longer escape ... responsibility'.[35] The *Manchester Guardian* believed it was 'a very severe test of the Government's sincerity towards reprisals',[36] while the *New York Times* published a front page story headlined 'Irish town burning'.[37]

Aside from its effect on the reputation of the British, Clarke's assurances to the *Daily Mail* meant Mallow also represented a serious blow to his personal credibility. He felt sufficiently let down to threaten to resign, though this threat does not seem to have been taken particularly seriously by his colleagues.

'I think it will blow over,' Mark Sturgis wrote in his diary. 'The CS [Chief Secretary] will jolly him out of it.'

He was right. Clarke withdrew his threat the next day.[38]

Notes

1   *Sheffield Independent*, 10 September 1919, p.4.
2   *Sheffield Independent*, 24 November 1919, p.4.
3   *Sheffield Independent*, 13 December 1919, p.6.
4   *Sheffield Independent*, 20 December 1919, p.4.
5   Ian Kenneally, *The Paper Wall – Newspaper and Propaganda in Ireland 1919–1921*, Cork, 2008, pp.16–18.
6   Ibid., pp.66–7.
7   Ibid., p.5.

8   Ibid., p.13

9   National Archives, Kew, 20120/1, Memo dated 12 March 1920.

10 For an example of a correction it published, see *Irish Bulletin*, 6 December 1920, p.4.

11 Nevil Macready, *Annals of an Active Life*, London, 1924, p.494.

12 Clarke to Alice, Dublin, 20 August 1920. The property of the Hartley family, its contents are published here for the first time.

13 National Archives, Kew, 20120/1, Memo dated 12 March 1920.

14 Hugh Oram, *The Newspaper Book*, Dublin, 1983, p.142.

15 *The Last Days of Dublin Castle: The Mark Sturgis Diaries*, edited and introduced by Michael Hopkinson, Irish Academic Press, Dublin, 1999, p.44.

16 *Manchester Guardian*, 26 October 1920, p.9.

17 *New York Times*, 26 October 1920, p.7.

18 *The Last Days of Dublin Castle: The Mark Sturgis Diaries*, edited and introduced by Michael Hopkinson, Irish Academic Press, Dublin, 1999, p.61.

19 *Manchester Guardian*, 29 October 1920, p.7.

20 *The Last Days of Dublin Castle: The Mark Sturgis Diaries*, edited and introduced by Michael Hopkinson, Irish Academic Press, Dublin, 1999, p.61.

21 *The People*, Wexford, 13 January 1934, p.4.

22 National Archives, Kew, CO 904/168/3/840-3, Clarke to Cope, 10 March 1921.

23 David Ayerst, *Guardian – Biography of a Newspaper*, Collins, London, 1971, p.421.

24 Scott to Clarke, 28 April 1923. Property of the Hartley family, its contents are being published here for the first time.

25 National Archives, Kew, CO 904/168/3/840-3, Clarke to Cope, 10 March 1921.

26 *Manchester Guardian*, 18 August 1920, p.7

27 David George Boyce, *Englishmen and Irish Troubles: British Public Opinion and the Making of Irish Policy, 1918–1922*, Cape, 1972, p.51.

28 Ian Kenneally, *The Paper Wall – Newspaper and Propaganda in Ireland 1919–1921*, Cork, 2008, p.22.

29 *New York Times*, 22 September 1920, p.1 and p.6.

30 Charles Townsend, *The British Campaign in Ireland 1919–1921: The Development of Political and Military Policies*, Oxford University Press, 1975, p.117.

31 *The Last Days of Dublin Castle: The Mark Sturgis Diaries*, edited and introduced by Michael Hopkinson, Irish Academic Press, Dublin, 1999, pp.48–9

32 Ian Kenneally, *The Paper Wall – Newspaper and Propaganda in Ireland 1919–1921*, Cork, 2008, p.31.

33 Parliamentary Archives, House of Parliament, LG/F/36/2/16, Macready to Miss Stevenson, 11 February 1921.

34 *The Times*, 20 September 1920, p.10.

35 *The Times*, 30 September 1920, p.11.

36 *Manchester Guardian*, 30 September 1920, p.7.

37 *New York Times*, 29 September 1920, p.1.

38 *The Last Days of Dublin Castle: The Mark Sturgis Diaries*, edited and introduced by Michael Hopkinson, Irish Academic Press, Dublin, 1999, pp.48–9,

15

Bloody Sunday

During a speech at the Lord Mayor's banquet in London on 9 November 1920, Lloyd George addressed the issue of Ireland. 'Unless I am mistaken,' the Prime Minister told the audience, 'by the steps we have taken we have murder by the throat'.[1]

Then just over a week later, the *New York Times* published a Dublin Castle statement that further reinforced the impression that the threat of violence was receding:

> The wave of violent crime which followed the death of the Lord Mayor of Cork appears to have spent its force. The number of outrages for the week is in fact lower than for any previous weeks during the last three months, indicating that the rise of the preceding fortnight was merely a temporary interruption of the steady decline in outrage and violence.[2]

If the British really believed the IRA's influence was waning, they were about to be shocked. Far from reducing its activity, it was actually in the final stages of preparing its most audacious operation of the whole conflict.

The man behind it was Michael Collins, the charismatic Republican who, after narrowly avoiding execution following the Easter Rising, had become an MP in 1918 and gone on to become a leading figure within Sinn Fein and the IRA. He was now best known as Sinn Fein's Minister of Finance, but had a wide range of responsibilities that included establishing an assassination unit called The Squad.

It was in this latter role that Collins identified the British intelligence network in Dublin as a threat that needed to be neutralised. His plan for doing this was as simple as it was brutal: to compile a list of men involved in British intelligence and target them in a coordinated wave of assassinations.

The original list of those to be targeted contained fifty names, but this was reduced to thirty-five because there was insufficient evidence that some of the men were involved in intelligence work. Then just after 8.00 a.m. on Sunday, 21 November, death squads arrived at the homes of the thirty-five officers. Some were still in their pyjamas when they were killed. Others were shot in front of their wives. The pregnant wife of one of the men jumped in front of her husband to try to shield him from his killers and gave birth to a stillborn baby a few days later. But while some of the British officers were ruthlessly dispatched, others escaped death either because they were not at home or because the operations were bungled by their would-be assassins.

In all, fourteen British were killed in the raid, including two Auxiliaries (the Auxiliaries were a paramilitary division of the police) who became involved after hearing the sound of gunfire from a nearby house. One IRA member, Frank Teeling, was wounded and arrested but later escaped from prison.

The violence struck at the heart of the British presence in Dublin and it fell to Clarke to prepare the British response to it. His department produced a long statement based on the witness statements of survivors, emphasising the callousness of the operation to try to create the impression that the IRA were cold-blooded killers rather than freedom fighters.

Clarke's work in responding to perhaps the greatest crisis the British had faced in Ireland since the Easter Rising seems to have been appreciated by his colleagues. 'Clarke is a great help on an occasion of this sort and handles the arrangements with regard to publication and distribution of news with an expert hand,' Sturgis recorded in his diary.[3]

The IRA operation against the British officers was not, though, the end of what became known as Bloody Sunday. A Gaelic football match between Dublin and Tipperary was scheduled for that afternoon at Dublin's Croke Park and, although there was some discussion of cancelling the match it finally kicked off about half an hour late at 3.15 p.m., in front of a crowd of between 10,000 and 15,000 people. The two sides had been playing for about 10 minutes when police and Auxiliaries arrived at the ground. What happened next is still disputed, but the events of the next few minutes left twelve people dead and many more injured.

★★★

Having spent the morning condemning the killings of the British officers, Clarke and his colleagues were suddenly faced with accusations that the British had themselves been guilty of atrocities against innocent people.

After getting reports of what had happened at Croke Park, Clarke hand-wrote a statement that was then amended by Sir John Anderson, the Under-Secretary at Dublin Castle who would later become Chancellor of the Exchequer during the Second World War.

The statement told how the police had believed that some of the killers from the morning were hiding in the crowd and so had planned to surround the field and for an officer with a megaphone to announce that the crowd was to be searched. But the police were fired on as they approached the ground and at the same time men sitting in the grandstand stood up and fired three shots into the air.

The statement speculated that these shots may have been a pre-arranged signal because people suddenly rushed forward, creating a stampede towards an iron railing. As the fleeing crowd started to climb over the railing it collapsed under their weight and a number of people were crushed. As this was going on, the armed men outside the ground were joined by gunmen from inside and they exchanged fire with the police for up to 3 minutes. About thirty revolvers were found on the ground afterwards, discarded by gunmen who then disappeared into the crowd.

Clarke's statement did not allow for any doubt about who was to blame for the deaths:

> The responsibility for [the casualties] rests ... upon those foul assassins whose existence is a ... menace to all law-abiding persons in Ireland.[4]

The next day, most London newspapers focused more on the killings in the morning than on events at Croke Park. This may have been partly because of the practical difficulty of the Croke Park tragedy occurring later in the day, but it is also likely that the deaths of British officers was considered more newsworthy than those of Irish civilians.

The Times described the killings as 'the most cruel and desperate of all outbreaks by the Republican murder gang' and, as Clarke's statement had led it to, highlighted the fact that 'in two or three cases officers' wives were pulled out of bed and their husbands were murdered before their eyes'.[5] The *Daily Mirror* and the *Daily Express* reported the killings along similar lines. All three newspapers relegated the events of the afternoon to second billing, with the *Daily Mirror* unable even to get Croke Park's name right and instead referring to it as 'Crow Park'.

So even though the *Daily Mail* connected the previous day's events to the Reprisals by describing them as 'the dreadful result of a policy of illegal violence to which the Government had for months past turned a blind eye',[6] it is not surprising that on the Monday Clarke told his colleagues the coverage in the English press was 'on the whole very good'.[7]

But as pleased as the British may have been with the initial coverage, on the Tuesday they began to face questions about the truthfulness of the Croke Park statement that have continued to this day. *The Times* reported that 'eye-witnesses declare that they heard no firing until the Crown forces were inside the ground', and also printed the Gaelic Athletic Association's claim that the allegation that Sinn Fein pickets had opened fire on the British was 'ridiculous'.[8]

On the same day, the *Manchester Guardian's* correspondent also challenged the veracity of Clarke's statement:

I find it unsupported by eye-witnesses in several important particulars ... The allegation of firing is strongly denied, and has no support except from the official reports. What did unquestionably happen is that the Auxiliary police rushed through the two main entrances carrying the turnstiles with them. They fired as soon as they got inside. This is the testimony of witnesses I have spoken to in all parts of the field ... It seems only too clear that the full story of Croke Park, when it can be told, will unveil one of the most awful incidents in the Irish trouble, and one for whose responsibility the authorities cannot be exonerated. The discipline of the forces evidently failed at the last moment.[9]

While suspicion about Clarke's statement may have taken two days to appear in the London press, it was present in Irish newspaper coverage from the beginning.

The *Freeman's Journal* set them out most forcefully. As early as the Monday it was already using the term 'Bloody Sunday', as it angrily described the deaths at Croke Park as the 'authorised answer' to the killings in the morning and Clarke's statement as 'a patent and infamous falsehood'.

'There were no proclamations, no warnings, no legalities defied by the assembly in Croke Park,' it continued. 'The slaughter was a classic example of a Government reprisal. The innocent were shot down in blind vengeance. The pretence that the firing was provoked by an attack upon the Government forces will deceive no one in Ireland. It is another base official lie.'[10]

The day after the *Freeman's Journal's* broadside, the *Irish Independent* added its voice to the claim that events at Croke Park were 'by way of reprisal for the sensational shooting of the officers earlier in the day'[11] and a week later it reported that Clarke's statement 'was not accepted by the public as an accurate representation of the facts'.[12] Even the *Irish Times*, which was so pro-British that its initial response to Bloody Sunday was to express concern that 'Great Britain's generous, almost romantic, attitude to Ireland will be laid aside',[13] was unconvinced by the statement, reporting that 'many of those who were present at Croke Park when the firing occurred stated that they did not hear any firing at the Auxiliary police or military'.[14]

In fact, by the Tuesday the *Daily Express*, which dismissed out of hand the 'suggestion that the Croke Park affair was in the nature of a reprisal for the murders in the morning',[15] seems to have been one of the few newspapers in either Ireland or England that still uncritically accepted Clarke's statement, and General Nevil Macready's memoirs later recalled bitterly how 'the press on both sides of the Channel and certain members of Parliament united in stigmatising this unfortunate business as a deliberate retaliation for the murders of that morning'.[16]

But whatever doubts existed, Clarke's statement was effective in so much as it helped ensure that, in England at least, the killings of the British officers were initially the main story of Bloody Sunday. It also gave a plausible version of events that those who did not want to believe the worst of the British could cling to. It is, though, very likely that it was substantially wrong. The historian Ian Kenneally has meticulously reconstructed events at Croke Park and shown that parts of Clarke's statement are contradicted by the evidence. Its claim that about thirty revolvers were found on the ground, for example, was later contradicted by the evidence of the senior police officer at Croke Park, who said that no weapons were found.[17]

'To read the mass of evidence ... renders the official version of what happened at Croke Park to be, most likely, false,' Kenneally concludes. 'There remains the possibility that a member of the IRA had fired warning shots into the air and that this was the first link in a chain of horrific events. We know that IRA members were in the crowd so that possibility cannot be completely ruled out, but the available evidence makes it very unlikely that this actually happened. Whether or not it happened, there was no justification for the actions of the police in firing on the crowd.'

★★★

While the killing of the British officers and the shootings at Croke Park ensured that 21 November 1920 would go down as one of the most brutal days in Irish history, there would be yet more death before the day was over. That night, three Irish prisoners being held at Dublin Castle died in what Sturgis admitted in his diary was 'a strange and possibly unpleasant affair'.[18]

Again, Clarke was responsible for producing a statement about what had happened. It set out how prison accommodation was full and so the three men were being held in a guard room that contained 'a large quantity' of army material such as rifles and ammunition. Without explaining why three dangerous prisoners were held in a room where guns and ammunition were lying around, his statement went on to claim that the prisoners were allowed to sit around a fire and during the night one of them found a grenade under a bed and, not realising it was not primed, threw it at the sentry guarding the door. In the confusion, the prisoners grabbed a rifle and a shovel and in the ensuing fight all three were killed.

As with the Croke Park statement, there are serious questions about the accuracy of Clarke's statement about the three deaths. As experienced IRA men, McKee and Clancy would have been expected to know that detonating a grenade in a confined space would almost certainly result in their deaths.[19] Also, the two Auxiliaries who arrested them were known for their use of violence while interrogating prisoners and a doctor who examined Clune's body concluded that some of his wounds did not fit with the version of events in the statement.[20] Sinn Fein's *Irish Bulletin* was in no doubt about what had happened, claiming that 'these three men were murdered'[21] and describing Clarke's statement as 'an invention from first to last ... which does even bear the most superficial scrutiny'.[22]

Clarke's statement was, though, reported largely uncritically by newspapers such as the *Daily Mail*,[23] *The Times*[24] and the *New York Times*,[25] although the *Manchester Guardian* was more sceptical. Its correspondent was allowed to see the guardroom for himself and, though he concluded that 'nothing in the general aspect of the room and its contents was inconsistent with the details given in the official story',[26] he could not understand why the prisoners would attempt to escape when, even if they got out of the guardroom, the position of the guard at the main gateway meant they would face 'the certainty of instant death'.[27]

Whatever suspicions may have existed, the deaths of the three men were different from events at Croke Park in that this time there were no independent witnesses. This meant most newspapers did not follow their initial uncritical reporting of it with more sceptical coverage of the kind that appeared in the days after Croke Park. It also meant that, even today, we do not know what really happened to the three men.

***

Bloody Sunday was followed a week later by an IRA ambush near Kilmichael in County Cork in which sixteen Auxiliaries were killed, and Clarke's office was involved in getting publicity for the allegation that some of the dead had been shot in cold blood and their bodies mutilated. Again, it is unclear what actually happened but the IRA bitterly contested the claims[28] and, at least with the mutilation claim, it appears to have had a point.[29] But the press in both Ireland and England uncritically reported the British statement about mutilation.

Taken in isolation, the media handling of Bloody Sunday and Kilmichael could be judged as successful because Clarke had managed to help present the IRA in an unfavourable light following Kilmichael, and at least minimised the reputational damage of Bloody Sunday. But in the longer term, being associated with statements that were almost certainly inaccurate damaged Clarke's reputation, as he came to be seen as a sinister hidden hand influencing the tone of newspaper coverage.

Actually, the handling of Bloody Sunday and Kilmichael were small and isolated victories. Looked at as a whole, the story of British public relations during Clarke's time in Ireland is not one of unseen manipulation but of chaotic management, internal division and lack of direction.

Notes

1   *New York Times*, 10 November 1920, p.1.
2   *New York Times*, 20 November 1920, p.15.
3   *The Last Days of Dublin Castle: The Mark Sturgis Diaries*, edited and introduced by Michael Hopkinson, Irish Academic Press, Dublin, 1999, p.77.
4   National Archives, Kew, CO 904/168/1/179–81.
5   The Times, 22 November, p.12.
6   Daily Mail, 22 November 1920, p.9.
7   *The Last Days of Dublin Castle: The Mark Sturgis Diaries*, edited and introduced by Michael Hopkinson, Irish Academic Press, Dublin, 1999, p.78.
8   *The Times*, 23 November p.12.
9   *Manchester Guardian*, 23 November 1920, p.11.
10 *Freeman's Journal*, 22 November 1920, p.4.
11 *Irish Independent*, 23 November 1920, p.4.
12 *Irish Independent*, 30 November 1920, p.4.
13 *Irish Times*, 23 November 1920, p.4.
14 *Irish Times*, 23 November 1920, p.5.
15 *Daily Express*, 23 November, p.1.
16 Nevil Macready, *Annals of an Active Life*, London, 1924, p.510.
17 Ian Kenneally, *Courage and Conflict: Forgotten Stories of the Irish at War*, Cork, 2009, pp.324–5.
18 *The Last Days of Dublin Castle: The Mark Sturgis Diaries*, edited and introduced by Michael Hopkinson, Irish Academic Press, Dublin, 1999, p.79.
19 Ian Kenneally, *The Paper Wall – Newspaper and Propaganda in Ireland 1919–1921*, Cork, 2008, p.41.
20 Ian Kenneally, *Courage and Conflict: Forgotten Stories of the Irish at War*, Cork, 2009, pp.324–5.
21 *Irish Bulletin*, 24 November, p.2.
22 *Irish Bulletin*, 26 November, p.3.
23 *Daily Mail*, 24 November 1920, p.7.
24 *The Times*, 24 November 1920, p.12.
25 *New York Times*, 24 November 1920, p.1.
26 *Manchester Guardian*, 24 November 1920, p.7.

27 *Manchester Guardian*, 24 November 1920, p.7.

28 Tom Barry, *Guerrilla Days in Ireland*, Dublin, 1989, p.51.

29 Peter Hart, *The I.R.A. and its Enemies: Violence and Community in Cork, 1916–1923*, Oxford, 1998, p.24.

16

'Propaganda by News'

Clarke's colleagues at Dublin Castle may have initially had doubts about him but, as Mark Sturgis's diary entry about his news management on Bloody Sunday suggested, it did not take long for him to win them over and Sir John Anderson reported back to London at the end of 1920 that Clarke was 'doing excellent work'.[1]

It was not just his professional ability they valued him for. The fact that most civil servants were largely confined to Dublin Castle for their own safety meant the atmosphere was tense and claustrophobic and so Clarke's colleagues appreciated both his good humour and his musical ability.

Sturgis described in his diary an evening when Clarke played 'the piano like a Trojan after dinner while we danced'.[2] 'What we should do without the good-tempered Basil I daren't think,' he wrote on another occasion. 'He and his piano are invaluable.'

A concert by local musicians that Clarke chaired at Dublin Castle gave a flavour of his sense of humour. The *Freeman's Journal* reported that when thanking the musicians, he described their performance as a gesture of friendship at a time 'when expressions of feeling towards Crown servants in Dublin took so many and varied forms, some of them quite explosive in their intensity'.[3]

It was on one of the evenings Clarke played the piano in Dublin Castle that General Nevil Macready, the head of the Army in Ireland, accompanied him by singing the words to the Rudyard Kipling poem 'Gunga Din'. Macready's son said it was the first time he had heard his father sing in ten years.[4]

But while they may have been prepared to socialise together, Macready and Clarke did not get on. This was partly because the Army did its own propaganda and Clarke was generally dismissive of it, writing in a memo to

Anderson that its 'journalistic values and word values, which count for so much in ultimate propaganda values, are not expertly weighed'. 'This is no reflection on those concerned,' he added, 'because they are soldiers first and the collection and editing of matter for Press and the handling of the Press generally is as much a craft as paper-hanging or horse-doctoring. We may all do a bit of these things in an amateur way but among fair judges it is generally admitted that the professional does it better.'[5]

An example of what he saw as the Army's ineffectual propaganda was an article it placed in the *Morning Post* in September 1920. Clarke wrote to a colleague that it had been a mistake to give it to a newspaper that already firmly supported Britain's policy in Ireland and had a relatively small readership. 'It is a poor job preaching to the converted,' he suggested. 'Such information could and should find a home in a much more neutral, more widely read paper.'[6]

Two months later Major Reginald Marians, who worked as a military press liaison, sent Clarke a copy of an article from the *Freeman's Journal* about two members of the RIC who had resigned just hours after arriving in Ireland. The *Freeman's Journal* had interviewed the men and used their comments as evidence of poor morale among the British.

The Army had responded by looking into the backgrounds of the men and discovered that one of them had previously been charged with assault, and in a separate incident had been fined for being drunk and incapable. Marians sent the information to Clarke with the idea of using it to discredit the source of the criticism.

Clarke added one handwritten sentence to Marian's note: 'The Freeman would promptly add: "But he was good enough for the RIC".'[7]

Clarke may have doubted the Army's ability to effectively manage the media, but Macready and his colleagues had an equally low opinion of him. In his memoirs, Macready did not even think Clarke worth mentioning by name:

> A gentleman was later imported from London into the Castle to give out news, and I believe plant literature here and there among the press, a good move in its way, but far short of what was required.[8]

Macready may have damned Clarke with faint praise publicly, but in private he was much more explicit in his criticism. He wrote to Anderson twice in March 1921 to complain about him, with his first letter urging that responsibility for propaganda be given to 'someone far more able than Basil Clarke',[9] and his second letter claiming 'Clarke has not the foggiest idea of how to set about propaganda from the point of view of a Military operation'.[10] There is also a suggestion that the Army was involved in press briefings against the civil administration, as Sturgis recorded in his diary that on a trip back to London

Clarke had 'been cruising down Fleet Street and says he finds what looks like an organised campaign afoot on the line that "Dublin Castle" is rotten and merely hampering the soldiers'.[11]

Macready also set out his concerns in a letter to Frances Stevenson, Lloyd George's secretary and mistress. He sent her a copy of one of his letters to Anderson and in his cover letter urged her to ask for the Prime Minister's intervention:

> Ever since I have been in Ireland, [I] have never ceased inveighing against the feebleness of our propaganda. If the PM could drop a word in Hamar [Greenwood]'s ear it would be, I think, a good thing.[12]

The lack of respect between Clarke and the Army was made worse by poor communication between them. Anderson raised this issue when he replied to Macready, accusing the Army of not giving Clarke enough information and adding that 'I do not think he or anyone else ought to be expected to create propaganda out of his own inner consciousness'.[13] At one point, Clarke's department even installed a trained journalist at army headquarters to try to improve the flow of information, but this does not seem to have made much difference.[14]

As to whether Macready or Clarke had the best case in questioning the competence of the other, perhaps the strongest piece of evidence is an interview Macready gave to the Associated Press following the Balbriggan Reprisal. In it, he implied that the behaviour of members of the RIC had been understandable in the circumstances:

> Inspector Burke … was very popular with the young police recruits he had trained, and when they heard that he had been murdered, it was human nature that they should feel they ought to avenge his death, knowing well that the organisation responsible for the crime would shelter rather than give up the culprits.[15]

Unsurprisingly, Macready's comments proved controversial and it would be easy to assume from their apparent naivety that they were the words of a man who did not take much interest in what journalists wrote. Actually, the opposite was true. But Macready seemed to think not in terms of the effect of newspaper coverage on public opinion but purely about its impact on the morale of British forces. He wrote in his memoirs that the Government's failure to put the true facts before the public 'rankled most deeply in the mind of every soldier'[16] and he even went as far as to suggest that, as much as they existed at all, a large proportion of the blame for the Reprisals lay with the way newspapers reported the conflict:

It can hardly be wondered if, after seeing himself and his comrades vilified and abused by the press or by the Kenworthys of Parliament [Joseph Kenworthy was an MP who was opposed to the Government's Irish policy], and no effort made to place the real facts before the public, he was inclined to see red when exasperated beyond endurance, and said to himself that he would give his maligners something they could talk about.[17]

While there were difficulties over personalities and communication, it was this fundamental difference in emphasis that was the greatest barrier to Clarke's department working well with the Army. Clarke wrote in a letter to Anderson that 'it is a difficult relationship, ours and theirs' and blamed this on the fact that 'one is conscious of a difference in outlook'.[18] In another memo, he admitted there was an 'inability on our part ... to impose our propaganda policy on men of a different service and different outlook who admitted quite frankly that they did not believe in that policy'.[19]

The problem was that while Macready wanted the Government to adopt a more aggressive approach to propaganda to show its support for the British forces, Clarke believed British statements should appear to be as impartial as possible. His approach, which he called 'propaganda by news', recognised that, as he put it in a memo to colleagues, 'every item of news tends to create some opinion, favourable or unfavourable'[20] and that Dublin Castle could make a story reflect better on the British simply through the careful selection of the information it released.

To illustrate to his employers how the approach worked, and perhaps with the Reprisals in mind, Clarke gave the fictional example of the police breaking into a man's house, opening fire indiscriminately, stealing whiskey and cigars and then setting the house alight. 'Such a news par would have a very real minus propaganda value,' Clarke wrote. 'But add to it, as a result of further inquiry, the fact that: "It was in this house three days ago that two unarmed police constables were murdered." And the minus propaganda effect of the news is lessened. In fact for simpler minds ... it is well-nigh removed.'[21]

This was a theory that was put into practice in the case of Kevin Barry, an 18-year-old Republican who was executed in November 1920 for his part in the deaths of three soldiers. When newspapers used his relative youth to present him as a sympathetic figure, Clarke asked Major Marians to find out the ages of the soldiers who had been killed and, when it emerged they too had been relatively young, this fact was publicised.[22] But in this case, the approach was wholly unsuccessful; Barry became widely considered to be a martyr of the Republican cause and a popular song was written in his memory.

Clarke realised the success of 'propaganda by news' depended on establishing the credibility of Dublin Castle, as this would, in Clarke's words, 'give us a hold over the press' and so enable him to influence the tone of coverage. To this end, it was so important to appear 'complete and candid' that it was sometimes even worth issuing news that reflected badly on the British because to 'appear deliberately to ignore it … is at once to reveal the wheels and works of the propaganda machine'.[23]

He also believed it was even sometimes necessary to include details in press statements that were detrimental to the British. 'An occasional partial concession of plus value for frankness sake, like an occasional bluff in poker, may be a sound propaganda investment,' he wrote in the same memo. 'The world is discerning and often sceptical and the report which reeks of rectitude is, like the too white life, often suspect by reason of its very appearance of blamelessness.'[24]

As part of this attempt to appear impartial, Clarke thought press statements should use the most neutral language possible. 'They should be no more than statements of facts,' he wrote. 'For any comment, no matter how justifiable, must be ex-parte and therefore liable to criticism as unseemly even if its justifiability and accuracy cannot be impugned. And facts can be so set forth as to bear in themselves their own comment.'[25]

This must have seemed like anathema to those who saw the role of a propagandist as simply to criticise the enemy as virulently as possible, but Clarke strongly believed they should stick to bare facts rather than opinion; the only way he thought a propaganda department should communicate views was through the factual reporting of the speeches of senior members of the administration.[26]

The most obvious reason for focusing on news rather than comment was that Dublin Castle was in a unique position as a source of news because of the large quantity of information that flowed into it. 'Views are the property of everyone, both sides alike, Sinn Fein and British,' Clarke explained. 'Journals can obtain either, but in news we have a monopoly.'[27] There was also the practical issue of newspapers generally being reluctant to publish comment pieces from outside sources, and Clarke also worried about being able to justify spending public money on comment pieces.[28] And while a comment piece would generally be limited to a single publication, an interesting piece of news had the potential to be published in hundreds of newspapers around the world.

But above all, Clarke explained to his colleagues in his memo, he believed that news was actually a more effective means of persuasion than comment:

Public and press opinion alike are more easily and more quickly and more widely influenced by news than by views.

News is … the raw material of views, which are after all no more than the direct product of mental (including emotional reactions) processes applied to that raw materials … if the news be right (from the point of view of one's propaganda project) then opinion, both public and press, may be left to look after itself.

Virtually every news item creates in the mind of the reader a reaction – either of emotion, pleasurable or unpleasurable, or of judgement, favourable or unfavourable or of both. This reaction may be conscious or sub-conscious; but it must occur.[29]

To illustrate his point, he gave his colleagues a fictional example of a piece of news that was likely to elicit an emotional reaction:

After leaving the "Blue Pig" at Tonypandy at 11pm on Saturday night John Jones, miner, a widower, went home and found his child on the doorstep, unable to open the house door before her father's arrival. He seized her by the hair, beat her with his fist and threw her into a neighbour's yard. She is aged 6 and from birth a cripple.

'This is a good propaganda-by-news paragraph against John Jones,' Clarke wrote. 'It contains no word of comment, no literary fluff or "sub stuff" such as might by clumsy hands have been put into it. Mr Jones nevertheless, would quite probably be lynched the next morning.'

He explained that the paragraph's lack of emotive language actually added to its power. 'Comment by the writer would mar its propaganda value,' he wrote. 'Pepper it with commentative adjectives, "brutal", "fiendish" etc. etc, and you rob simple folk of the very comment they would themselves delight to supply for all to hear, thereby advertising your news.'[30]

Clarke also understood how including as much detail as possible could enhance a story's news value. A full account of the wounding of one man, he wrote, might have greater news value than a sparse report of the killings of six people, and the statement could be valuable as a piece of propaganda if these extra details were calculated to better dispose the reader to the British.

'There are really quite few items in which the minus factor cannot be lessened by careful inquiry and treatment,' he concluded. 'For there is hardly any mistake, mishap or misconduct for which at least some excuse or reason or explanation calculated to win sympathy cannot be found if it be intelligently searched for.'[31]

★★★

The ideas Clarke set out in his 'propaganda by news' memos are not dramatically different to how large organisations approach public relations today. For one thing, most press releases do not contain emotive language in the main body of the text and confine any comment to a quote from a representative of the organisation. And governments, in particular, carefully select from the large amount of information at their disposal to try to influence the news agenda. But while Clarke's approach might seem obvious today, he was unable to convince the Army of its merit, and as late as April 1921, just three months before the end of the fighting, he was still trying to persuade Macready and his colleagues to support his way of doing things.

Yet though Clarke's relationship with the Army caused him most angst, it was not the internal relationship that posed the biggest threat to his chances of success. His relationship with the RIC may have been relatively smooth, but the work of its publicity department seriously undermined the credibility that Clarke's 'propaganda by news' approach so depended on.

It was run by Hugh Pollard, a firearms expert who one acquaintance later remembered 'looked and behaved like a German Crown Prince and had a habit of letting off revolvers in any office he happened to visit' and who later became known for flying Franco from Tenerife to Morocco in preparation for a fascist uprising in Spain.[32] Together with William Darling, Pollard was responsible for the *Weekly Summary*, a publication that was intended to raise morale within the RIC but which became notorious for the way it appeared to actively encourage Reprisals.

One soldier in Ireland described it as a 'weekly incentive to murder indiscriminately'[33] and former Prime Minister Herbert Asquith told the House of Commons that the copy he had seen was 'one of the most extraordinary documents I have ever read' and 'contained a number of the most inflammatory extracts you could possibly take from most extreme organs of one section of opinion in this country'. Asquith was particularly appalled by the way it recalled ('not with disapproval', he noted) an American Civil War General who on entering Kentucky had warned that if any of his men were killed then local people would be shot, regardless of their innocence or guilt.[34]

Clarke did not escape association with the *Weekly Summary*, as in April 1921 a Parliamentary question asked whether he 'admitted or denied' being the editor of it.[35] But there is no evidence he was involved and in fact Greenwood told the House of Commons that Clarke had nothing to do with it as it was 'published by the police, and for the police'.[36]

As well as editing the *Weekly Summary*, Pollard and Darling orchestrated attempts at black propaganda that were so ill-conceived that, according to the historian Ian Kenneally, they could be more accurately described as 'slapstick propaganda'.[37]

Perhaps their most ridiculous effort was an attempt to capitalise on the death of Kevin Barry. The RIC produced a report about a medium who had supposedly been contacted by Barry's spirit and was told that Heaven had 'melted his wicked heart' and that he wanted his friends and the people of Ireland 'to stop their wicked deeds'.[38]

Around the same time, Pollard was involved in the production of photographs of the aftermath of the so-called 'Battle of Tralee' in southwest Ireland, where a group of Auxiliaries were said to have bravely fought off an IRA ambush. It quickly emerged that the whole thing was an invention; there had been no 'Battle of Tralee' and the photographs had actually been taken in County Dublin. The *Irish Independent* exposed the deception by publishing the fake photograph alongside another photograph of the same location.[39]

The fictitious 'Battle of Tralee' was an embarrassment for the Government and Greenwood's attempts to distance himself from it did little to lessen the damage because, in the words of the *Manchester Guardian*, 'in … disclaiming any part in the deception, he [Greenwood] must be held as admitting that the soldiers who posed for the photograph, as well as the motor-lorries, guns, and other military accessories utilised to make up the battle-piece, had been used for the purpose without authority.'[40]

If this were not bad enough, Pollard and Darling outdid themselves after Auxiliaries seized the equipment and distribution list for the *Irish Bulletin* during a raid in Dublin. Rather than simply announcing the success of the raid, they decided to try to damage Sinn Fein's reputation by producing bogus editions of the *Irish Bulletin* and sending them to the people on the distribution list.

The aim of the faked editions seems to have been to raise doubts about the political beliefs of Sinn Fein – one of them included the report that 'there is less crime in Ireland than in any country in Europe, except Bolshevik Russia'[41] – and to undermine the *Irish Bulletin*'s credibility by making allegations against the British that were so outlandish that almost no one could possibly have believed them to be true. These included the implausible suggestions that the British had murdered thousands of Irish people; ruined millions of homes; and that there was no evidence that a single policeman had been killed by the IRA.[42]

Producing fake copies of the *Irish Bulletin* was a ridiculous plan and one which it must have been obvious was doomed to failure from the start. One article calling on Republicans to invent stories about British brutality, which was presumably written to create the impression that Sinn Fein claims could not be trusted as a source of information, stretched the boundaries of plausibility to breaking point:

Where true statements can be secured this should be done, but if because of enemy aggression it is impossible for members of the Dail to visit their constituents suitable statements can be prepared from any other sources at their disposal. The well-authenticated and unvarying brutality of enemy forces is now so well established that it is only necessary that events described by members should be attached to a place and to an individual.

It did not take long for people to realise what was happening. 'One may well ask would any Sinn Fein propagandist, however insane, issue such nonsense to an English and foreign public whose sympathy for his national movement he seeks to invoke,' the *Manchester Guardian* suggested, adding that the fake editions were 'too clumsy to deceive anyone'. It finished its article by demanding to know who had commissioned them and how much public money it had cost.[43] The episode further descended into farce when the real *Irish Bulletin* reappeared and denounced the forgery, to which the British version responded by claiming it was the real one that was in fact the forgery.[44]

We do not know if Clarke took part in or was aware of these attempts at black propaganda, but it seems unlikely given that their effect was to undermine the credibility of Dublin Castle that his 'propaganda by news' so depended on. As the MP Walter Elliot said in the House of Commons in response to the photographs of the 'Battle of Tralee':

One faked photograph might do more harm than 50 genuine photographs could do good.[45]

Added to the apparent inaccuracies in the work of Clarke's own department, the RIC's risible efforts at propaganda meant journalists had good reason to question the veracity of British statements. The *Manchester Guardian* reported in October 1920 that Dublin Castle was 'not precisely a crystal well of truth',[46] and there is no evidence to suggest this perception changed during Clarke's time there.

★★★

As well as being sceptical about the truthfulness of Clarke's statements, journalists began to question the very idea of having a publicity department at Dublin Castle. When Greenwood was forced to defend Clarke's work in the House of Commons in March 1921 – he memorably described him as an 'official truth-disseminator' – Clarke became perhaps the first person in British public relations history to break what has become one of the industry's golden rules: to never become the story.

The *Manchester Guardian* responded to the statement by arguing that 'Sir Hamar Greenwood's regime is under strong suspicion of overstepping the line' and that 'the public here is left in a state of uneasy suspicion that it is being fed with false news by two propaganda factories, a Sinn Fein one and a Government one',[47] while *The Times* believed Clarke's very presence at Dublin Castle undermined the credibility of the British. 'There is no reason why skilled journalists should be employed for the purpose of communicating news to the Press,' it stated. 'Plain statements of fact would suffice, and ordinary officials are surely competent to make them … The confidence of independent organs in the Government's news [will not] be restored by the knowledge that such news reaches them only after passing through a professionally staffed propaganda department. The country … will strongly resent the idea that it is being told only what the Irish Government may consider good for it.'[48]

The *Westminster Gazette*, meanwhile, was not against the principle of employing a public relations officer at Dublin Castle but questioned the effect of this in practice. 'In view of the world-wide interest in Ireland, there would be no intrinsic objection to the Government's employment of a trained journalist to assist those in search of information, were it not for the fact that the Government stands convicted of suppressing essential information on every possible occasion,' it suggested. 'In such circumstances official publicity is merely a waste of money. Much of the information disseminated is received with suspicion, and everyone knows that the facts which are really wanted are being withheld.'[49]

None of these newspapers mentioned Clarke by name, but the *Irish Bulletin* identified him as the 'official truth-disseminator' Greenwood had referred to. It reported:

> The 'trained journalist' to whom Sir Hamar Greenwood referred in his statement in the House of Commons is Mr Basil Clarke, late of the Daily Mail. His place of training explains the embellishments which are so much more frequent than accuracy in the official reports.[50]

This was the start of a series of *Irish Bulletin* articles that tried to undermine trust in the British by targeting Clarke personally. Over the next few months, it repeatedly accused him of wilfully including lies in British press statements. In May 1921, it blamed him for 'the issue of fantastic reports' that it claimed were 'being industrially maintained by the Dublin Castle Publicity Department'[51] and used a statement about how soldiers had driven off attackers from a barracks after two and a half hours of fighting as an example of his deceit. The truth, it claimed, was that there had been no attack and all that had happened was that a mentally ill man in a nearby house had thrown slates into the street and onto the adjoining building. The following month, another *Irish Bulletin* article headlined 'One of Mr Basil Clarke's "ambushes"' alleged that a Dublin Castle statement about an ambush in County Kerry was 'an invention from first to last'.[52]

★★★

When Clarke talked to the journalist Wilfrid Ewart in April 1921, he blamed the failure to reach a negotiated peace on 'an extremist wing of Sinn Fein' that had undermined any peace initiatives by committing 'some particularly violent outrage'.[53] But privately, he was critical of the Government's unwillingness to compromise, as well as jaded by the futility of the seemingly never-ending cycle of violence.

On the day that six IRA prisoners were executed, for example, Clarke wrote a letter home to Alice in which he wearily described the effect of the executions on the mood at Dublin Castle:

> Nobody likes them and it makes us all very grumpy; though nobody will admit the reason to anybody else. Breakfast this morning was like a funeral party – no one saying a word.

> I suppose there will be a reprisal by the Shins of some sort and six other poor devils who had nothing to do with it at all will be hooped off into eternity … Damn silly business all round. Some of our chaps are getting fed up and if the Govt don't settle they'll get out … [Things] might have been very different if the Govt had only accepted the advice they have received from here all along. Lots of effort has been spent by our crowd here to make them settle. They'll have the whole caboodle toppling about their ears if they don't look out.[54]

His sense of disillusion would have been made worse by the fact that around the same time his competence was once again called into question, and this time not by the Army but by a colleague in the civil administration.

On 6 March 1921, both the Mayor and the ex-Mayor of Limerick were murdered in their homes and suspicion immediately fell on the British. The details of the Dublin Castle response are sketchy, but what is clear is that Clarke was given information about the men – probably intelligence that they had previously tried to prevent IRA actions – that suggested the IRA may have been responsible.[55]

Clarke decided not to release this information and instead issued what the *New York Times* called a 'bare statement of the murders'.[56] It was a decision that has been vindicated by history, as it is very likely that the British were in fact responsible for the deaths,[57] but it went down so badly at Dublin Castle that Andy Cope, one of the senior civil servants there, wanted Clarke to stop issuing statements about incidents in Ireland and to limit his activities to answering journalists' questions and making statements about policy issues.

This would have ruined any lingering hope Clarke may still have had of 'propaganda by news' being successful and he was forced to write a memo defending both his decision not to release the information and also his wider approach to propaganda.

Clarke's explanation for not having made a fuller statement on the killings of the Mayors of Limerick offered a startling insight into the dysfunction within the British propaganda machine. He had come to believe he could no longer trust the information he was given to release to the press.

'I have in mind some half dozen or more cases in which in good faith I have accepted … statements and at the wish of responsible officials have worked them into statements to the Press with a view to clearing the Government and its agents of definite charges,' he wrote. 'The results were so unfortunate as to lead me to determine never again on my own authority to accept and issue ex-parte statements relating to matters which were sub-judice or which in their nature must sooner or later be explored judicially. My feeling is that such advance statements, even if true, have, through past mishaps and through no other reason, lost much of their propaganda value, and if untrue, are … deadly destructive of Government credit.'[58]

He defended his statement about the Mayors of Limerick as having been 'a sound measure of propaganda' because his only other options had been to issue information he did not trust; to simply confirm the murders had happened; or to refuse to comment altogether.

Having dealt with the specifics of his response to the murders, Clarke went on to robustly defend his general approach, arguing that it allowed the British to 'maintain the propaganda initiative and attack' and that merely confirming news would mean 'we lose this initiative and take up a position of defence'.[59]

He went on to write that his previous statements had been successful in making newspaper reports less damaging to the British than would have otherwise been the case, and he pointed to the number of journalists who attended his Press Bureau and the failure of the boycott of it as evidence of the success of his approach.

But as persuasive as this argument may have been, Clarke could not escape the fact that it was included in the same memo as an acknowledgement that his department had issued a number of statements that had later been shown to be untrue. Given the extent to which 'propaganda by news' depended on Dublin Castle's credibility, this perhaps gives a better measure of his success than his boasts about how much journalists valued his work.

Notes

1 National Archives, Kew, MH 107/23, Memo from Sir Arthur Robinson, 4 December 1920.

2 *The Last Days of Dublin Castle: The Mark Sturgis Diaries*, edited and introduced by Michael Hopkinson, Irish Academic Press, Dublin, 1999, p.158.

3 *Freeman's Journal*, 12 Mar 1921, p.5.

4 *The Last Days of Dublin Castle: The Mark Sturgis Diaries*, edited and introduced by Michael Hopkinson, Irish Academic Press, Dublin, 1999, p.123.

5 National Archives, Kew, CO 904/168/3/877, Clarke to Anderson, 18 April 1921.

6 National Archives, Kew, CO 904 168 521, Clarke to Loughnane, 22 September 1920.

7 National Archives, Kew, CO 904 168 1178, Marians to Clarke.

8 Nevil Macready, *Annals of an Active Life*, London, 1924, p.465.

9 National Archives, Kew, CO 904/188/692. Macready to Anderson, March 1921.

10 National Archives, Kew, CO 904/188/733. Macready to Anderson, 28 March 1921.

11 *The Last Days of Dublin Castle: The Mark Sturgis Diaries*, edited and introduced by Michael Hopkinson, Irish Academic Press, Dublin, 1999, p.151.

12 Parliamentary Archives, Houses of Parliament, LG/F/36/2/17.

13 National Archives, Kew, CO 904/188/740. Anderson to Macready, 29 March 1921.

14 National Archives, Kew, CO 904/168/3/877, Clarke to Anderson, 18 April 1921.

15 *The Times*, 27 September 1920, p.10.

16 Nevil Macready, *Annals of an Active Life*, London, 1924, p.471.

17 Ibid., pp.454–5.

18 National Archives, Kew, CO 904/168/3/844, Clarke to Anderson, 23 June 1921.

19 National Archives, Kew, CO 904/168/3/877, Clarke to Anderson, 18 April 1921.

20 National Archives, Kew, CO 904/168/3/869–70, Memo from Clarke: Points about Press Propaganda.

21 National Archives, Kew, CO 904/168/3/917, Basil Clarke, Press Propaganda memo, 4 April 1921.

22 National Archives, Kew, CO 904/163/2/1167, Marians to Clarke, 29 October 1920.

23 National Archives, Kew, CO 904/168/3/840–3, Clarke to Cope, 10 March 1921.

24 National Archives, Kew, CO 904/168/3/919, Clarke's memo on Press Propaganda.

25 National Archives, Kew, CO 904/168/3/918, Basil Clarke, Press Propaganda memo, 4 April 1921.

26 National Archives, Kew, CO 904/168/3/921–2, Clarke's memo on Press Propaganda.

27 National Archives, Kew, CO 904/168/3/869, Memo from Clarke: Points about Press Propaganda.

28 National Archives, Kew, CO 904/168/3/904, Memo from Clarke, 4 April 1921.

29 National Archives, Kew, CO 904/168/3/905, Memo from Clarke, 4 April 1921.

30 National Archives, Kew, CO 904/168/3/918, Basil Clarke, Press Propaganda memo, 4 April 1921.

31 National Archives, Kew, CO 904/168/3/917, Basil Clarke, Press Propaganda memo, 4 April 1921.

32 *The Historical Journal*, Volume 49, Issue 01, March 2006, pp. 277–80.

33 Brigadier-General F.P. Crozier, CB, CMG, DSO, *Ireland For Ever*, Bath, 1971.

34 Hansard, H.C. Deb, 24 November 1920, vol 135, p.487–601.

35 Freemans Journal, 30 April 1921, p.5.

36 *Morning Post*, 21 March 1921, p.4.

37 Ian Kenneally, *The Paper Wall – Newspapers and Propaganda in Ireland 1919–1921*, Cork, 2008, p.32.
38 Ibid., p.34.
39 Ibid., p.33.
40 *Manchester Guardian*, 21 March 1921, p.12.
41 D.G. Boyce, *Englishmen and Irish Troubles; British Public Opinion and the Making of Irish Policy 1918–1922*, London, 1972, pp.87–8.
42 *Irish Bulletin*, 30 March 1921, p.1.
43 *Manchester Guardian*, 5 April 1921, p.9.
44 D.G. Boyce, *Englishmen and Irish Troubles; British Public Opinion and the Making of Irish Policy 1918–1922*, London, 1972, pp.87–8.
45 *Manchester Guardian*, 21 March 1921, p.12.
46 *Manchester Guardian*, 23 October 1920, p.8.
47 *Manchester Guardian*, 21 March 1921, p.6.
48 *The Times*, 21 March 1921, p.13.
49 *Westminster Gazette*, 21 March 1921, p.7.
50 *Irish Bulletin*, 1 April 1921, p.3.
51 *Irish Bulletin*, 17 May 1921, p.1.
52 *Irish Bulletin*, 16 June 1921, p.1.
53 Wilfrid Ewart, *A Journey in Ireland*, Milton Keynes, 2009, p.12.
54 Clarke to Alice, Dublin. The letter is undated, but was probably written on 14 March 1921, due to the reference to six executions. This was the date six IRA prisoners were hanged at Mountjoy Prison.
55 Nevil Macready, *Annals of an Active Life*, London, 1924, p.546. It is not certain that this information is the same information that Clarke was given following the murders, but it seems very likely.
56 *New York Times*, 8 March 1921, p.1.
57 D.M. Leeson, *The Black and Tans: British Police and Auxiliaries in the Irish War of Independence*, Oxford, 2011, P.189.
58 National Archives, Kew, CO 904/168/3/840-3, Clarke to Cope, 10 March 1921.
59 National Archives, Kew, CO 904/168/3/840-3, Clarke to Cope, 10 March 1921.

17

Truce to Treaty

As much as both the British and Sinn Fein may have talked in public only in terms of total victory, there had been secret negotiations between the two sides since the end of 1920, and by the middle of 1921 there was a real willingness to reach a compromise. As well as the financial cost and the rising number of casualties, the effect on public opinion had serious implications for the British Government given that its popularity was waning. On the Irish side, there was a growing realisation that they could not continue their armed struggle indefinitely.

So after George V made a conciliatory speech in Belfast on 22 June – his call for 'all Irishmen to pause, to stretch out the hand of forbearance and concilia-tion' was welcomed by both sides – the British offered to negotiate with Sinn Fein. The offer was accepted and these talks quickly led to an agreement for a truce that would allow more substantial negotiations on the terms of a treaty between the two sides. The truce was signed on 9 July and came into effect two days later.

For Clarke, the truce meant that what he described as the 'heavier Press work' was now done and so he volunteered to tour the country to act as a liai-son between Sinn Fein and the British in areas where peace was threatened by, as he put it, 'folly or misunderstanding on one side or the other'.[1] The details of his liaison activities are unknown, though Clarke's son Alan later wrote that it was dangerous work that involved meeting trigger-happy men who did not necessarily want the war to be over.[2]

As well as meaning the end of British rule in most of Ireland was now in sight, it came at the right time for Clarke professionally. This was because the British had finally decided to adopt a more co-ordinated propaganda approach, but it was the Army and not Clarke that was chosen to lead it. Charles Foulkes, an expert on gas warfare who had played hockey for Britain at the 1908 Olympics and had been transferred to Dublin in May 1921 to focus on army propaganda, was selected to become the overall Director of Propaganda.

Foulkes believed Clarke's approach was too narrowly focused on newspapers, though he was sufficiently impressed by him to have planned to keep him on. 'I have a much bigger conception of this task [propaganda] than the present man at the Castle (whom I hope to retain in charge of his own little branch, namely the Press),' Foulkes wrote in a memo.[3]

Rather than concentrating on issuing news, Foulkes wanted to focus on arranging for the 'right sort of people' to visit Ireland in the hope that they would then make speeches praising the British administration there. These speeches might then be reported in newspapers.

As much as he thought about working directly with newspapers at all, Foulkes fell into the trap of trying to engage with newspapers that already supported the British, as he tried to arrange meetings with the editors of the *Morning Post* and the *Pall Mall Gazette* to get their advice on why British propaganda was not more successful.

Foulkes's appointment meant that if the War of Independence had not ended, then Clarke would have had to both take orders from the Army and accept working under a completely different propaganda system.

★★★

As well as his work liaising between Sinn Fein and the British, Clarke spent the second half of 1921 dealing with the repercussions of a Dublin Castle press statement about a Sinn Fein document that had been seized during a raid in May 1921.

The document, which was dated 28 March, contained the admission that some Sinn Fein units were demoralised and Dublin Castle used it as evidence that support for Sinn Fein was declining. Before the document was issued to the press, someone had added '1921' to the end of the date. But the document had actually been written in 1920.

It is unclear whether this was a genuine error but, given previous British propaganda efforts, it is unsurprising that some people saw the addition of the wrong year as another example of deceit. The *Irish Bulletin* accused Clarke of personally altering the date to try to gain extra propaganda value. It pointed out that the document referred to the recent capture of an IRA member who had by then been in prison for over a year, adding that Clarke 'does not seem to have altered the letter more than was necessary to make it ridiculous'.[4]

But Clarke had an alibi. He had been in England when the document was captured and issued to the press and so, on this occasion at least, there is good evidence that the *Irish Bulletin* was wrong to blame him personally. There was not, though, much he could do about it. As libellous as the article was, he could hardly take legal action against an illegal newspaper.

But then Eleanor Acland, the wife of the former Under-Secretary of State for Foreign Affairs, Francis Dyke Acland, repeated the allegations in a letter to the *Westminster Gazette*.

'Mr Basil Clarke should have taken pains to make sure there was no internal evidence in the letter to expose his little ruse,' she wrote. 'Who and what are these inept beings, such as this Mr Basil Clarke, whom the commotion of war has tossed up from their recent obscurity into the unbecoming glare of salaried Government posts?'[5]

Mrs Acland was essentially accusing Clarke of forgery and Clarke responded with a writ for defamation against her and the *Westminster Gazette*. Francis Dyke Acland was also named in the writ, as husbands could be held accountable under civil law for the actions of their wives, a legal anomaly that would not be changed until 1935.

When Mrs Acland learned Clarke had been in England when the document was altered, she wrote to his solicitors and offered to publish an apology in whatever way he chose. The *Westminster Gazette* also wrote to Clarke to apologise for publishing Mrs Acland's letter. Whether it was because he was angry at being accused of dishonesty or because he still harboured ill-will towards the *Westminster Gazette* for its coverage of the blockade five years earlier, the apology did not bring an end to it and the case went before the High Court on 7 December 1921.[6]

The defence admitted to the court that, far from the 'inept being' described in Mrs Acland's letter, Clarke had 'had an exceptionally brilliant career as a man and a journalist, and had given every satisfaction to the responsible Government in Ireland'. The judge accepted that Mrs Acland had 'made all the amends possible and withdrawn what she had said' but still awarded Clarke a substantial amount of money that left him with 400 Guineas, or about six months' salary, even after he had covered his costs.

'The sum, in the circumstances, I had no scruple in taking,' Clarke wrote to a friend.[7]

★★★

The day before Clarke's libel case was heard in the High Court, negotiations between the British and Sinn Fein had finally reached a conclusion.

Michael Collins and Sinn Fein founder Arthur Griffith signed a treaty in the early hours of 6 December 1921, but only after Lloyd George reportedly threatened the renewal of a 'terrible and immediate' war if they refused.

The Treaty included the agreement for an Irish Free State that would be self-governed but still retain the British Monarch as its head of state, and it also gave the mainly pro-British Northern Ireland the chance to opt out. The Treaty was passed overwhelmingly by both Houses of the British Parliament, though the concessions it made angered the right wing of the Conservative Party and this was one of the reasons Lloyd George's Coalition Government fell apart ten months later.

But the opposition to the Treaty among British MPs was nothing compared to the division it created on the Irish side. Collins's comment on signing it that he had just signed his own death warrant would prove prophetic, as he was killed nine months later during the Irish Civil War that was caused by disagreements within Sinn Fein about the terms of the Treaty.

Given the opposition to it from prominent figures among the Republicans, including from the Dáil Éireann's President Éamon de Valera, it was far from certain the Treaty would be ratified by the Dáil Éireann. Clarke reported back to London that while the result was likely to be close, he thought the Treaty would be passed. 'The whole business gives me a pain but I think it will come out right,' he wrote.[8]

The date for the Dáil Éireann vote was set for 7 January, which meant Clarke's career had once again conspired to keep him from his family at Christmas. 'This letter is to wish you a Merry X'mas and to hope Santa Claus will bring you something nice,' he wrote to his son, Ian, who was by now almost 5 years old.

Being in Ireland in the run up to the vote did, at least, give him a small role in a footnote in newspaper history after Richard Eccleston of the Press Association (PA) asked for his help.

With hundreds of journalists arriving in Dublin, it was clear there would be fierce competition to get the result of the vote out first. PA's private wire did not extend to Ireland, and because long-distance telephone lines were not yet easily accessible – it had only been seven years since the first transcontinental telephone call between New York and San Francisco – it was not possible to simply phone the result through to London.

Unable to compete with the budgets other organisations had to spend on trying to get the news out first, Eccleston asked Clarke for permission to use the Government's private line between Dublin Castle and the Irish Office in London to relay the result of the vote across the Irish Sea. Eccleston's plan was for a PA journalist inside the Dáil Éireann chamber to run to a nearby public telephone as soon as he heard the result. Eccleston would already be on the telephone to another colleague at Dublin Castle and would give him the news. It would then be relayed via the castle's private line to another PA employee at the Irish Office in London, who would in turn telephone the result to PA's London office.

Whether it was because he had previously worked for PA as a war correspondent or because the plan would ensure the British got the news quickly, Clarke persuaded his colleagues to agree to the plan. So on the day, Eccleston watched the debate and then when they were getting ready to vote he left his colleague in the debating chamber and made his way to a nearby telephone and called his other colleague at Dublin Castle.

The two men did not want the telephone operator to know what they were doing and so they chatted about sports news and gossip while they waited for the result. Eventually, Eccleston was interrupted by the operator.

'Haven't you finished on this line?' she said.

'Just give me time to talk about my troubles,' Eccleston pleaded with her.

'You men are worse than any women; you just can't stop talking,' the operator told him, but she let him stay on the line.

Eccleston used up more time by talking about anything he could think of until eventually, his colleague from inside the chamber came running down a flight of stairs with the news of the result. The Dáil had ratified the Treaty, he shouted.

Just as Eccleston heard the news, the operator came back on the line.

'You'll have to finish with this line,' she said.

The entire plan depended on Eccleston being able to convince her to let him continue talking. He pleaded with her to let him have one more second and she reluctantly agreed, little realising that a second was all he needed.

'Treaty accepted,' he said, and then hung up.

The news was quickly passed from Dublin Castle to the Irish Office in London and then on to PA's London office. Within 3 minutes of the result, PA was flashing the news all over the world. The Irish War of Independence was over and, thanks to Clarke, PA had beaten the rest of the world's media to the story.[9]

★★★

The Irish Free State created by the Treaty did not come into being for almost another year, but there was now little left for Clarke to do but prepare to return to the Ministry of Health.

'I think I shall soon be coming to live at home again,' he wrote to his son Ian a few days after the vote. 'We will have some larks if I do and fires in the garden.'[10]

As well as looking forward to spending more time with his family, Clarke must have been relieved from a professional point of view that his time in Ireland was coming to an end as it had been fraught with difficulty and he had little to show for his efforts. He might have been able to point to isolated propaganda successes and could even have made the case that public opinion towards the Government's Irish policy might have been even more hostile if he had not been there. But taken as whole, it is difficult to see his time in Ireland as anything other than a failure.

It did not matter that 'propaganda by news' showed a real understanding of how newspapers worked, or that he provided a template that would be followed by thousands of public relations practitioners in the decades to come. Ultimately, his inability to persuade colleagues to support his approach or to stop the flow of inaccurate information meant success was almost impossible. Clarke is far from alone in this; the history of public relations is littered with examples of people who identified the right approach but were then unable to win support for it within their organisation.

But even if Clarke had succeeded in convincing Macready and the RIC of the merits of 'propaganda by news', there would still have been the issue of the Reprisals. He correctly identified that the British would never win public sympathy while its soldiers and police officers were indiscriminately burning buildings and terrorising innocent people. Clarke's son Alan later wrote that the experience taught Clarke 'how weighted are the scales against an advocate whose case would not completely stand up to the test of public opinion'.[11]

Even Lloyd George, despite some evidence that he condoned the Reprisals,[12] understood the effect they were having and wrote to Greenwood in February 1921 to complain that 'indiscipline, looting and drunkenness in the RIC is alienating great numbers of well-disposed people in Ireland and throwing them into the arms of Sinn Fein'.[13]

Despite this, the British lacked either the collective will or the ability to stop them. This was always likely to be fatal to any propaganda efforts. As Clarke himself put it in one of the memos he wrote justifying his approach:

If, after every care in the accumulation of plus results and the lessening of minus results, the balance of result on public opinion is not plus, the fault is not that of the propaganda but of the subject of the propaganda. It is a bad case, and no propaganda will win a public sanction for it.[14]

For many years after the Irish War of Independence, Clarke's role was largely forgotten. As much as he was mentioned at all, it was in passing, along with the other civil servants at Dublin Castle.

Then in the early 1990s, this began to change. The Irish journalist Kevin Myers wrote that Terence MacSwiney, whose death by hunger strike in 1920 had helped win sympathy for Sinn Fein's cause, had been part of a group that had planned to kidnap and possibly murder the Bishop of Cork. The allegation angered MacSwiney's family and they complained to Myers that it was untrue.

Myers agreed to write another article to make this clear and in this article, published in the *Irish Times* in January 1992, he blamed Clarke for the deceit:

> Terence s's family understandably are upset that this allegation should have been printed. The least I can do is to accept willingly and fully that it was a lie, and express utter regret that I did not recognise it for what it was.

> It is one of the perils of journalism that the skilled liar is always at an advantage; and perhaps in the regions where Basil Clark [sic] currently resides he permits himself a small smile that his lies live after him; a lamentable achievement.[15]

It was a crass piece of journalism, but it seems to have resurrected the idea first established by the *Irish Bulletin* that Clarke was a sinister hidden hand behind the British propaganda campaign.

This was followed in 2006 by a pamphlet by Brian P. Murphy called *The Origins and Organisation of British Propaganda in Ireland 1920*, which accused Clarke of bringing with him to Dublin Castle a 'knowledge of all the propaganda skills that had been developed during the War: censorship of the press; the fabrication of special articles; the use of photographs, sometimes faked; and above all the feeding to the press of "official" news'.[16]

Murphy highlighted Clarke's use of the word 'verisimilitude' in a memo in which he explained how journalists 'take our version of the facts – which I take care are as favourable to us as may be, in accordance with truth and verisimilitude – and they believe all I tell them'. Clarke also used the word in a memo about how it was important for any press statement about an incident to 'detract to the fullest extent from its unfavourable factors (compatible with verisimilitude)'.[17]

Murphy saw Clarke's use of the word as evidence of deceitfulness because he defined 'verisimilitude' as meaning 'a statement having the air of being true, while not, in fact, being so'.

In Murphy's defence, Clarke had used the word to imply deceit in a 1914 article he wrote for the *Daily Mail* in which he suggested the motive behind German shelling of Dunkirk was more about creating a false impression than in gaining military advantage.[18] But while some dictionaries do state that 'verisimilitude' implies deceit, most simply define it as 'having the appearance of truth'.

The context in which Clarke used the word in one of the Dublin Castle memos – 'in accordance with truth and verisimilitude' – strongly suggests his understanding of the word's meaning was different to Murphy's.

Murphy's pamphlet also accused Clarke of being 'engaged in the more secret process of black propaganda' and being responsible for the work of Hugh Pollard, the RIC propagandist who was involved in the fake photographs of the 'Battle of Tralee' and the forged editions of the *Irish Bulletin*. But Murphy does not give any evidence for this, and the nearest he comes to making a convincing case against Clarke is when he suggests Clarke's statement about the killings of the British officers on Bloody Sunday downplayed the intelligence roles of the officers to try to maximise public sympathy.

It is certainly true that Clarke's department issued statements that were factually inaccurate. For example, Murphy makes a strong case that the Republican Thomas Hales was tortured by the British despite Clarke's statement to the contrary,[19] but there is no real evidence to suggest that this, or indeed any other incorrect statement issued by Clarke, was done knowingly. Given how 'propaganda by news' relied on building the trust of newspapers and how Clarke complained to colleagues about being given inaccurate information, it seems unlikely.

The historian Ian Kenneally offers a more credible assessment of Clarke's role in Ireland:

> While he [Clarke] was not an outright deceiver, his job was to portray the Crown forces in as positive light as possible.[20]

Clarke may not have been guilty of the kind of black propaganda practised by Pollard and Darling, but his reputation has been damaged over the past twenty years because of his association with Ireland. In some cases, he has almost been portrayed as representing all that was bad about the British policy there.

Clarke was long dead by the time Myers and Murphy made their allegations and so was unable to defend himself, but a letter he wrote to *The People* newspaper in Wexford in January 1934, some twelve years after leaving Ireland, gives a good idea of what his reaction would have been. Responding to an article that criticised the propaganda issued by his Dublin Castle Press Bureau, he wrote:

> It is a fact that I never gave, or authorised the giving, to the Press of any information that was not substantiated by official reports … That early reports, wired in code to the Castle, and handed on by me to the Press, sometimes proved inaccurate, cannot be laid at the door of my department.

My mind is so clear of guilt on the matter that I was surprised and rather sad to see myself handed on by you to present-day Ireland as something of a scheming villain, one who had set a precedent to be avoided in official administration.[21]

Notes

1   *The People,* Wexford, 27 Jan 1934, p.11.
2   Alan Clarke, *The Life & Times of Sir Basil Clarke – PR Pioneer, Public Relations,* 1969, Vol. 22 (2) pp.8–13.
3   Kings College London's Archives and Special Collections, London, Foulkes, 7/15, Foulkes to Sprot, 12 July 1921.
4   *Irish Bulletin,* 20 May 1921, p.1.
5   *Westminster Gazette,* 8 December 1921 (quoting the original article).
6   *Manchester Guardian,* 8 December 1921, p.11.
7   Parliamentary Archives, Houses of Parliament, S/31/3/56, Clarke to Strachey, 20 December 1920.
8   Parliamentary Archives, Houses of Parliament, LG/F/20/1/10, Clarke to Street, 16 December 1920.
9   George Scott, *Reporter Anonymous – The Story of the Press Association,* London, 1968, pp.162–4.
10 Clarke to Ian, 11 Jan 1922. The property of the Hartley family, its contents are being published here for the first time.
11 Alan Clarke, *The Life & Times of Sir Basil Clarke – PR Pioneer, Public Relations,* 1969, Vol. 22 (2) pp.8–13.
12 Ian Kenneally, *The Paper Wall – Newspapers and Propaganda in Ireland 1919–1921,* Cork, 2008, p.20.
13 Parliamentary Archives, Houses of Parliament, LG/F/19/3/4, Lloyd George to Greenwood, 25 February 1921.
14 National Archives, Kew, CO 904/168/3/840-3, Clarke to Cope, 10 March 1921.
15 *The Irish Times,* 29 January 1992, p.13.
16 Brian P. Murphy, *The Origins & Organisation of British Propaganda in Ireland 1920,* Aubane History Society and Spinwatch, 2006, p.28.
17 National Archives, Kew, CO 904/168/3/843, Clarke to Cope, 10 March 1921
18 *Daily Mail,* 11 December 1914, p.5.
19 Brian P. Murphy, *The Origins & Organisation of British Propaganda in Ireland 1920,* Aubane History Society and Spinwatch, 2006, pp.33–6.
20 Ian Kenneally, *Courage and Conflict: Forgotten Stories of the Irish at War,* Cork, 2009, p.323
21 *The People,* Wexford, 27 January 1934, p.7. This also included a response from the journalist who had written the original article, who stated that it had not been meant as a personal criticism of Clarke, who had always been courteous, but a criticism of the system.

18

Back at the
Ministry of Health

A t the beginning of April 1922, Clarke returned to a Ministry of Health[1] that was very different to the one he had left in the summer of 1920.

The Conservatives in the Coalition Government had become exasperated by Christopher Addison's lack of budgetary restraint and this had led to him being replaced as Minister of Health by Alfred Mond, a Liberal who is best remembered today for being mentioned in a T.S. Eliot poem.

It was not just the political leadership that had changed. Just a month after Clarke left for Dublin, in September 1920, a new structure was proposed for the ministry's publicity branch that meant the head of the Press Bureau would report to a director who would also oversee advertising and administrative functions. It meant Clarke's position was effectively being downgraded and, as well as being dissatisfied with the diminution in his professional standing, he was unhappy with the choice of a Captain Townroe as the new director.

Shortly after Bloody Sunday, Clarke met with Sir Arthur Robinson, a civil servant at the Ministry of Health, to discuss his future prospects. Robinson assured him it was not yet clear whether Townroe's position would be a long-term solution.

'I added that Captain Townroe is unestablished and it will probably be impossible to establish him,' Robinson wrote somewhat cryptically to colleagues after his meeting with Clarke. 'The contingency of Mr Clarke having to return and serve under Captain Townroe was however one that had to be faced. This contingency was the worst which Mr Clarke had to contemplate. Mr Clarke did not pretend to appreciate the position but seemed prepared to accept it if it arises.'[2]

He may have been prepared to tolerate it, but Clarke saw Townroe's promotion over him as an injustice and he confirmed this view to Robinson in a letter he sent following their meeting:

> I could not pretend to welcome the prospect of working under a colleague who was not only junior to me in rank, years and salary, but who was also considerably lower in professional status and attainment and of less experience – using this term to cover not only journalistic, literary and Press experience, but also experience of Governmental methods and practice.[3]

Clarke may have been justified in believing Townroe's promotion over him was unfair. Certainly, a Treasury memo from April 1920 supported his view that he was better qualified:

> Mr Basil Clarke is, I gather … regarded by the Ministry as having a bigger job than Capt T, and also as being a bigger man.[4]

But whatever Clarke's view of Townroe's abilities, Townroe himself seems to have been well-disposed towards Clarke. When *The Times* published an article in 1944 that was less than flattering about how press enquiries had been handled during the early days of the Ministry of Health, Townroe wrote a letter that came to the defence of his former colleague:

> [I] was impressed with the way Sir Basil Clarke … and the late Mr W Haslam Mills [who filled the position while Clarke was at the Sheffield Independent] scrupulously limited their activities to circulating honest and objective news and to explaining official documents.[5]

As Clarke settled back into life at the ministry, he discovered the changes in structure had not led to any greater clarity about what sort of publicity work it should be doing.

A memo from September 1920 by the civil servant Sir Aubrey Simmons argued that the department should not just be sending reports to journalists but producing articles that newspapers could then publish. But success, Simmons believed, depended on convincing the press that the aim of any publicity work was to benefit the public rather than promote the department. 'Any notion that the Department is trying to use the Press simply to play its own game or to cover its own faults would be disastrous,' he warned.[6]

Whatever plans there may have been, a memo from November 1922 admitted that 'at present we do nothing but inform the Press spasmodically when anything awakening their interest brings them to Mr Clarke'.[7]

Just as Clarke had struggled to persuade colleagues at Dublin Castle to believe in 'propaganda by news', six months after returning to the Ministry of Health he was still having to make the case for how he thought the ministry's propaganda could be improved.

'Much money and effort alike are being wasted in bad propaganda methods,' he wrote in a memo. 'Ill-conceived, ill-considered and I think in some cases even destructive appeals are being made to the public under the name of public health.'[8] He used a recent report into the causes of blindness as an example of a missed propaganda opportunity, arguing that in its current state it was 'virtually useless as a propaganda instrument' but that it could be easily converted into a popular leaflet or booklet on how people should look after their eyes.[9]

He wanted the ministry to improve its propaganda by establishing a group of experts from a range of disciplines such as psychology and advertising to look at how health publicity was conducted in the UK and abroad. This group could develop guidelines for the most effective approach and then a smaller group of experts could be maintained to give advice on an on-going basis.[10] But there is no evidence that the ministry made any plans to put this structure in place.

★★★

Clarke's return to the Ministry of Health seems to have been as frustrating as his two previous stints there but, outside his work at the ministry, there were other things to occupy his mind.

Just before the truce in Ireland, in May 1921, the prospect of Clarke being recognised in the Honour's List had first been mentioned. Andy Cope, the civil servant who had wanted him to stop issuing news after the murders of the Mayors of Limerick, asked him if he would be interested in a knighthood as a reward for his work in Ireland.

Clarke was initially ambivalent and asked Mark Sturgis for his advice; Sturgis recorded in his diary that he advised Clarke to 'take whatever was going'.[11] Yet even when Sir John Anderson later confirmed to him he was being recommended for a knighthood, Clarke was still unsure.

'Thank you, but I don't know what I've done to deserve it,' he told Anderson.

'Why my dear Basil,' Anderson replied, 'haven't you played the piano most delightfully for us every night during our long siege?'[12]

On 1 January 1923, it was announced that Clarke was to be awarded a knighthood for his work in Ireland;[13] he was one of a number of people, including Macready and Anderson, to be included in the New Year's Honours List and he was knighted on 15 February.[14] But while the knighthood represented an impressive achievement for the grandson of a shepherd, the experience may have been tainted by the fact that it coincided with Clarke once again being forced to defend himself against a personal attack.

This time, it came from the *Morning Post*. In November 1922, its Dublin correspondent wrote a critical article about the administration at Dublin Castle and its most savage criticism was directed at Clarke. Describing him as an 'obtuse and egregiously self-satisfied ex-Civil Servant', it alleged that he had only worked for 2 or 3 hours a day and had given 5 per cent of the information at his disposal to 'his cronies' and suppressed the rest.[15]

The article did not mention Clarke by name but it would have been obvious to anyone with knowledge of Dublin Castle that he was the civil servant in question. And in a second article, the same journalist responded to the announcement of the New Year's Honours List by claiming that 'Basil Clark [sic] spent most of his time making a fuss because various enterprising journalists got good news stories from the military, the police, and other good sources of information in the Castle, which he considered should have been permitted to filter exclusively through his own office'.[16]

It is not certain who was behind these articles, but the British Army seems the most likely culprit because of its connections with the *Morning Post* and because Clarke had previously complained that the Army had bypassed him by sending material there. Whatever the motivation, the two articles were clearly libellous and Clarke, perhaps emboldened by his success against Mrs Acland and the *Westminster Gazette*, instructed his lawyers.[17] This time it did not go to court, with the *Morning Post* agreeing to compensate him for his costs and publishing an apology for the allegations, expressing its 'sincere regret that they should have been published in this journal'.[18]

As preoccupied as he may have been by his knighthood and his legal action, at around the same time Clarke was also personally affected by the fact that, faced with recession and deflation after a number of years of spiralling public expenditure, the Government was under severe pressure to cut costs. In 1921, Lloyd George had tasked a committee of businessmen led by Sir Eric Geddes to find large savings within government, and this drive to save money continued after Lloyd George was replaced as Prime Minister in November 1922 by Andrew Bonar Law. Overall, the 'Geddes Axe' saw the number of civil servants cut by 35 per cent[19] and Clarke was one of those who lost their job.

A memo from December 1922, a month after Lloyd George was replaced by Bonar Law, suggested the decision was taken because there was not enough propaganda work planned[20] and a civil servant at the Ministry of Health wrote to the Treasury that 'it is not necessary to continue the post at present filled by Sir Basil Clarke' and so 'this post should be abolished as from the end of the present financial year'.[21] But a memo from a civil servant to Sir Arthur

Griffith-Boscawen, who replaced Alfred Mond as Minister of Health when Bonar Law became Prime Minister, gave the impression that Clarke's redundancy was due to cost cutting.[22]

Clarke's departure from the Ministry of Health may not have been his choice, but he seems to have left on good terms because of a 'gratuity settlement' of over £300, or about £6,000 today; in a letter to a colleague he described it as 'too good to be true'.[23]

And with that, Clarke's civil service career ended. His ideas about how publicity could be used by the Ministry of Health died with it.

'Sir Basil Clarke suggests a Committee to consider the whole question, to develop into a small permanent staff attached to the Ministry,' an internal memo explained. 'In the current atmosphere, I do not think any Commission could prudently be convened – it all means more money.' A hand-written note is added to the memo confirming Griffith-Boscawen agreed with it.[24]

As well as being unfortunate to be working in government at a time when public spending was being reduced, Clarke and his ideas were victims of the growing feeling within Whitehall that public relations was an inappropriate use of public money, a view summed up in a memo from an unnamed civil servant to the Minister of Health:

> The Chancellor has set his face firmly against the policy of spending the taxpayers' money to tell the taxpayer how his money is being spent.[25]

Clarke's work at the Ministry of Health does, though, seem to have been appreciated by journalists. Some months after he left, the *Manchester Guardian* praised his work there in an article about government publicity departments:

> Most journalists who had to go to Government departments for information would speak gratefully of the assistance they received from Sir Basil Clarke when he was in charge there ... It is clear that this kind of service is of great value to newspapers and of great value to the public.[26]

Notes

1   National Archives, Kew, MH 107/23, letter from the Undersecretary at Dublin Castle to the Secretary of the Ministry of Health, 28 March 1922.
2   National Archives, Kew, MH 107/23, memo from Sir Arthur Robinson, 4 December 1920.

3 National Archives, Kew, MH 107/23, letter from Clarke to Sir Arthur Robinson, 8 December 1920.
4 National Archives, Kew, T162/23, handwritten addition to letter from Treasury, 22 April 1920.
5 *The Times*, 18 April 1944, p.5.
6 National Archives, Kew, MH55/27, memo from Sir Aubrey Simmons, 12 September 1920.
7 National Archives, Kew, MH55/27, note from Heseltine, 6 November 1922.
8 National Archives, Kew, MH 55/27, minute from Basil Clarke to Sir George Newman, not dated. Hand-written note was added on 6 November 1922.
9 National Archives, Kew, MH 55/27, minute from Basil Clarke to Sir George Newman, 7 November 1922.
10 National Archives, Kew, MH 55/27, minute from Basil Clarke to Sir George Newman, not dated. Hand-written note was added on 6 November 1922.
11 *The Last Days of Dublin Castle: The Mark Sturgis Diaries*, edited and introduced by Michael Hopkinson, Irish Academic Press, Dublin, 1999, pp.170–1.
12 Alan Clarke, *The Life & Times of Sir Basil Clarke – PR Pioneer, Public Relations*, 1969, Vol. 22 (2) pp.8–13.
13 *Manchester Guardian*, 1 January 1923, p.7.
14 *The Times*, 16 February 1923, p.13.
15 *Morning Post*, 8 Nov 1922, p.10.
16 *Morning Post*, 11 January 1923, p.8.
17 *Freeman's Journal*, February 1923, p.6.
18 *Irish Independent*, 24 April 1923, p.10, quoting article in the *Morning Post*.
19 Institute for Fiscal Studies, 'Public Spending in Hard Times', Christopher Hood, Carl Emmerson and Ruth Dixon, 2009.
20 National Archives, Kew, MH 55/27, minute dated 6 December 1922.
21 National Archives, Kew, 20120/1, A. Woodgate to Treasury, 18 January 1923.
22 National Archives, Kew, MH 55/27, memo from civil servant to Sir Arthur Griffith-Boscawen, 10 January 1923.
23 National Archives, Kew, 20120/1, Clarke to Leggett, 12 March 1923.
24 National Archives, Kew, MH 55/27, memo from civil servant to Sir Arthur Griffith-Boscawen, 10 January 1923. Hand-written note added on 16 January.
25 National Archives, Kew, T162/23, William Graham to John Wheatley, 10 September 1924.
26 *Manchester Guardian*, 30 July 1923, p.12.

19

Editorial Services Ltd

After almost five years in the Civil Service, Clarke was once again unemployed. But while being out of work at the age of forty-three may have been a daunting prospect, it was to be the impetus for another career move of real significance.

This did not, though, happen immediately. A month after leaving government he wrote an advertorial for the food and restaurant company J Lyons and Co that appeared in *The Times*. He spent a day at its Cadby Hall bakery in Hammersmith and in his article he explained how he had compiled a list of interesting facts that might give an idea of the bakery's vastness and then showed Alice the list to 'get a woman's view on the matter'. After interrogating Clarke about whether he had managed to make it through the almond-drying room without dipping his fingers in the tray, she decided that Cadby Hall's use of 5 tons of butter a day was the single fact that best illustrated the scale of the operation. 'That's the most tell-tale item of all,' she told him. 'It gives the imagination quite a bump.'[1]

He wrote another article for Lyons the following month about the Lyons Corner House in London's Piccadilly; this one appeared in the *Daily Mirror*.[2] And when Lyons was chosen to do the catering for the British Empire Exhibition at Wembley the following year, it commissioned Clarke to write a thirty-six-page pamphlet about how great a technical feat this was. Clarke explained how catering for what was perhaps the biggest exhibition ever held involved the logistical challenge of building fifty-four separate restaurants that had to cater for customers ranging from monarchs to 'a shopman from Oldham or a farm labourer from Old Meldrum'.[3]

This new line of work may have paid well, but for someone who had until recently been an important figure in the British administration at Dublin Castle and whose articles for the *Daily Mail* had been reprinted all over the world, writing this kind of advertising copy must have seemed like a backward career step. It was not limited to Lyons. Around the same time he wrote *The World's Greatest Adventure*, a pamphlet promoting a mural decoration of the Quest of Columbus by the maritime painter Frank Mason. He described the mural in epic terms that were embarrassingly over-the-top considering its subject was essentially just an alternative to wallpaper:

> The folly of fear, the justification of hope, the vindication of faith and the joy of achievement – all are reflected therein. And there is everything to be said in these times for a wall-covering that revives in us these basic truths.[4]

But just as he seemed to be treading water professionally, Clarke was about to create another landmark in public relations history to add to his claim of being Britain's first public relations professional. He decided to set up the UK's first public relations agency, establishing Editorial Services Ltd in 1924 partly with his own money and partly with investment from Reginald Sykes of the London Press Exchange and James Walker of the advertising agency Winter Thomas.[5] It was based near Embankment tube station in London in a building in Buckingham Street that had once been the home of the diarist Samuel Pepys.

The public relations agency was already an established business model in the United States. The world's first ever public relations firm, the Publicity Bureau, had opened its doors in Boston as early as 1900 and there were at least eight companies there by the time Clarke set up Editorial Services Ltd.[6] But in Britain, the idea was certainly new and as well as being generally thought to be the UK's first public relations agency,[7] Editorial Services Ltd was also the leading British firm throughout the 1920s.

★★★

Much of the detail of Editorial Services Ltd's work are sketchy, but early clients included the National Milk Publicity Council, for which it secured an average of 135 newspaper cuttings per month,[8] the National Union of Teachers and the greyhound racing industry.[9]

It also worked to promote motorcycling for the Manufacturers' Union[10] and the use of the telephone for the Telephone Development Association (TDA), which declared itself pleased with the 'combination of enthusiasm, originality, and persistence' that Editorial Services Ltd displayed. Its publicity work, the TDA's 1927 annual meeting heard, was part of the reason 'telephone development is undoubtedly a topic of the day, and both the Press and the public are now genuinely interested in the subject'.[11]

While Clarke would later attempt to intellectualise public relations, the evidence of how Editorial Services Ltd secured coverage for the telephone industry suggests the practice was often more prosaic than the theory. For example, Clarke wrote a letter to *The Times* setting out how Britain was close to Holland in terms of telephone density, but his letter failed to disclose that he was writing on behalf of the industry.[12]

The early days of Editorial Services Ltd did, though, include innovations still used today. Clarke possibly invented the concept of the press trip while working for the Ulster Tourists' Development Association. Now a key part of travel industry media relations, they rely on the understanding that journalists are generally willing to set aside critical thinking in exchange for a free holiday. It certainly seems to have worked with the *Irish Times*'s correspondent, who proclaimed the 'wonderful beauties of the "Diamond of Ireland"' and reported that the five-day trip had shown him 'how much more narrow is the gulf between our neighbours and ourselves than some politicians would have us believe'.[13]

According to his son Alan, Clarke also notched up another landmark in British public relations by becoming the first outside publicist to work for a political party by promoting the Conservative Party.[14] There is no suggestion this was done out of political conviction, later in life he would joke that 'no man can do six years hard labour on the M.G. [*Manchester Guardian*] and emerge as anything other than a good Liberal' and in 1927 he was interested enough in the Liberal Party to attend a meeting about what he was told were 'matters of the most vital importance to the future of Liberalism in London'.[15] But the meeting left him so angry that he wrote to the organisers to complain that it had 'proved to be nothing but a money-cadging affair'.[16]

Working for the private sector represented different challenges to those of the public sector, though many of the issues were the same. He still had difficulty in convincing clients to take his advice and he once complained that 'many otherwise capable business men go "right off the hooks" on questions of what the Press want … and on the question of public relations particularly they may be as innocent as children'. When it came to representing the National Playing Fields Association in 1927, for example, he recommended that the announcement of a £200,000 donation from the Carnegie United Kingdom Trust should be delayed until after the launch of a national appeal because this would enable the campaign to get back into the news once the initial momentum had been lost.[17] But the Carnegie United Trust worried this might detract from the importance of its donation and felt it was 'inconsistent with the responsibilities of the Trust to come in at the fag-end of the first fortnight'. Clarke was overruled and the trust's donation was announced at the start of the appeal.

As well as the frustration of having his advice ignored, Clarke was one of only a few people working in a new and poorly understood industry and this meant he often had to convince people of the concept of public relations as much as of his ability to deliver it effectively. While companies today generally see public relations as important for success, one of Clarke's challenges was demonstrating that it did more than duplicate the service offered by advertising agencies.

He believed the fundamental difference was that public relations focused more on long term reputation-building rather than short-term sales. 'While our Press work will sell nothing and does not aim to sell,' he wrote, 'it nevertheless creates an atmosphere of greater and more enlightened public interest in a commodity, or idea, or service, generically – in other word, creates an atmosphere in which sales are much more easily effected.'[18] Editorial coverage also had the advantage of being understood by the public to be more likely to be impartial than advertising, the essence of which he described as 'a man saying something more or less eulogistic about his product or services and paying to say it'.[19]

In a speech to the Royal Society of Arts in 1926, Clarke used George V's recent purchase of a British car as an example of the advantage public relations held over advertising:

> Can the Motor Trade Association dash into print an advertisement proclaiming the fact? They would very rightly fear a rap on the knuckles if they did. Yet a paragraph in the news columns announcing the purchase with fullest detail, including even what the King said, would not be inappropriate, and such a paragraph would be an enormous help to the British motor industry. Can an industry be blamed for seeking expert help to get the very widest publicity for such a fact?'

Clarke seems to have been successful in making the case that public relations offered something outside the reach of advertising: he even convinced the advertising industry to use Editorial Services Ltd to promote its work.

★★★

Around the time Editorial Services Ltd was established, Clarke collaborated with the economist Joseph French Johnson on a self-help book for aspiring businessmen called *Business and the Man*. The book is long-forgotten but is significant because it offers an insight into how Clarke believed public relations could be used in the private sector. Even though it is unclear which parts of the book Clarke wrote, he is almost certain to have had a hand in its section on marketing, even in the unlikely event that he did not actually write it.

His ideas do not seem to have changed dramatically from his time at Dublin Castle, though they had shifted slightly towards a greater emphasis on the importance of appealing to people's emotional reactions. Perhaps showing that Clarke was influenced by Edward Bernays, the nephew of Sigmund Freud who used psychological techniques in his public relations work in the United States, *Business and the Man* advised that 'men are a good deal like children – bundles of habits and instincts' and that an 'appeal to their reason often leaves them unmoved, while a subtle appeal to their emotions, prejudices or ambitions often drives them into conduct utterly irrational'.[20]

Business and the Man also argued that as well as often being more powerful than rational argument, appeals to the emotion were likely to resonate with a broader group of people:

At a theatre the downfall of the villain and the rescue of the heroine get equal applause from the boxes and the gallery, but at a lecture on some abstract topic there is no applause because there is no common response; perhaps only a few of the audience understand and appreciate all that is said, and it may be that not a single hearer is in agreement with all the speaker's arguments.[21]

Clarke expanded on the theme in his Royal Society of Arts lecture. While he still believed in the power of news to persuade people, he now acknowledged that simply presenting facts was not always enough:

A man who comes to a conclusion by his own reasoning on facts presented to him is usually firmer in that opinion and more active upon it than a man who accepts an opinion ready-made. But the world is made up of both sorts of people; and many folk need, unfortunately, to have not only the facts, but the conclusion also, presented to them before their minds will arrive at that conclusion and accept it as their own.

Propaganda and publicity are concerned, therefore, with the dissemination of facts and conclusions – not necessarily together, but both facts and conclusions may be sown like two different sorts of seeds, careful selection being made as to whether the one seed or the other, or both, can best be sown in a particular soil.[22]

While Clarke may have been influenced by Bernays's use of psychology in public relations, he did not share his American counterpart's enthusiasm for stunts. Bernays famously challenged the taboo on women smoking in public by getting women to light up during a 'Torches of Freedom' parade in 1929 and in doing so provided a template for how stunts can be used to highlight issues and campaign for change. But Clarke generally avoided them. His only known stunt was the relatively modest idea of persuading a group of influential businessmen to arrive on motorbikes at the Ritz hotel in London to promote the motorcycle industry. Clarke arrived in the sidecar of Raleigh chairman Sir Harold Bowden's motorcycle, his dress coat blowing in the wind. He decided to take a taxi for the journey home.[23]

The reason Clarke was generally happy to leave stunts to others may have been that his confidence in his ability to find the inherent news value in clients' work meant he felt he did not have to resort to gimmicks. Clarke had worked in and around newspapers for twenty years by the time he established Editorial Services Ltd and he thought deeply about news value, the ill-defined concept editors use to decide which stories to publish and how prominently. He was so interested in the theory of it that he intended to write a book about it[24] (which he never got around to completing) and his lecture to the Royal Society of Arts gave an insight into how he believed a story's 'news value' came from four sources: its importance; its human interest factor, the authority (including credibility) of the source, and timeliness.

For a daily newspaper, Clarke thought 'time factor', as he called it, was 'the greatest instrument of propaganda that we have'. This was because news quickly loses its value. 'Even a day's lateness is a tremendous handicap to any news item,' he explained. 'Note how the morning paper struggles to get "yesterday" or "last night" into its news; the evening paper "today"'. But all four were important, and an Editorial Services Ltd document from 1933 highlighted the human interest factor – or 'entertainment value' – as being particularly useful because the fact that 'a love drama of real life or a hen with three legs is as interesting to Durham as to Devon' meant it had the potential to appeal to a wide range of people.[25]

Clarke realised, though, that every piece of news did not have to contain all four factors. He used the example of how news of the method of Tsar Nicholas II's execution had been a big story despite the authority for the story being weak and the details only emerging many months after the news of his death. The political importance and the human interest value of the story were both large enough to overcome its lack of authority and timeliness.

Clarke thought this understanding of news and the ability to accentuate the news value of a story were what set Editorial Services Ltd apart, as he did not believe these were shared by many of his competitors. He told his audience at the Royal Society of Arts that 'news-value factors are woefully ignored' in publicity departments across the country, with the result that 'quite 99 per cent of the propaganda copy on innumerable subjects sent to newspapers is doomed *ab initio* [from the beginning] to the waste paper basket'.[26] He also believed in Editorial Services Ltd's ability to produce the kind of clear and concise copy that would appeal to journalists; when it came to offering clients advice about how to write for newspapers, he passed on the three rules for news writing – covering completeness; unambiguity; and simplicity – that his friend Herbert Sidebotham had given him when he had started out as a young reporter. And reflecting the fact that the ultimate goal of public relations is persuasion, Clarke added a fourth rule he had presumably developed himself: 'Could I have written it so as to make a deeper impression on his [the reader's] mind?'[27]

Editorial Services Ltd also offered a broader service than just securing newspaper coverage. On one occasion it even produced a publicity song that Clarke himself played on the piano. One of his colleagues later remembered him 'sitting at the piano on the stage of a West-end theatre and knocking out the accompaniment while the composer sang his head off'.[28] It seems Clarke also worked as a speechwriter for George V, though the Royal Archives are secretive about the work of royal speechwriters and so it is not clear whether he did this in a private capacity or during his time as a civil servant.

His son Alan would later recall an anecdote about his father visiting Buckingham Palace and finding the King leaning against a marble mantelpiece, reading a draft of a speech Clarke had written for him. The King turned to him. 'Clarke, I like the speeches you write for me,' he said. 'You don't make me sound too bloody pompous.'[29]

Clarke also promoted 'industrial propaganda', which was the idea that organisations could become more effective by changing the way they communicated with their employees. Clarke believed this was 'the most difficult and delicate type of propaganda work that can be imagined',[30] but he told the Royal Society of Arts that he believed 'a great deal of good would accrue from giving all workers a better and wider conspectus of the part that they and their work play in their firm's affairs than they are able to obtain from the narrow viewpoint of their own bench or loom or machine or desk'.

Like internal communications theorists in recent years, Clarke understood that workers were rarely motivated purely by financial gain and so he believed industrial propaganda could help take the 'joy of the worker expressed in his work' that had existed in the old crafts that were then dying out in Britain and recreate them in an industrial setting. He thought this should involve showing employees how their productivity benefitted them and their company, as well as comparing their work to that of their competitors.

He thought this sort of pride could be instilled in workers through an understanding of how a company's product was superior to that of its competitors. And if this were not the case, then fear could also be used as a motivating factor. Clarke gave the example of a Midlands firm that had placed competitors' adverts around its own site. 'I venture to think that the British worker, who is as cute as any other, would take in that little implication that he would see what his firm was up against in selling in that market,' Clarke said.

There was, of course, nothing new in the idea that good morale in a work-force is important. But Clarke suggested this should be seen as a branch of public relations and today this view is widely accepted, with most large organisations now having a post dedicated to internal communications. The history of internal communications is even less well chronicled than that of public relations generally, but the fact that Clarke was promoting industrial propaganda as early as 1926 means he has a good claim to having invented it. Certainly, his ideas about industrial propaganda pre-date by seven years the more famous internal communications work of Sir Stephen Tallents, the other main figure of early British public relations, at the General Post Office.

★★★

The innovations Clarke made as the head of Britain's first public relations agency are likely to be mainly of interest to those working in the media, but his work also led to his involvement in two of the biggest news stories of the inter-war period.

The first involved the pioneering aviator Amy Johnson, who sought Clarke's help in getting the financial backing for her flight to Australia. Johnson worked in the office of William Charles Crocker, a solicitor who was Clarke's friend and a director of Editorial Services Ltd. Perhaps aware of Clarke's interest in aviation, Crocker suggested to Johnson that she should have lunch with him in the hope that he might be able to introduce her to his contacts at the *Daily Mail*.

It is unclear whether Clarke and Johnson actually met, though her father wrote to her warning her to be wary about meeting 'big men' such as Clarke.[31] Whether it was with or without Clarke's help, Johnson managed to complete the flight, in doing so becoming the first woman to fly solo to Australia.

Clarke's friendship with Crocker also led to his involvement in solving one of the most notorious crimes of the time. As part of his work as a solicitor for the Cornhill Insurance Company, Crocker investigated a life insurance claim following the death of an elderly woman called Rosaline Fox in a fire at a hotel in Margate in October 1929. Rosaline's son, Sidney, told the inquest into her death that he had been staying at the hotel with his mother and had tried to rescue her from the fire. The inquest accepted his account and recorded a verdict of death by misadventure. But Crocker became suspicious when, on examining the paperwork, he discovered that Sidney's life insurance policy for his mother had been due to expire just half an hour after her death.

Crocker asked Clarke to publicise the case in the hope it might lead to new evidence. The resulting newspaper coverage led to people coming forward who claimed Sidney owed them money and Sidney was arrested and charged with obtaining credit by fraud. It was while he was awaiting trial for fraud that his mother's body was exhumed and a post-mortem concluded she had not died in the fire but had actually been strangled. Sidney Fox was convicted of her murder and hanged.[32]

Notes

1 *The Times*, 23 April 1923, p.17.
2 *Daily Mirror*, 26 May 1923, p.4.
3 Sir Basil Clarke, *Two Great Undertakings*, J. Lyons, 1924, pp.11–12.
4 Sir Basil Clarke, *The Quest of Columbus in Mural Decoration*, London, no date but probably published in 1923 or 1924, p.8.
5 Alan Clarke, *The Life & Times of Sir Basil Clarke – PR Pioneer*, Public Relations, 1969, Vol. 22 (2) pp.8–13
6 Larry Tye, *The Father of Spin: Edward Bernays and the Birth of Public Relations*, New York, 1998, pp.245–7.
7 Patrick Robertson, *The Book of Firsts*, Crown Publishers, 1974, p.142; and Richard West, PR: The Fifth Estate, London, 1963, p.119.
8 Alan Jenkins, *Drinka Pinta – The Story of Milk and the Industry that Serves It*, Heinemann, London, 1970, p.92.
9 Alan Clarke, *The Life & Times of Sir Basil Clarke – PR Pioneer*, Public Relations, 1969, Vol. 22 (2) pp.8–13.
10 David Thomas, Len Holden, Tim Claydon, *The Motor Car and Popular Culture in the 20th Century*, Ashgate, 1998, p.168.
11 *The Times*, 31 January 1927, p.21.
12 *The Times*, 22 July 1925, p.10.
13 *Irish Times*, 18 May 1925, p.7.
14 Alan Clarke, *The Life & Times of Sir Basil Clarke – PR Pioneer*, Public Relations, 1969, Vol. 22 (2) pp.8–13.
15 Churchill Archives Centre, THRS VI 19/2, Clarke to Lord Weston, 16 December 1927.
16 Churchill Archives Centre, THRS VI 19/2, Clarke to Sir Archibald Sinclair, 16 December 1927.
17 William Robertson, *Welfare in Trust: A History of the Carnegie United Kingdom Trust 1913–1963*, Dunfermline, 1964, p.89.
18 Sir Basil Clarke, *The Public and its Institutions*, p.4. This is a previously unknown publication produced by Editorial Services, probably in 1934, and the only known copy is the property of the Bibbings family. Its contents are being published here for the first time.
19 *Advertiser's Weekly*, 10 December 1931.
20 Joseph French Johnson in collaboration with Sir Basil Clarke, *Business and the Man*, London, 1924, p.66.
21 Ibid., pp. 66–7.
22 *Journal of the Royal Society of Arts*, 1926, pp.491–2.
23 Alan Clarke, *The Life & Times of Sir Basil Clarke – PR Pioneer*, Public Relations, 1969, Vol. 22 (2) pp.8–13.
24 Journalism By Some Masters of the Craft, London, Isaac Pitman & Sons Ltd, 1932, p.115

25 National Union of Teachers, Press Correspondence for the use of Publicity Committees and Press Secretaries. The document, produced by Editorial Services Ltd, probably in 1933, was kept by Alan Clarke and is the property of the Bibbings family. Its contents are being published here for the first time. It is not certain that Clarke actually wrote it, but the fact that this document includes his views on news value and news writing suggests he at least had a hand in it.

26 Journal of the Royal Society of Arts, Vol. 74, 1926, p.493–4.

27 National Union of Teachers, Press Correspondence for the use of Publicity Committees and Press Secretaries.

28 Alan Clarke, *The Life & Times of Sir Basil Clarke – PR Pioneer, Public Relations*, 1969, Vol. 22 (2) pp.8–13.

29 Ibid.

30 Journal of the Royal Society of Arts, Vol. 74, 1926, p.485–6.

31 Constance Babington Smith, Amy Johnson, London, 1977, p.170

32 Alan Clarke, *The Life & Times of Sir Basil Clarke – PR Pioneer, Public Relations*, 1969, Vol. 22 (2) pp.8-13. I have repeated the story as Alan Clarke related it, though it seems strange that William Charles Crocker does not mention Clarke's involvement in the account of the Fox case in his autobiography, despite devoting a whole chapter to it. There is nothing in Crocker's autobiography, however, to contradict Alan Clarke's account of his father's involvement.

20

Business

Given that he had jointly produced a book about business and was running a company of his own, it is not surprising that in the late 1920s Clarke decided to expand his business interests. But while he made a success of Editorial Services Ltd by using his understanding of the newspaper industry, when he became involved with companies outside the world of journalism he quickly discovered that running a company was significantly more difficult than writing about it.

The highest profile of a number of forays into the world of business involved the cinema, a subject he had long been interested in. While editor of the *Sheffield Independent*, he had overseen a leader column complaining about the lack of realism in film acting:

> If the man on the street meets with an acute grief he will, at the most, merely look unhappy in a dull stolid way. If the cinema star strikes an unlucky patch he will work his throat five times and indulge in a whole series of facial gymnastics. The result is to give an air of unreality to film stories, and an exaggerated sentimentality.

> We have full sympathy with the difficulty of the cinema actors in expressing their feelings without talking, but we are sure they give audiences credit for too little imagination. In their anxiety to convey the state of their feelings accurately to the audience they overdo the expression. We certainly think it is time there was an improvement.

Another *Sheffield Independent* leader column during his editorship had expressed confidence in the so far untapped potential of British cinema, suggesting there was no reason Britain's film industry could not be as successful as its theatre.[1]

In 1927, Clarke got the opportunity to put these ideas into practice. Adelqui Millar, a Chilean actor and director who has been described by the film historian Rachael Low as having 'a leaning towards the exotic which sometimes slipped over into the absurd',[2] joined with Charles Lapworth, who claimed to have been Charlie Chaplin's personal representative, and film publicist Norman Pogson to form a new company called Whitehall Films, and Clarke was given the chance to become a company director.[3]

While he may have believed the British film industry had the potential to compete with the rest of the world, Whitehall Films's business model was altogether more cynical in that it was a response to the Cinematograph Films Act 1927. Apparently intended to help nurture the British film industry by requiring for a certain proportion of films shown in Britain to be British-made, the Act was actually just a crude piece of protectionism. Millar, Lapworth and Pogson were presumably among those who realised that, rather than improving the quality of British cinema, this would simply result in an increase in demand for cheaply made and poor quality British films (they became known as 'quota quickies')[4] that they hoped Whitehall Films would be able to meet.

The prospectus for Whitehall Films was published in November 1927 and set out how it planned to buy 2,000 acres of land in Borehamwood, a Hertfordshire town that later became known as the British Hollywood, and build a studio capable of producing films that would be popular around the world. But the prospectus also mentioned that the six films it planned to make in its first year would cost an average of no more than £10,000 each, a relatively small amount that Rachael Low has identified as an early sign that Whitehall Films was actually more intent on exploiting the quota system by being preoccupied with keeping its costs down.[5]

Despite concerns in the trade press that the plan was over-ambitious, Whitehall Films captured the public's imagination; the share issue sold out in a matter of hours and by the end of the year 1,500 people had applied for acting roles with the company.[6]

At a shareholders meeting in February 1928, Clarke gave the chairman's report in the chairman's absence. The report claimed that after just a few months, Whitehall Films was already making a 'very fair measure of progress' that included the start of work on the Borehamwood studio. The studio, Clarke told the meeting, was scheduled to be finished by the following June and would be 'probably the most up-to-date and efficient studio in this country', with the added advantage that its position near the train station would mean its sign was 'a permanent advertisement of no small value'.

While the building work was progressing, Clarke added, Millar had gone to Spain to direct and star in *Life*, a film based on the Spanish novel *Juan José*, while Pogson was about to leave for China to make a film about the adventures of Marco Polo. They had also acquired the British rights to three foreign films.

The chairman's report also addressed criticism that had been levelled at Whitehall Films:

> Some kind charitable souls have seen fit to invent and spread some malicious aspersions on this company and the prospects of this company. So indeterminate were the charges and so well camouflaged was their source, that no legal action was possible. We had to leave these statements alone. But they did our shares harm and frightened many shareholders. For that we are sorry. But the Board would like you all to know that they are far more concerned about making Whitehall Films a commercial success than in the immediate market price of the shares of the company. We are satisfied with the progress and see excellent prospects of success.[7]

Clarke's performance in selling the company's vision for the future certainly impressed the *Financial Times*. 'Sir Basil's account of the progress made reads more like a novel than a formal record of the Board's activities during a very busy period,' it reported, 'and there seems no reason to believe that, with such a beginning, the company will have difficulty in living up to its joint aim — namely, money and reputation.'[8]

Following *Life*, Whitehall Films produced another film called *The Inseparables*. Starring the Italian actress Elissa Landi, who would later become famous as one of the stars of *The Count of Monte Cristo*, it told the story of a smuggler who falls in love with a gypsy girl he rescues from a storm.

But these outward signs of good progress masked the fact that, behind the scenes, things were going badly wrong at Whitehall Films. The company was beset by arguments, the most serious of which involved Clarke accusing Pogson of stealing hundreds of pounds from a charity event in aid of the Middlesex Hospital.[9] This seems to have led to Pogson's resignation. And though Clarke succeeded in forcing Pogson out, he did not last much longer himself. By November 1928, both he and Lapworth had also resigned from the board.[10]

Then in June 1929, with the company deeply in debt, Millar was removed from the board and had his contract cancelled[11] and a few months later the company went into liquidation, blaming, among other things, the unexpected rise in the popularity of talking cinema. The *New York Times* reported that Whitehall Films was the first of the numerous British film companies inspired by Cinematograph Films Act to go out of business, estimating that total investments in these companies had depreciated by some £12 million.[12]

The collapse of Whitehall Films must have been a difficult experience for those involved. Millar returned to his native Chile, where he continued directing films until his death in the 1950s, while Lapworth seems to have disappeared from the film industry. As for Pogson, the next time he and Clarke would meet, the outcome would be even more acrimonious.

★★★

Clarke's involvement in Whitehall Films was not his most bizarre business venture. He also became a director of Radium Springs, a company that marketed radioactive water as a health-giving drink.[13] The company prospectus of 1928 made a series of extraordinary claims about the health benefits of its water, including that it prevented cancer, obesity and the hardening of the arteries, and that it could 'remove the ill-effects of alcohol and tobacco, prevent and cure neuralgia [a condition that causes severe facial pain] and insomnia, and stimulate and invigorate the heart'.[14]

As ridiculous as all this may sound today, Radium Springs was not alone in promoting the supposed health benefits of radioactive water and even some doctors seem to have believed in the fad. Even so, Clarke displayed poor judgement in associating himself with such wild claims, particularly given his former position at the Ministry of Health. He resigned as a director in 1931,[15] though the company continued to operate for another decade before being wound up.[16]

Around the same time, Clarke became a director of British Booklet Matches (1928). As the name suggests, the company was established in 1928 and its stated aim was to 'carry on the business of manufacturers and dealers and all other articles or contrivances for obtaining ignition etc'.[17] Its big idea was the 'Disk', which comprised fifty-four matches arranged in a circle along the same lines as the spokes of a wheel. The company prospectus hailed the 'Disk' as a 'triumph of modern invention' that would be 'commonly adopted as well in domestic circles as in hotels, clubs, restaurants, and on ships and railway trains'.[18]

The reality was very different. British Booklet Matches (1928) proved no more successful than Whitehall Films or Radium Springs and by the time Clarke resigned as a director just over a year later,[19] it had already lost over £26,000 (the equivalent of over £850,000 today). This was blamed on poor administration in its early days, compensation for cancelling unsuitable contracts and, ironically given the nature of the product, a fire in the factory.[20]

For most people, being involved in three disastrous companies would be enough to convince them they were unsuited to the world of business. Clarke, though, seems to have been undeterred. He was also involved in a gold mining company in Ireland,[21] a company in London that worked as 'editors and compilers of literary matter'[22] and a steel company.[23] He may have even tried his hand at business overseas, as he and Alice spent time in Argentina in 1927 and in Egypt in 1929. While in Cairo, they dined with the children's author Arthur Ransome and Ransome's diary entry about the dinner suggests Clarke was in Egypt on business. 'Cheerful couple but he wants watching,' Ransome wrote. 'Suggested a job for me, which made me doubt very much. He wants money from the Egyptians.'

While the details of some of Clarke's business dealings are unknown, there is no evidence that any of them were successful. His son Alan later admitted his father was 'a poor business man' and that 'his enthusiasms led him to make some very bad investments'.[24]

Notes

1 *Sheffield Independent*, 6 November 1919, p.4.
2 Rachael Low, *History of British Film*, Vol 4, London 1997, p.196.
3 *The Times*, 7 November 1927, p.24.
4 Scott Anthony, *Public Relations and the Making of Modern Britain: Stephen Tallents and the Birth of a Progressive Media Profession*, Manchester University Press, 2012, p.63.
5 Rachael Low, *History of British Film*, Vol 4, London 1997, p.196.
6 *Manchester Guardian*, 27 December 1927, p.4.
7 *Financial Times*, 6 February 1928, p.2.
8 *Financial Times*, 6 February 1928, p.4.
9 *Daily Express*, 17 July 1930, p.9.
10 National Archives, Kew, BT 31,32870/225546/31.
11 Rachael Low, *History of British Film*, Vol 4, London 1997, p.196.
12 *New York Times*, 13 November 1929, p.24.
13 *The Times*, 24 November 1928, p.24.
14 *Daily Express*, 24 November 1928, p.14.
15 National Archives, Kew, BT 31/33852/234 947/23, Radium Springs annual returns, 31 December 1933.
16 National Archives, Kew, BT 31/33852/234 947/26, High Court of Justice Chancery Division, Companies Court, Mr Justice Crossman, 20 February 1942.
17 *Financial Times*, 31 March 1928, p.8.
18 *Financial Times*, 2 April 1928, p.14.
19 *Daily Express*, 30 April 1929, p.14.
20 *Financial Times*, 29 October 1929 p.8.
21 *Irish Independent*, 26 September 1935, p.11.
22 *Financial Times*, 21 August 1928, p.7.
23 *The Foundry*, Volume 41, 1929, p.208.
24 Alan Clarke, *The Life & Times of Sir Basil Clarke – PR Pioneer*, Public Relations, 1969, Vol. 22 (2) pp.8–13.

The 'Publicity Journalist'

I n 1929, the Prince of Wales visited mining communities in the north of England to highlight the plight of the miners in the area. Clarke agreed to manage the publicity for the visit free of charge and it attracted newspaper coverage around the world, so much so that the prince wrote to Clarke to thank him for what he thought were among the best press arrangements he had experienced.

Clarke later recalled that the journalists who covered the story had also praised his handling of it. But the Newspaper Society did not agree. It was so angered by Clarke's involvement that it wrote to the prince to complain that it had been an 'interference with the liberties of the press'.

'I do not know how near this vendetta is going to restriction of trade,' Clarke said shortly afterwards, 'but I am not much concerned, since the actual attitude of editors as a whole is nothing but friendly. They publish my copy whenever they think it worthy of publication and put it into the waste-paper basket when they do not – and that is all I ask of any editor.'[1]

Whatever he might have said about not being bothered, as a former journalist the idea of being portrayed as an enemy of press freedom must have rankled, and the Newspaper Society's criticism was not an isolated case. One weekly newspaper editor in the Midlands wrote to Clarke to complain that a press notice about a Dairy Workers' Carnival Dance at Covent Garden was 'none other than an advertisement very carefully disguised as reading matter'.[2] Lord Riddell, who had acted as liaison between the press and the Government during the First World War, was also a critic, despite having himself managed public relations for the British delegation to the Paris Peace Conference in 1919. Clarke complained that Riddell's attitude towards public relations officers could be summed up as: 'Kill off the lot of them; blackball every bit of their copy.'[3]

It was partly in response to these criticisms that during a lecture in 1929 Clarke offered a robust defence of public relations as a 'useful and perfectly honourable calling',[4] explaining how he thought that, far from stifling the press, public relations simply made life easier for newspapers because it offered journalists another source of newsworthy information:

> Even the little newsboy who dashes to the newspaper office with word of a fire or a murder receives fair words and his half-crown. No single soul in this world is really an enemy of the editor or unwelcome if he has fresh, live news to tell.

> Why, then, is the press agent to be condemned if he offers, free of all charge, some "copy" or information which the editor may like to publish and which he can always throw away into the WPB [wastepaper basket] if he does not? Does the fact of its being a press agent's copy, and therefore publicity copy, automatically condemn it, destroy its news-value, vitiate its interest for the public? Of course not. For it is one of the truths the editor knows from his editorial cradle that virtually every single item in the paper is publicity for some person, cause, or thing. From the law reports and book reviews, which help barristers and authors to fame, to the football reports which help to make a footballer worth paying £9,000 for, the whole paper is publicity for something or somebody ...

> Here, then, is the position: on the one hand, newspapers and editors striving for that vital spark, news-value; on the other hand, many quite worthy people – governments, institutions, industries, movements and businesses, advertisers and others – striving for objective publicity in the only place in which it is to be found, namely, the columns which our editors command.

> There are two sorts of intermediaries between these two sets of people. The first and most important is the journalist ... The second intermediary is the press-agent. He digs as wide and as deep as he can into his clients' affairs in search of the same valuable commodity, news-value, and offers his findings free of cost to the editor.[5]

The large number of people working in public relations today is proof that Clarke was right about the usefulness of public relations. But he was wrong to see it as just another source of news and many people today argue that the media's reliance on public relations has become extremely damaging. As he himself had recognised during his time in Ireland, effective public relations might increase the amount of news an editor has to choose from, but it will not necessarily mean the newspaper is better equipped to reflect the truth of an issue.

Clarke, though, was unable to see how anyone with knowledge of newspapers could be opposed to properly conducted public relations. Instead, he blamed the hostility he faced on a tendency to lump all press agents together and the resulting failure to distinguish between reputable public relations practitioners and the older form of press agents who were often either incompetent or dishonest. 'Perhaps it is that, as one of the bigger press agents of the country, I am catching on my back the blows which should fall on other shoulders,' he told the audience.[6]

If he really was being stigmatised for the sins of others then he was justified in feeling aggrieved, as there was certainly a strong ethical dimension to his work. Perhaps as a result of his time in Ireland, he was opposed to what he called the 'hidden persuaders' who practised black propaganda and he was so committed to high ethical standards that he once rejected the chance to represent the spirits industry because he was already trying to convince the British public that 'beer is best' on behalf of the brewing industry and worried about the potential conflict of interest.[7]

He also refused to work for causes and products he did not believe in, writing that 'we cannot hope to secure public support or help for anything which is anti-social; which has not within it some aspect of definite public interest or worthwhile public service, greater or less.'[8] This approach was pragmatic as well as idealistic. 'You can turn the limelight on one particular aspect of a problem or thing,' he explained, 'but that limelight will always enable people to peer into any shadows there may be around.'

One way to help the public distinguish the good public relations practitioners from the bad, Clarke decided, was to change what they were called. He thought the reputation of press agents was so tarnished that a new name was needed to describe those working in public relations who, like him, took their profession seriously and who had proper training in journalism, publicity and advertising. The new name he came up with was 'publicity journalist'.[9]

In attempting to rebrand those who worked in public relations, Clarke was several years behind Edward Bernays, who was referring to himself as a 'public relations counsellor' as early as 1920.[10] As well as being earlier with the idea, Bernays was also much more successful with it; while the term 'publicity journalist' has only been used occasionally, many people working in public relations in America today still refer to themselves using the term Bernays coined.

Clarke was, though, ahead of Bernays, and indeed everybody else, when it came to ideas for how public relations might be regulated. He saw the need for an ethical framework that those willing to be held account to could point to as evidence of their professionalism and integrity and so, at some point during the mid-1920s,[11] he developed the industry's first real code of conduct.

The issue of ethics was not new to public relations. The American Ivy Lee (who Clarke's son Alan claimed was a friend of Clarke's)[12] had included an ethical element in his 'Declaration of Principles for Public Relations' in 1906. Lee's own ethics, though, were so questionable that he was known as 'Poison Ivy' and when he died in 1934 he was being investigated by Congress for his links to Nazi Germany. Also, in 1927 Bernays chaired a committee of fifteen American public relations men with the aim of creating an organisation to 'clean up the evil practices in publicity'[13] and his 1928 book *Propaganda* included a code of ethics.[14]

But Lee only included ethics as a small part of a wider document, while Bernays' code of ethics was as much a description of how public relations practitioners already behaved as it was an attempt to codify standards of behaviour that could be used to hold people to account. As for the committee of PR men, it fell apart after Bernays alienated the other committee members by issuing a statement about their work to a magazine.

Clarke's code was the first of its kind anywhere in the world in that the whole document was about ethical standards, and it set tough and credible standards that those working in public relations were expected to conform to.

The Code[15] called for an end to anonymity in public relations. All public relations copy was to be marked with the sender's name and clearly labelled as publicity copy, while the press agent would be obliged to disclose the name of his client if asked to do so by an editor. The question of transparency also featured in Bernays's *Propaganda*, which, in an echo of Clarke's code, argued that publicity material should be 'clearly labelled as to source' and that newspaper editors should know 'from whom it comes and what its purpose is'. It is unclear whether it was Bernays or Clarke who first developed this idea, though Bernays was hardly in a position to moralise about the importance of transparency given that obfuscation – and particularly the creation of apparently objective front organisations – was central to his success in public relations. With the Torches of Freedom parade that promoted cigarettes to women, for example, Bernays went out of his way to hide the fact that a tobacco company was behind it.[16]

As well as highlighting the importance of transparency, Clarke's code set out that press agents should not accept fees from newspapers or 'suborn' newspaper staff to publish stories, while they should also be responsible for satisfying themselves of their clients' bona fides. It also judged canvassing for business to be inappropriate because it could lead to press agents over-promising about the levels of coverage they were likely to achieve. And work should be paid for by professional fee, rather than by the number of articles secured.

Its other provisions included that stunts should not be used if they were intended to deceive either an editor or the public; that press releases should include footnotes giving the source for any claims; and that, except in 'special circumstances', editorial publicity was to be offered alongside advertising rather than instead of it. The code also stipulated that press agents should not offer to place advertising with a newspaper on condition that it agreed to give editorial coverage, as this was 'degrading alike to the maker of the threats and to the paper'.

Clarke hoped his code would force deceitful press agents to either change their ways or go out of business, and that this would enhance the professional reputations of those who remained. He also called for an industry-wide approach where a new 'Vigilance Committee' would monitor adherence to these rules and punish those who broke them, which he thought 'would rid editorial publicity work of many abuses and leave unimpaired the useful functions'.

As visionary as Clarke's code may have been, it does not seem to have had an immediate effect on the public relations industry, and a decade later Clarke was lamenting that 'there is still no knowing who is, or may be, a press agent, or what he may do … [and] nor is there any limit, except those imposed by his natural decency, to which a press agent may descend to get his publicity or propaganda across'.[17] It was not until the 1960s, some forty years after he published his code, that the Institute of Public Relations (IPR) finally established a British public relations code. In the United States, the Public Relations Society of America published its first code in 1950.[18] As well as being first with the idea, the content of Clarke's code has stood the test of time. According to the public relations historian Jacquie L'Etang, every point in it has been included in the IPR's code at some point.[19]

★★★

In 1963, the journalist Richard West looked back at Clarke's code as part of a book about the public relations industry. He concluded that while it was 'admirable as far as it goes',[20] the vast majority of 1960s public relations firms were consistently breaking at least some of Clarke's rules. 'A few break all of them except number 10,'[21] West wrote, referring to the point about payment being by professional fee rather than based on the results.

One rule West claimed was being routinely ignored was the one about 'suborning' journalists, which he thought included asking journalists to see a copy of their article before publication and so making 'the journalist reluctant to be critical in his writing'.[22] But in this, West may have misunderstood what Clarke meant, as he is more likely to have been referring to the practice he had witnessed in Bucharest during the First World War, where journalists were bribed not to send reports of Austrian atrocities.

West also gave the example of public relations practitioners regularly posing as ordinary members of the public when writing to the letters page of newspapers as evidence of a failure to be transparent. But to be fair, Clarke had himself been guilty of this when he had written to *The Times* on behalf of the telephone industry.

West believed Clarke's rule about disclosing the identity of clients was particularly important because of the practice, which had been pioneered by Bernays, of creating apparently impartial organisations for the sole purpose of promoting the work of a particular company.[23] This is still a contentious issue today, and it is to Clarke's credit that the ethical issues he identified in his code are still relevant almost ninety years later. The fact that some firms have been able to get away with not disclosing clients in recent years reflects the fact that the Chartered Institute of Public Relations (CIPR) code of conduct,[24] which today's public relations practitioners are expected to follow, is less exacting than Clarke's code. This may be because the content of Clarke's code was solely a matter for him, while the CIPR's code has to have the support of the whole industry.

Another element of Clarke's code still being debated today, and something that is not included in the CIPR's code, is the issue of payment by results. Some argue that it ensures clients get value for money, while its detractors see it as incentivising unethical behaviour and being an inappropriate payment model for a respectable profession.

As for Clarke, he apparently only ever broke his rule on payment by results once, when a client insisted he would only pay for the newspaper coverage Editorial Services Ltd actually secured. Clarke reluctantly agreed a rate and at the end of the campaign the client was shocked to find that the bill was five times higher than the fee Clarke had originally proposed. Content to have taught the client a lesson, Clarke eventually let him off the difference for the price of a lunch.[25]

Notes

1   *Journalism By Some Masters of the Craft*, London, Isaac Pitman & Sons Ltd, 1932, pp.118–9.
2   *Advertisers' Weekly*, 23 January 1931.
3   *Journalism By Some Masters of the Craft*, London, Isaac Pitman & Sons Ltd, 1932, pp.118–9.
4   Ibid.
5   Ibid., pp.115–6.
6   Ibid., p.119.
7   Alan Clarke, *The Life & Times of Sir Basil Clarke – PR Pioneer*, Public Relations, 1969, Vol. 22 (2) pp.8–13.

8   Sir Basil Clarke, *The Public and its Institutions*, p.2.
9   Journal of the Royal Society of Arts, 1926, p.493.
10 Larry Tye, *The Father of Spin: Edward Bernays and the Birth of Public Relations*, New York, 1998, p.53.
11 While the exact date Clarke developed his Code is unclear, 1924 seems to be the most likely date. In an interview with *Advertisers' Weekly* on 13 September 1934, Clarke said: 'Ten years or so ago … I suggested … establishing some higher standard of practice'.
12 Alan Clarke, *The Life & Times of Sir Basil Clarke – PR Pioneer, Public Relations*, 1969, Vol. 22 (2) pp.8–13. However, Jacquie L'Etang (*Public Relations in Britain: A History of Professional Practice in the Twentieth Century*, New Jersey, 2008, pp.48–9) has questioned whether this was actually the case.
13 Larry Tye, *The Father of Spin: Edward Bernays and the Birth of Public Relations*, New York, 1998, pp.250–1.
14 Ibid., p.99.
15 *The British Advertiser*, April 1930, p.139, sets out the code; it was also published in *Journalism By Some Masters of the Craft*, London, Isaac Pitman & Sons Ltd, 1932, pp.120–1.
16 Larry Tye, *The Father of Spin: Edward Bernays and the Birth of Public Relations*, New York, 1998, p.33.
17 *Advertisers' Weekly*, 13 September 1934.
18 A. David Gordon, John Michael Michael Kittross, John C. Merrill, *Controversies in Media Ethics*, New York, 2011, p.170.
19 Jacquie L'Etang, *Public Relations in Britain: A History of Professional Practice in the Twentieth Century*, New Jersey, 2008, p.147.
20 Richard West, *PR: The Fifth Estate*, Mayflower Books Ltd, London, 1963, p.121.
21 Ibid.
22 Ibid.
23 Ibid.
24 The Chartered Institute of Public Relations's Code of Conduct is available online at http://www.cipr.co.uk/content/about-us/about-cipr/code-conduct (accessed December 2012)
25 Alan Clarke, *The Life & Times of Sir Basil Clarke – PR Pioneer, Public Relations*, 1969, Vol. 22 (2) pp.8–13

'What Really Matters'

Clarke was walking through Dulwich one night with one of his sons in early 1927 when they heard a police whistle. They followed the sound and found a police officer outside a house that was in the process of being burgled, and Clarke and his son waited at the front of the house while the officer went to arrest the intruder. Clarke went with them back to the police station but the burglar became violent on the way and the police officer later admitted that he would have got away had it not been for Clarke stopping him.[1]

This willingness to restrain a burglar who was almost twenty years younger than him showed that Clarke's becoming part of the establishment – his position in the Anglo-Danish Society led to him being given the Order of the Dannebrog (roughly the equivalent of a knighthood) by the King of Denmark[2] and he was also a member of several London clubs – had not diminished his physical bravery. Neither did entering middle age mellow his temper. His quickness to anger had already caused him to lose at least two jobs, and in 1930 it resulted in two incidents that led to his public humiliation.

The first occurred on 4 June when he was watching the Epsom Derby from the top deck of a bus that was being used as a viewing platform. Clarke sat behind Admiral Sir Henry Bruce, who had commanded the HMS *Hercules* during the early part of the First World War, while a Major Victor Beaufort stood between the front two seats to watch the race.

The trouble began when Bruce asked Beaufort to move because he was restricting his view and Beaufort reportedly responded angrily to repeated requests to sit down and told Bruce to 'shut up'.[3]

The race was so close that the spectators were left unsure which horse had won and so Beaufort stood on the seats to try to see the number of the winner. At this point, he fell forward and only just managed to stop himself going over the edge of the bus. It is unclear whether he had been pushed by Bruce, but when he had steadied himself he turned to Bruce and asked him what he thought he was doing.

It was at this point that Clarke intervened. Believing Beaufort was about to hit Bruce, he leapt forward and hit Beaufort with what he later described as a 'right and a left'. One of the punches was so hard that it apparently cut the inside of Beaufort's mouth against his false teeth and gave him a black eye for a week. Beaufort later claimed Clarke then came at him with a raised leg and tried to throw him off the top of the bus. Clarke denied this and accused Beaufort of trying to pull his ear off. The fight only ended when Beaufort managed to get Clarke in a headlock and hold him until he calmed down.

Beaufort pressed charges and Clarke stood trial at Epsom Police Court on 24 June, accused of unlawfully assaulting and beating Beaufort. 'If a man of his [Clarke's] position behaved in a ruffianly way he should be treated as if he was a ruffian,' the prosecution suggested.

Clarke was unrepentant and the defence told the court that 'Sir Basil was of the opinion that it was his duty as a gentleman, and in law, to prevent an unjustifiable assault' and that 'he did what any decent Englishman would have done, and hit Major Beaufort'.

The chairman of the court seems to have accepted that Clarke had only been trying to defend Bruce, as he dismissed the case. But the chairman may not have known that just two weeks after Clarke's fight with Beaufort and barely a week before his court appearance, Clarke had been involved in another violent confrontation.

By 1930, Clarke was living in a large house at Eton, the grounds of which backed onto the River Thames. On 15 June, he saw a man and a woman tying up a boat in a backwater and told them they were not allowed to moor there because it was private property. By extraordinary coincidence, the man was Norman Pogson, the co-founder of Whitehall Films who had resigned after Clarke accused him of stealing charity money. Despite their history, Clarke later claimed not to have recognised Pogson and to have spoken to him 'in quite a friendly voice'.[4]

Pogson, who was out boating with his wife, complied with the request and instead moored the boat at an exit of the backwater. But Clarke believed they were still on private property and, now angry, he got into a dingy and rowed towards them.

'Now then, Pogson,' Clarke said as he approached the couple in his dingy. 'I asked you nicely to go away and you came sneaking down here again.'

Pogson challenged Clarke to point to a sign that indicated it was private property, but Clarke was in no mood to discuss the matter and told him to 'clear out'.[5]

At this point, Pogson and Clarke's accounts of the incident diverge. In Pogson's version, Clarke swung at him so fiercely with an oar that 'if it had hit me it would have killed me',[6] but Pogson managed to use his paddle to ward off the blow. Clarke then pulled the oar back behind his head and brought it down with 'frightening violence' on the paddle. The blade of the oar snapped as it hit the paddle, flying off and hitting Mrs Pogson in the head.

'Oh, my head,' Mrs Pogson cried. 'You shan't murder my husband.'[7]

Clarke was left holding the shaft of the broken oar and his boat had started to drift away, but he still managed to swing two more blows at Pogson before he floated out of reach.

'You have made yourself a beastly nuisance in my life before, Sir Basil,' Pogson apparently shouted as his adversary drifted away. 'I did not expect you could do it at this part of the river.'

Clarke's account was very different, though he was quite open about having threatened Pogson with violence.

'If you are impudent to me I shall smack your face,' he claimed to have responded when Pogson questioned whether he really was on private property.

'Will you repeat that?' Pogson asked. Clarke said it again and he claimed that at this point Pogson grabbed his oar, which pulled his boat onto its side and caused water to start pouring in. Clarke then hit Pogson's arm with the other oar and the oar snapped when it hit the side of the boat.

He admitted he and Pogson had exchanged three or four blows, but insisted 'it was nonsense to say that anything from the broken oar could have gone within 5 yards of Mrs Pogson'.[8]

Clarke was summoned to Slough Police Court on 27 July to answer a charge of 'causing common assault and grievous bodily harm'. Pogson told the court he had pressed charges because 'I believe if a man behaves as he has behaved then he should be stopped'.[9]

Mr Fox-Andrews, representing Clarke, accused Pogson of bringing the charge in revenge for Clarke forcing his resignation from Whitehall Films. 'I suggest that you brought these proceedings purely and solely out of spite,' he said.

Pogson denied even being aware of the allegation of theft, which he said was a lie.[10] But Mr Fox-Andrew's expert questioning quickly succeeded in undermining Pogson's credibility and the case against Clarke was dismissed. He walked out of court a free man for the second time in barely a month.

Clarke may have escaped punishment, but the two court cases were widely reported in the press and caused Clarke great embarrassment. Yet when his son

Alan put it to him that these sorts of incidents were bad personal public relations, Clarke was unrepentant.

'Yes, my boy, of course they are,' he said. 'But it doesn't really matter what the world thinks. What really matters is what you think of yourself.'[11]

★★★

The two court cases and the failure of his business investments meant that the late 1920s and early 1930s was a difficult time. Yet neither the ineptness of his investments nor the shortness of his temper seemed to have had any significant impact on Editorial Services Ltd. By 1933, two of his sons were on the company payroll, with Basil Camden a director and Alan also finding work there after Clarke unsuccessfully tried to get him a job at the *Manchester Guardian*.[12]

By this time, the company had moved to offices in Chancery Lane near Holborn to accommodate a staff that had expanded to sixty employees and which secured about 50,000 press cuttings a year for 400 clients.[13] 'There is no worthwhile paper which has not used our copy ... [and] Editorial Services copy is respected as the best of its kind that reaches newspaper offices, both in conception and workmanship,' Clarke once boasted.[14]

Among its new clients was the Halifax Building Society, which enlisted it to promote the idea of building societies generally and the work of the Halifax in particular. It secured 250 editorial references a month for the Halifax and also wrote speeches for its directors.[15] Editorial Services Ltd also successfully campaigned to have imported skimmed milk marked 'unfit for babies', was credited with increasing the popularity of Nottingham lace curtains, and was commissoned by the Blue Star line to promote the idea of taking cruises.[16]

Clarke also worked to secure coverage for the 400th anniversary of the *Passion Play* at Oberammergau in Germany in 1934. He commissioned Winston Churchill – then in the middle of his 'wilderness years' but still a well-known public figure – to write a 1,000-word article encouraging people to attend. By this point, Clarke had a flat in the same block near Victoria Station as Churchill, and Clarke invited Churchill to visit him in his flat one evening. There is no record, though, of whether this happened.

In a company brochure, Clarke set out Editorial Services Ltd's 'specialist aptitudes' as being 'knowledge of the public and its institutions' and the ability to identify 'which part ... of a client's objectives is, or can be made, capable of help from any of these quarters', together with the 'experience and skill' and the 'necessary contacts' to bring about change.[17]

Clarke's knowledge of the newspaper industry was still the bedrock of the company's work, though he now saw the handling of newspapers as part of a wider approach to public relations. He wrote that while it was possible to make a 'plain living' from being able to see things from the point of view of a newspaper editor, this was unlikely on its own to bring either wealth or great influence, as the public relations practitioner also needed to be able to create 'news stimuli to which the Press and public will respond'.[18]

Editorial Services Ltd claimed to be able to work with every institution that might 'rightly be used to shape public opinion and thereby achieve commercial, social or political objectives'. Of these, Clarke wrote, 'the Press though the chief is only one'.

He bought into the view, advocated by Bernays in the 1920s, that public relations was about not just directly promoting a cause or product but about changing society to increase the chances of that cause or product's success. 'Many a selling problem or production problem remains imperfectly solved because the client regards the legal or social framework into which his policies have to fit as being unalterable,' Clarke wrote. 'The idea that this steel frame can be reshaped or enlarged either does not occur to them or presents itself as an object unattainable ... [when, in fact,] given right public relations work no good case is unattainable'. He seems likely to have borrowed this idea from Bernays. While there is no record of Clarke referring to the American by name, the use of the term 'the crystallisation of public opinion' in an Editorial Services Ltd document[19] – almost directly lifted from the title of Bernays's book *Crystallizing Public Opinion* – strongly suggests he was influenced by him.

Clarke certainly seems to have enjoyed public relations success outside of simply getting articles in newspapers. He apparently secured government funding for boots for disadvantaged children while working for the leather industry, and a ban on harmful additives in processed foods on behalf of Heinz.[20] He also claimed to have won a last-minute change to the Chancellor of the Exchequer's annual budget on behalf of an unnamed industry to help it against foreign competition.[21]

All this meant Editorial Services Ltd was much more successful than Clarke's other businesses, though this is not necessarily because it was any better run.

Clarke certainly believed in the importance of recruiting high-calibre people; he thought that only the most talented people could succeed in public relations. In a 1929 lecture, he set out the qualities required of a new recruit:

He must be an expert in news-value – in finding news, preparing it in different journalistic forms to secure the best and widest Press reflex for it, also in distributing it to best advantage. He must be expert in news treatment, also the capacity to impart to a cold static fact some warm and dynamic news quality, a 'time' factor, an 'authority' factor, a 'human interest' factor, and all the other factors that go to the make-up of news-value...

I do think, however, that the duties of a press agent who is directing or advising in the public relations of a big undertaking or movement demand something more than ordinary journalistic qualifications. They demand a knowledge of men and affairs more comparable with an editor's knowledge; a certain aptitude for, and knowledge of, business and administration which a journalist need not necessarily possess.

However high his standards were in theory, he failed to apply them when it came to the practice of hiring his own staff. Alan Clarke described Editorial Services Ltd as 'a clearing house for all kinds of people needing a job'. Just as Clarke's optimism had led him into poor business investments, Alan later remembered how 'Fleet Street spongers', as he called them, found that it also meant he was an 'easy touch' when it came to looking for a job.[22] 'Few lasted, but all were given a chance,' wrote Alan.

***

At the end of 1933, Clarke suffered a terrible personal tragedy.

His son, Ian, attended Canford School, a boarding school in Dorset, and he suffered so badly from earache that he would sometimes be unable to sleep and so would spend nights wandering the school grounds.

On 3 December, the school called Clarke to tell him Ian was feeling depressed and had asked for a visit from his father, who Ian's housemaster said he held in the 'greatest regard'. Clarke left for Dorset immediately and the two of them spent some time together at the school.

At the end of the visit, Clarke and Ian parted on what the housemaster described as 'affectionate terms' and the housemaster accompanied Clarke back to Bournemouth Station.[23] When the housemaster returned from the station, he found Ian lying on a bed next to a test tube and the remains of some white powder. He had taken a dose of arsenic oxide that he had access to for a chemistry experiment. Doctors spent nine hours trying to save his life[24] but he died in the early hours of 4 December.[25]

It must have been extraordinarily difficult to cope with the suicide of his youngest son, coming fifteen years after George's death from scarlet fever. But somehow, Clarke's positive outlook on life, perhaps combined with a lack of introspection, seems to have enabled him to overcome the tragedy. Certainly, by the start of 1935 he seems to have been enjoying his life with Alice at their large house in Eton.

The house was next to a bend in the river where Izaac Walton, the author of the *Compleat Angler*, had spent time fishing in the seventeenth century, and Clarke regularly swam in it and hunted for pike. The property also had a couple of acres of land that included a tennis court and a barn where Clarke busied himself with carpentry.

It was in the barn that he developed the unusual hobby of painting bright patterns on empty jars that had contained the preserved ginger he and Alice had with their breakfast. He once overheard his daughter Margaret telling a friend that the jars were 'a wanton but cheerful eyeful' that represented 'the Pater at his worst'.[26] To add to the slight impression of eccentricity, Clarke stopped wearing his glass eye after deciding it was an 'empty vanity'. He later wrote that his 5-year-old granddaughter was the only person who seemed to notice he was not wearing it, though in reality she is likely to have been exceptional in her lack of tact rather than in her observational skills.

The cheery optimism that helped sustain Clarke through difficult times was also the reason why people found him good company. He gave an insight into his approach to life when he attended a boxing match at Wembley between the British heavyweight champion Jack Petersen and the German Walter Neusel in June 1935. He was in good humour despite the fact it was raining heavily and he was wearing his evening dress and did not have a hat or coat.

He had a theory: he enthusiastically explained to his fellow spectators that if you have the glow of excitement from within, the weather cannot harm you.[27]

Notes

1   *Daily Mirror*, 8 January 1927, p.19.
2   *The Times*, 17 May 1927, p.17.
3   *The Times*, 24 June 1930, p.11.
4   *The Times*, 17 July 1930, p.16.
5   *Manchester Guardian*, 17 July 1930, p.6.
6   *Daily Express*, 17 July 1930, p.9.
7   Ibid.
8   *The Times*, 17 July 1930, p.16.
9   *Daily Express*, 17 July 1930, p.9.
10 Ibid.
11 Alan Clarke, *The Life & Times of Sir Basil Clarke – PR Pioneer, Public Relations*, 1969, Vol. 22 (2) pp.8–13.
12 Manchester University: John Rylands Library, A/C55/11, Edward Taylor Scott (C.P. Scott's son and his successor as editor) to Clarke, 6 November 1931.
13 Alan Clarke, *The Life & Times of Sir Basil Clarke – PR Pioneer, Public Relations*, 1969, Vol. 22 (2) pp.8–13.
14 Sir Basil Clarke, *The Public and its Institutions*, p.4.
15 Halifax Archive, Acc. 2004/013/131 Minute Book of Advertising & Advances Committee, Feb 1939-45, Apr 1958 [Loc. SH/36/A/2].

16 Alan Clarke, *The Life & Times of Sir Basil Clarke – PR Pioneer, Public Relations*, 1969, Vol. 22 (2) pp.8–13.

17 Sir Basil Clarke, *The Public and its Institutions*, pp.1–2.

18 *Advertisers' Weekly*, 28 July 1932.

19 National Union of Teachers, Press Correspondence for the use of Publicity Committees and Press Secretaries.

20 Alan Clarke, *The Life & Times of Sir Basil Clarke – PR Pioneer, Public Relations*, 1969, Vol. 22 (2) pp.8–13.

21 Sir Basil Clarke, *The Public and its Institutions*, p.6.

22 Alan Clarke, *The Life & Times of Sir Basil Clarke – PR Pioneer, Public Relations*, 1969, Vol. 22 (2) pp.8–13.

23 *Manchester Guardian*, 5 December 1933, p.11.

24 *Daily Mirror*, 5 December 1933, p.2.

25 *The Times*, 5 December 1933, p.16.

26 Basil Clarke, *Unfinished Autobiography*, p.2.

27 *Daily Mirror*, 27 June 1935, p.9.

The 'Doyen' of
Public Relations

Just a few weeks after the boxing match between Jack Petersen and Walter Neusel, Clarke, by now 55 years old, was lying in bed at his home in Eton one morning and contemplating how to spend the day ahead of him.

Having decided to start with a morning swim in the river, he got out of bed. But as his foot touched the floor, he was shocked to find he had almost no control over his body. He lurched forward, hitting his head with a 'terrific crack' on a chest of drawers as he fell to the floor. He tried unsuccessfully to get up and with a feeling of fear rising within him he realised he could not move his left arm or left leg.[1]

Clarke called for help and two of his sons helped him back into bed while he waited for a local doctor to arrive. This doctor examined him and then called for Bertrand Dawson, the President of the Royal College of Physicians, who is best known today for hastening the death of George V so it could be announced in the morning papers rather than in what he viewed as the less appropriate evening journals.[2]

After examining Clarke, Dawson told him he had suffered a stroke and recommended that he should travel to Burma to aid what he warned was likely to be a slow recovery. Clarke accepted the advice about the merits of a foreign trip, but instead chose South Africa because one of his brothers worked as a doctor in Kenya and, having not seen him for over twenty years, Clarke thought it would be a good opportunity for a reunion. So in September 1935, Clarke, Alice and Margaret boarded a boat for Cape Town.

Among their fellow passengers were the South African cricket team, who were returning home after a successful tour of England. Clarke got on well with them, as he appreciated the way they were 'always ready to lend a kindly hand or shoulder to an old crock when a gangway or stairway had to be negotiated'. The cricketers also made a positive impression on the Clarke women, with Alice describing them as a 'nice lot of lads' and the now 16-year-old Margaret declaring herself impressed by their dancing skills. The family got on so well with them, in fact, that two of the players, Herbert Wade and Bob Crisp, invited them to visit their homes in Cape Town.

Clarke spent his first two months in South Africa at a nursing home and then joined Alice and Margaret at the Queen's Hotel in Sea Point. It was at this hotel that he was reunited with his brother and he also met the singer Gracie Fields there. He found her to be a 'bright, cheery lass' and as a native of Lancashire she seemed impressed to learn Clarke had once worked for the *Manchester Guardian*, which she called 'the newspaper with all the long words in it'.

Clarke enjoyed aspects of the trip, which included he and Alice buying a Chrysler and going for drives through the countryside around Cape Town, though it did not herald the beginning of the return to health he had hoped for. He had to have his left leg amputated soon after returning to England the following May, probably as a result of the smoking-related illness Buerger's disease. But as distressing as the loss of the limb must have been, Clarke managed to retain a semblance of good humour; as he examined what he described as the 'wretched remnant of the limb' he turned to his doctor and announced that he would call it 'Mein Stumpf' in parody of the title of Adolf Hitler's Mein Kampf. The joke, Clarke later remembered, was 'the only smile I got out of the whole grim affair.'

Clarke's amputation exacerbated the loss of mobility that had been caused by the stroke. He discovered with frustration that even the relatively sedate pursuits of fishing and carpentry required a surprising degree of balance and so he was unable to do much except read books and listen to the radio. Partly to relieve the boredom, he began to write an autobiography.[3] He wrote about 200 pages of a first draft – taking him up to his second stint at the Ministry of Health – but he never finished it.

Clarke spent the rest of his life as what his son Alan described as 'more or less an invalid',[4] though the courage with which he endured his ill-health earned the respect of his peers. 'He bore his heavy physical troubles with high humour and never lost his humour and hope,' the *Manchester Guardian* reported.[5]

His friend Herbert Sidebotham died in 1940. Clarke saw him near the end and would later remember the last words Sidebotham said to him: 'Doesn't it strike you, Basil, that friendship is about the best thing that life has to offer?'[6] Clarke sent a representative to attend the funeral on his behalf, presumably because he was not well enough to go himself. He also wrote a tribute for the *Daily Sketch* in which he described Sidebotham as 'the greatest that British journalism has produced in a generation' and 'a great and loveable friend'. 'I am devastated by his loss,' he wrote.[7]

Despite his health problems, Clarke continued to produce occasional articles. He wrote a review of a book about the River Mersey in 1944[8] and when Lloyd George died in 1945 he wrote an article about his memories of him for the Institute of Journalists' Journal. With three of his sons in the armed forces, Clarke also took a close interest in the Second World War. Its greatest personal impact on him came in 1942 when Margaret's husband was killed in action just eight months after their wedding. She was a widow at the age of twenty-two.

Clarke lived long enough to see the Allies win the war. He died on 12 December, 1947,[9] at his home in Highgate, his son Basil Camden by his side. He was sixty-eight.

Newspapers from *The Times* to the *New York Times* reported his death, while his old employer the *Daily Mail* paid tribute to him as the 'doyen' of public relations officers, who had been a 'great correspondent' for the *Daily Mail*.

But it was perhaps the *Manchester Guardian*, where his career had really begun, that best summed him up when it described him as 'an impetuous, warmly social, talented recorder of events and tendencies to whom every day was a new day'.[10]

★★★

Clarke left Alice £3,046 in his will. The equivalent of about £80,000 today, it was a relatively modest sum that was probably the result of the failure of his business ventures and the cost of twelve years of medical care. Alice lived for another twenty years, dying in 1968.

Today, Clarke's name is mentioned in passing in accounts of the history of public relations and the First World War. But outside of Ireland, where his time in charge of propaganda at Dublin Castle is still controversial, he has mostly been forgotten.

Despite this lack of personal fame, his influence is still felt today. For one thing, Editorial Services Ltd continued after Clarke's death and, after changing its name to CS Services, was sold to the American public relations firm Burson-Marsteller in the 1960s. The acquisition was an important step in Burson-Marsteller becoming the biggest public relations agency in the world.

But the real measure of Clarke's legacy is that as the UK's first public relations officer, he started an industry that now has an annual turnover of £6.5 billion[11] and has a profound impact on all of our lives. From him being the only public relations practitioner at the end of the 1910s, the profession has mushroomed to the point where it now employs almost 50,000 people, and there are now thought to be more people working in public relations than in journalism.[12]

The huge growth in public relations has, at its best, given organisations the confidence to engage with the media and the public in a way that has made for a more open and transparent society. At its worst, the fact that it produces vast quantities of copy that can be readily slotted into articles and bulletins has helped mask a decline in the kind of quality journalism that can meaningfully hold those in positions of authority to account. It has also fuelled a corrosive cynicism that those in public life are more concerned with presentation than with substance.

What is almost as astonishing as how fundamentally public relations has transformed the media landscape and changed society more generally is the extent to which public relations itself has stayed the same. For all the attempts by academics to theorise about it and the efforts of the industry itself to become more respectable, and despite the rise first of 24-hour news and then social media, it is remarkable just how little change there has been in the tactics used in public relations and in the ethical dilemmas facing those who use them. This means that even though just a tiny proportion of those working in public relations today have even heard of Basil Clarke, all of them are walking down the trail he blazed.

Notes

1   Basil Clarke, *Unfinished Autobiography*, pp.2–3.
2   Max Watson, Caroline Lucas, Andrew Hoy, Jo Wells, *Oxford Handbook of Palliative Care*, Oxford, 2009, pp.10–11; includes extract from British Medical Journal (1994); 308: 1445, by J.H.R. Ramsay.
3   Basil Clarke, *Unfinished Autobiography*, pp.4–7; the story about 'Mein Stumpf' is also included in James Lansdale Hodson, *Home Front*, London, 1944, pp.118–19.
4   Alan Clarke, *The Life & Times of Sir Basil Clarke – PR Pioneer*, Public Relations, 1969, Vol. 22 (2) pp.8–13.
5   *Manchester Guardian*, 22 December 1947, p.6.
6   Basil Clarke, *Unfinished Autobiography*, p.145.
7   *Daily Sketch*, 20 March 1940, p.10.
8   *John O'London's Weekly*, 22 September 1944, p.243.
9   *The Times*, 13 December 1947, p.1.
10 *Manchester Guardian*, 22 December 1947, p.6.
11 Centre for Economics and Business Research Ltd, *The Economic Significance of Public Relations*, London, 2005.
12 Nick Davies, *Flat Earth News*, London, 2009, p.85.

Index

If you enjoyed this book, you may also be interested in…